'IMMORTAL

AUSTRIANS IN EX

THE YEARBOOK OF THE RESEARCH CENTRE FOR GERMAN AND AUSTRIAN EXILE STUDIES

8

INSTITUTE OF GERMANIC AND ROMANCE STUDIES
UNIVERSITY OF LONDON

Editorial Board

Charmian Brinson, Richard Dove, Anthony Grenville, Andrea Hammel, Bea Lewkowicz, Marian Malet, Jutta Raab-Hansen, Andrea Reiter, J. M. Ritchie, Jennifer Taylor, Ian Wallace

Amsterdam - New York, NY 2007

'IMMORTAL AUSTRIA'?

AUSTRIANS IN EXILE IN BRITAIN

Edited by

Charmian Brinson, Richard Dove
and Jennifer Taylor

Cover Image: The Austrian tenor, Richard Tauber, in a scene from the film "Heart's Desire" (1935), The British Film Institute. ©Canal Plus Images

The paper on which this book is printed meets the requirements of 'ISO 9706: 1994, Information and documentation - Paper for documents - Requirements for permanence'.

ISSN: 1388-3720
ISBN-13: 978-90-420-2157-0
©Editions Rodopi B.V., Amsterdam - New York, NY 2007
Printed in The Netherlands

Table of Contents

Acknowledgements

The editors would like to thank both the Leo Baeck Institute (London) and the journal *German Life and Letters* for their generous financial support for this publication. They are also grateful to David Newton for invaluable technical assistance in the production of this volume. Thanks are due to Michael Roeder for specific advice. Finally, the editors would like to express their thanks to the Austrian Cultural Forum and the Institute of Germanic and Romance Studies for their support of the conference 'Austria in Exile', held in September 2005, at which the papers published in this volume were originally given.

Introduction

The essays contained in this volume were originally given as papers to a conference on 'Austria in Exile', held by the Research Centre for German and Austrian Exile Studies in London in September 2005. The volume's title – 'Immortal Austria' – is taken from the name of a 'British-Austrian Rally and Pageant', devised and staged by Austrian émigrés in war-time London in March 1943. It was a title which summarized the Austrian refugees' collective memory of their homeland, evoking an image of mountain pastures, historical grandeur and cultural refinement. It was a picture which bore little relation to the final years of the First Republic, whose death throes were still vivid in the minds of most émigrés – and which bore even less relation to the materially and morally shattered homeland to which some of them would eventually return.

Although reliable figures are hard to find, there were probably around 30,000 Austrian refugees from National Socialism in Britain at the outbreak of war, of whom some 10-15 % were political or intellectual exiles and some 85-90% were of Jewish origin, though there was naturally a degree of overlap between these two groups. There were in fact three successive waves of Austrian refugees who arrived in Britain, corresponding to the course of political events in Germany and in Austria itself. The first came in 1933, after Hitler's seizure of power in Germany. The second wave arrived in the wake of the Austrian civil war in 1934, when the Dollfuß government had used troops to crush Socialist and Communist opposition, forcing many party activists into exile. However, it was the Anschluss, Hitler's annexation of Austria on 11 March 1938, followed a few months later by the 'Reichskristallnacht', which caused the greatest number of Austrian refugees to seek sanctuary in Britain, a flow continuing unabated until the outbreak of war.

Austrians in Exile

Studies of German-speaking exile have frequently failed to make any distinction between Germans and Austrians or to consider the experience of emigration from an Austrian-specific standpoint. Anthony Grenville, in his survey of Austrian emigration to Britain, sets out to remedy this deficiency. He examines, *inter alia*, the way in which British immigration policy and practice determined the composition of the Austrian emigration to Britain, as well as the self-image of the body of Austrian refugees that was to prove central to the development of their collective identity and of their wartime and post-war community.

Austrian exiles in London included such well-known literary figures as Stefan Zweig and Elias Canetti: Zweig from 1933, Canetti from 1938. Tatiani Liani considers the case of Stefan Zweig, an unwilling émigré who nonetheless preferred the anonymity of London to the threat of impending Fascism in his home country. Her article records Zweig's extraordinary literary productivity in London, and shows how the course of historical events transformed him from an émigré into a refugee and finally into an 'enemy alien'. Anne Peiter examines Elias Canetti's ambivalent attitude to some of the key themes of his work - exile, Jewishness and the German language. Her article contrasts various reflections contained in his unpublished notebooks with those appearing in later published works such as *Masse und Macht* and *Die Provinz des Menschen*.

The Austrian author Bruno Adler, who in exile specialized in creating typical Berliners to star in his radio features, is the subject of Jennifer Taylor's study of the 'Kurt und Willi' radio series. By examining a selection of the roughly two hundred scripts which were prepared, the paper shows how Adler, then working for the Political Intelligence Department of the Foreign Office, successfully incorporated Government propaganda into these scenes for broadcast to Germany.

While most of the Austrians seeking refuge in Britain went on to settle here, the Viennese cabaret artist and writer Georg Kreisler had only the briefest taste of life in wartime Britain, arriving in 1944 not primarily as an exile but as a soldier serving in the American army. His is a situation which Colin Beaven defines as 'multiple exile'. Beaven investigates Kreisler's experience of British life, and considers his image of Britain as well as its significance for his later British-based novel *Der Schattenspieler*.

Renate Feikes considers the fate of the Jewish medical practitioners who fled to Great Britain after the Anschluss. She examines the difficulties they faced in becoming accepted in their profession, including the inferior status accorded to dentists in Britain in comparison with Austria, and concludes by noting the lukewarm reception afforded to those who wished to return to Austria after the war.

Representations of Austria

During the years of exile, Austria frequently assumed a near-mythical form in the cultural output of Austrian émigrés. Charmian Brinson considers the work of the journalist and writer Eva Priester in which, true to the tenets of the Communist-influenced Austrian Centre, of which she was a key member, and the Free Austrian Movement, she promoted the idea of Austria as a nation culturally and historically separate from Germany and indeed as Germany's 'victim', well before the Moscow Declaration of November 1943 gave Austrian 'victimhood' its official Allied backing.

The mythologizing of Austria was particularly notable in the film industry. Tobias Hochscherf's study examines the substantial contribution made by German-speaking film-makers from central Europe to the British film industry before and after 1933. Hochscherf illustrates the cosmopolitan nature of film-making by reference to film-makers such as Paul Czinner, Alexander Korda and Josef Somlo and examines the extent to which it was possible to counteract the mythical representation of Austria as a Ruritanian idyll in films funded by an international film industry. The films that Paul L. Stein shot in London with the renowned tenor Richard Tauber, both of them refugees, traded unashamedly in nostalgia for a mythical 'Gay Vienna'. Christian Cargnelli examines such films as *Blossom Time*, *Heart's Desire* and *Waltz Time* and discovers beneath the artificiality and sentimentality of the popular genre some of the central concerns of exile: rootlessness, foreignness, loss of language.

The most prominent film critic of the First Republic, Fritz Rosenfeld, forms the subject of Brigitte Mayr and Michael Omasta's contribution, which surveys his work prior to exile in Great Britain, concluding with his informed view of the shortcomings of the depiction of Austria in contemporary films, the potential of the Austrian film industry and his assessment of its future.

The historical novel became one of the most popular literary genres amongst exiled writers. Andrea Hammel's study deals with two historical novels by women writers, Hermynia zur Mühlen's *Ewiges Schattenspiel* and Hilde Spiel's *Die Früchte des Wohlstands*, showing how each of these narratives deals with historical turning-points, illustrating both the failures in Austria's history, and the missed opportunities for alternative social developments and considering particularly the questions of multiculturalism, Jewish emancipation and gender relations.

It is remarkable that Austria as myth should also figure so strongly in the work of a representative of the second generation of exiles; indeed, Eva Ibbotson was still a child when she arrived in Britain and her vision of Austria has remained strikingly childlike. Deborah Vietor-Engländer considers the novels and short stories that feature Ibbotson's mythologized Austria and her 'Golden City of Vienna', and contrasts aspects of her imaginary and romanticized landscape with the more realistic representations of exile which also feature in her work.

Austria Re-visited

'Zurück oder nicht zurück?' was the title of a speech delivered in March 1942 by F. C. West, President of the London Austrian Centre, in which he appealed to his compatriots to return to Austria after the war and take part in the task of reconstruction. It demonstrates the importance for refugees, even in the midst of war, of the question of an eventual return. In fact, some 90% of Austrian refugees would choose to remain in Britain, preferring to keep the toehold they had acquired there to the political and economic uncertainties of life in Austria. Those who did return were generally the politically committed or those, such as writers or actors, whose allegiance to Austria was primarily cultural and linguistic.

One writer who did not return to Austria was the novelist Robert Neumann. Maximiliane Jäger evaluates Neumann's career during the years 1946-65. Her study discusses the post-war perception and reception of Neumann's work in Austria and Germany, his vigorous re-entry into the West German literary scene from 1959 onwards, and above all his journalistic and literary works dealing with Germany's failure to confront the Nazi past, culminating in the novel *Der Tatbestand*.

Anthony Bushell's article examines the prevailing attitudes to exile in post-war Austria through the medium of the literary and cultural journals which were so influential in the early post-war years. His study shows that exile was often disregarded and that the debate as to what precisely constituted Austrian literature and culture was in the main conducted without reference to the work produced by émigrés.

The cultural and psychological gulf between returning émigrés and those who had remained in Austria did not lessen with the passage of time. With the emergence of the Cold War, in which Austria's borders constituted part of the front line, former exiles encountered growing suspicion. In a cultural agenda increasingly dominated by the political Right, they became, in Hans-Albert Walter's telling phrase, 'the victims of a political situation for the second time'. Even 'Spätheimkehrer', such as the writer Hilde Spiel, who finally returned to Vienna only in 1963, were forced to note the distance between them and their compatriots. As late as 1976 Spiel could observe:

> Wer aber allzu lange gezögert hatte und sich erst nach Jahrzehnten entschloß, an den Ort seiner Kindheit zurückzukehren, merkte nach einer Zeit der Euphorie, daß der Bruch nicht mehr heilbar, daß er in der Heimat mehr als in der Fremde ein Außenseiter war.

In fact, the cultural consequences of the Cold War were to delay any serious consideration of exile in Austria for over forty years. Only in the last decade and a half has Austrian exile become a legitimate subject for academic research and debate, a development which finally led to the establishment of the Österreichische Gesellschaft für Exilforschung in March 2002. It is to be hoped that this volume, containing contributions by Austrian, British and German scholars, will be seen very much as a contribution to the current debate.

Charmian Brinson, Richard Dove and Jennifer Taylor
September 2006

Austrians in Exile

The Emigration of Austrians to Britain after 1938 and the Early Years of Settlement: A Survey

Anthony Grenville

This article seeks to provide a framework for a social history of the Austrian refugees from Hitler in Britain, distinguishing them as far as is possible from the refugees from Germany, with whom they are almost invariably grouped together. It analyses the social composition of the community of the mostly Jewish refugees from Austria, by considering the community from which they came, the impact of British immigration policy in determining those likely to gain entry, and the principal characteristics and collective identity of the refugee community in the post-war years of settlement in Britain.

Few of the historians who have written about the forced migration of Austrians after the Anschluss take proper account of the fact that Britain ranked alongside the USA as one of the two most important countries of refuge for Austrians fleeing the Nazis in the pre-war period. Wolfgang Muchitsch gives the figures for those Austrians who found refuge in Britain before the war as 27,293 (the figure given by Jewish organizations to the Nazi authorities in November 1941) or, more reliably, as 30,850 (the figure arrived at by a post-war study).[1] More pre-war Jewish refugees from Austria came to Britain as their *first* country of refuge than to any other, with just over 30,000 coming here and just under 30,000 going to the USA, though subsequent movements meant that the final number in America exceeded that in Britain. Nevertheless, it is a fact that something like one in six of Austria's 180,000 or so Jews found refuge in Britain, and that of those who survived the Nazi years (some 120,000) about one in four survived by fleeing to Britain.

It is generally accepted that Jews made up some 90% of the refugees from Nazism, though it is impossible to arrive at an exact figure. The non-Jews were mostly political opponents of the Nazis, and many of them returned to Austria after 1945; they played only a small part in the story of the post-war settlement of refugees from Austria in Britain, unlike the Jewish refugees, most of whom chose not to return to Austria. After the war, Britain, along with Israel and the USA, was one of the three countries that played host to a substantial settled community of former Austrian Jews; the concentration of Austrian Jews in Britain was far greater than that of the Jews from Germany, who began to emigrate earlier, from 1933, when their range of options was considerably wider than that facing their Austrian counterparts in 1938/39. To this day, Britain remains home to one of the largest contingents of former Austrian Jews in the world, as the lists of those eligible for compensation from Austrian government funds show.

The first condition determining the very existence of an Austrian emigration to Britain was British immigration policy, which enabled the refugees from Austria to enter Britain in the first place. The shift in British immigration policy and practice that took place in 1938 allowed the entry of hitherto unprecedented numbers of refugees from Nazism.[2] Prior to the Anschluss, the number of refugees from the Reich admitted to Britain had been under 10,000, as Britain was neither a favoured nor a particularly welcoming country of refuge. It was the Anschluss and its aftermath that transformed the situation. The anti-Semitic excesses that accompanied the installation of the Nazi regime in Austria were fully documented at the time by journalists like Shirer and Gedye,[3] and they have remained a prominent feature in the autobiographies and memoirs of refugees. The level and intensity of anti-Semitic violence and open terror in Vienna clearly distinguished it from the situation in the German cities. George Clare's vivid description in *Last Waltz in Vienna* of the orgiastic outburst of anti-Semitic violence in that city is the more striking for the contrast with Berlin, where to his amazement Jews could still walk around freely, at least until November 1938.[4]

The result was that foreign consulates in Vienna were besieged by Jews desperate to emigrate. Where Britain was exceptional was in the loosening of its immigration practice that took place in 1938/39, at a time when almost all other countries were tightening the restrictions that they imposed on refugees from Nazi-controlled territory. Whereas Britain had accepted fewer than 10,000 refugees in the five years from 1933 to 1938, in the eighteen months between the Anschluss and the outbreak of war it admitted over 50,000, a remarkable rate of increase. It was, obviously enough, the Jews from Germany and Austria who benefited from this, and of these the Jews from Austria benefited most, for they were pressured to emigrate by extreme levels of anti-Semitism from March 1938 and their German fellow Jews only from November 1938: this difference of eight months represents almost half of the precious period of grace before the outbreak of war during which it was possible, though never easy, for Jews from the Reich to enter Britain. This goes a long way to explaining the high proportion of Jews from Austria to be found among the Jewish refugees from the German-speaking lands who settled in Britain.

After the Anschluss the British government introduced a visa system to control the flood of refugees seeking to enter the country from Austria. The visa system, as already noted, certainly did not cause the number of refugees from the Reich to diminish. In one way, it facilitated entry to Britain. For now refugees arriving at British ports could no longer be turned back on embarkation by immigration officers if they had visas; though visas were not easy to obtain, possession of one did guarantee the owner entry. Take the case of Hanne Norbert, later to marry the famous refugee actor Martin Miller. She was acting in Innsbruck at the time of the Anschluss and swiftly took a train for England, only to be refused entry and returned to France, where she remained until her parents reached Britain. They had a visa that included her, however, and she was then admitted to Britain without any difficulty.[5]

The visa system also played a key role in determining the composition of the Austrian emigration to Britain, as it favoured some groups of potential refugees while disadvantaging others. Obvious beneficiaries were the Jewish children who were admitted to Britain without visas on Kindertransports, of whom over 2,000 came from Vienna. Visas could be obtained relatively easily by those few who were perceived as having special value for the host country, international celebrities like Sigmund Freud, performing artists like Richard Tauber, academics and scientists brought over by the Society for the Protection of Science and Learning, or entrepreneurs willing to create new industrial enterprises; one can add to them famous people like the writer Stefan Zweig, who had already been admitted to Britain before the Anschluss. Those who could show that they would not become a financial burden on the British state were another, and larger, group who were granted visas more readily. These included those who found British citizens willing to provide a financial guarantee for them, and those who could finance themselves – the latter being few indeed, given the near-impossibility of bringing material assets out of the Reich. But quite a number of Austrians were able to avail themselves of private or business contacts with British citizens or firms to secure a guarantee.[6]

It was the affluent, middle-class sections of Austrian Jewry who were more able to take advantage of such contacts, while poorer Jews tended to lack the life-saving benefits of wealth, contacts abroad, bankable qualifications and familiarity with the mechanics of foreign travel. Although the British authorities issued regulations to passport officers intended to keep out small businessmen, agents, shopkeepers and those in similar occupations, they were less than successful in doing so.[7] Indeed, one of the features of the German- and Austrian-Jewish refugee community in Britain was precisely the number of small businessmen and entrepreneurs it contained, as a walk in the post-war years up the Finchley Road in North-West London, the area around which refugee shops, cafés and businesses clustered most densely, would have demonstrated. Two groups whose entry was resisted not only on paper by the British government, but also more robustly by British professional associations defending the interests of their members, were lawyers and medical and dental practitioners; despite the barriers they faced, however, they arrived in some numbers, presumably reflecting, as did the businessmen, the patterns of employment and vocational choice common among middle-class Austrian Jews. Considerable numbers of medical practitioners from Austria eventually practised in Britain; fewer lawyers were able to practise, on account of the two countries' differing legal systems, but their skills still enabled many of them to build careers in commerce, industry and management, and later in dealing with the legal side of restitution claims.

A large group of women came to Britain on domestic service visas, to meet a perceived shortage of domestic servants in British households. A smaller number also came to work as nurses; some of these subsequently went on to become doctors, showing the initiative and drive often associated with the refugees, though others, one should not forget, saw their career aspirations shattered for life. Many of the domestic servants endured poor treatment and harsh conditions, though most were able to escape into better forms of employment once war broke out and their labour was in demand elsewhere. It seems that those who worked in the households of British Jews often carried a lasting sense of grievance, perhaps because they had expected better from co-religionists.[8] At any rate, the treatment of domestics by Anglo-Jewish families does seem to be one of the factors contributing to the abiding distance between the Jews from Central Europe and established Anglo-Jewry, a factor of very great importance for the entire character and development of the German- and Austrian-Jewish refugee communities in Britain, which were not, as expected, smoothly absorbed into Anglo-Jewry.[9]

The British authorities were also prepared to admit on a temporary basis 'transmigrants' who could be expected to emigrate on from Britain to another country; several thousand men came to Britain as transmigrants, of whom about 4,500 were accommodated in Kitchener Camp, at Richborough in Kent. Well over a third of the camp inmates were Austrians. The admission of transmigrants was also used as a device to save the lives of Jewish men who had been sent to concentration camps after Kristallnacht and whom the German authorities would agree to release if they had the necessary documents for emigration to a foreign country. In practice, the 'temporary' admission of transmigrants proved to be something of a fiction, as they were never obliged to move on and following the outbreak of war were allowed to stay permanently in the same way as other refugees. Also permitted to stay were those already living temporarily in Britain, like the future Nobel Prize winning chemist Max Perutz, who had come to Britain from Vienna for research purposes in 1936 and for whom return became impossible after the Anschluss.

The Austrian Jews who fled to Britain in 1938/39 were not representative of Austrian Jewry as a whole; this again is of the greatest importance for the development of the Austrian refugee community in Britain, for that community would have been very different if it had reflected more exactly the social and occupational structure of Austrian Jewry. Like Austrian Jewry, however, the refugees were overwhelmingly Viennese. Austrian Jews in Britain who originate from towns and cities outside Vienna are relatively rare. (I have interviewed only one, an observant Jew from the village of Lackenbach in the Burgenland, one of a group of Jewish settlements long established on Esterhazy land.) Emigration was easier from Vienna, given the proximity of foreign consulates and also the Nazi offices from which permission and documentation had to be secured.

That the emigration from Vienna was unrepresentative of Viennese Jewry as a whole and drew disproportionately on middle-class groups is easily demonstrated. The largest concentration by far of Jews in any district of Vienna was to be found in the Leopoldstadt or 'Mazzesinsel', the Second District, where the Jewish population tended to be poorer, working-class, Orthodox and closer to the traditions and customs of the shtetls of the East; the same was true to some extent of the Twentieth District, Brigittenau, which contained a sizeable Jewish population. But the refugees in Britain tended to come far more heavily from the more prosperous inner districts of Vienna, where the Jews were assimilated, secularized, bourgeois in their lifestyle, well educated and wedded to the German-speaking culture of the city to which they had contributed so notably.

It is a common perception that one only had to scratch a Viennese Jew to discover a Freud, a Schnitzler, a Popper or at the very least a budding member of the Amadeus Quartet. This is, however, a false perception, resulting not least from the fact that the non-assimilated, working-class Jews from the poorer districts of Vienna, though more numerous, were far less successful than assimilated, middle-class, 'culture-bearing' Jews in overcoming the obstacles to emigration in the short period between the Anschluss and the outbreak of war. In the lapidary phrase of Georg Stefan Troller, describing in his autobiographical volume *Selbstbeschreibung* the Leopoldstadt and the fate of its Orthodox residents, 'Waren wir Assimilanten nach Westen emigriert, so die frommen Chassidim geschlossen nach Auschwitz'.[10]

To take an example: of the nine Jews interviewed for the book *Changing Countries* who grew up in Vienna and came to Britain, only one came from a working-class area; though the interviewees for the book cannot be seen as a representative sample of the Jewish refugees in Britain, this is nevertheless a striking figure.[11] Even those refugees from Vienna whose families lived in modest circumstances were often more middle-class than proletarian in their values, lifestyle and aspirations, and their fathers were rarely manual workers. I have interviewed very few Viennese refugees whose fathers were manual workers; one is Otto Deutsch, who grew up in a municipal housing block in the working-class Tenth District, Favoriten, the classic background for the proletariat of 'Red Vienna'.[12] Otto Deutsch's relatives still mostly lived as Orthodox Jews in the Leopoldstadt, and he remained drawn to the working-class and traditionally Jewish ambience with which he was familiar long after emigrating to Britain – though he subsequently settled in Southend-on-Sea, made a career as a tour manager and guide, and is now chairman of the Essex branch of the Association of Jewish Refugees (AJR).

The Second World War greatly disrupted the process of the settlement and integration of the refugees from Austria into British society, through the restrictions imposed on 'enemy aliens' at the start of the war, the internment of many thousands of refugees in May/June 1940, the dislocation caused by the bombing of British cities, and the geographical dispersion of the many refugees who served in the British forces, often overseas, or contributed to the war effort in other ways. From a scholar's point of view, the war had the advantage of separating out the Austrian from the German component of the refugee community in Britain, since the wartime period brought about a flowering of specifically Austrian organizations dedicated to the establishment of an Austrian presence in Britain. This has enabled scholars like Wolfgang Muchitsch and Helene Maimann to research the wartime period fully, and for that reason it will not be dealt with at length here.[13] The Austrian Centre, the largest and most important of the wartime organizations set up by Austrian refugees in Britain, is the subject of a study by members of the London-based Research Centre for German and Austrian Exile Studies.[14]

One point relating to the impact of the war on relations between the refugees and their British hosts does merit closer consideration. The war greatly disrupted the refugees' lives, and the refugees often had in these early years to endure the ugly underside of prejudice, intolerance and deep-seated British suspicion of foreigners, especially Jews – and German-speaking Jews at that. But from a psychological point of view, it appears that in the longer term the war years contributed significantly to the readiness of the refugees to integrate into British society and to build their future lives in their country of refuge. The experience of British society in wartime, the behaviour of ordinary British men and women during the Blitz and during the long years of privation, danger, losses and hardship, left a deep impression on many refugees, as did Winston Churchill's inspiring leadership. They saw in the quiet determination to win through to victory at all costs and in the refusal to contemplate defeat a unity of purpose notably lacking in pre-war Austria, a unity that transcended political divisions in the battle against the common foe and that bound the nation willingly into the war effort that would ensure its survival, while still preserving a measure of consideration for others, of fair-mindedness, civilized manners and, not least, humour. This was a cause in which the Jewish refugees, the erstwhile pariahs and victims, could once again take part actively and as equals; they could take pride in contributing to the defeat of Nazism, in the armed forces, the factories or as fire-watchers or nurses.

Though it is hard to measure, the psychological impact of the wartime years on the refugees' view of Britain is difficult to overestimate, and it goes a long way towards explaining the extremely – one might almost say undeservedly – favourable image of Britain common among the refugees. This view of Britain, related to the general mythologization of the war in post-war British society, was strengthened by the revelations of Nazi crimes and the extermination of Austria's Jews that emerged at the war's end and that for many refugees ended their sense of identification with their former homeland. The refugees often had reason to shake their heads at the behaviour of the British, but, once the misconceived policy of interning refugees in 1940 was abandoned, they increasingly did so with reluctant admiration and a slightly baffled, but enduring affection.

This is not to minimize the hardships and perhaps especially the isolation and emotional insecurity that beset so many refugees. One only needs to think of the children and young people who came over on Kindertransports or as domestic servants and had to fend for themselves, in orphanages and foster families or in menial positions, and with little or no support; or of the elderly, unable to make the transition to a strange new life and subsisting in much reduced circumstances. On the other hand, a surprising number of the former did succeed in making careers for themselves in middle-class professions: for example, Richard Grunberger, editor of the AJR's journal from 1988 to 2005 and historian, and Ernst Flesch, secretary of Club 1943 (the venerable refugee cultural forum founded in 1943 and still active today) and a former college lecturer, came over as boys on Kindertransports and spent their early years in Britain in very unpropitious circumstances.

Almost all the specifically Austrian organizations set up during the war ceased to exist once it had ended, including the Austrian Centre, the

Free Austrian Movement, Young Austria, the newspaper *Zeitspiegel*, the Austria Office and others, since their leading spirits mostly returned to Austria; such specifically Austrian institutions as the units in the British armed forces manned by Austrians also ceased to exist, while the BBC's Austrian Section was eventually wound up. Those that remained were often devoted to particular purposes, like the Anglo-Austrian Music Society. The Anglo-Austrian Society (originally Anglo-Austrian Democratic Society) still exists, but it has a membership of both nationalities. It is at this point that the difficulties inherent in the task of tracing the specifically Austrian element in the now predominantly Jewish community of refugees from the German-speaking lands in Britain become plain, as no scholarly work has been done on the refugees from Austria in Britain after 1945 as a distinct group.[15]

Even the number of Austrians who settled in Britain is unknown. From the register of naturalizations for the post-war years, it emerges that 8,626 certificates of naturalization were granted to Austrians in the period 1946-51, over 7,000 of them in the years 1947-49.[16] A certificate under one name, usually the husband's, often covered an entire family, so at a conservative estimate the total of Austrian-born refugees naturalized in those years could have reached 17,000. To these must be added those who had, exceptionally, been naturalized during the war; those few who took British citizenship after 1951; those, very few, who happened to hold British nationality before they left Austria; the far larger number who reapplied for Austrian nationality (lost under the Nazis) and never took British citizenship; those who came on to Britain after 1945 from Palestine and who were listed as originating from there; and those who refused to state their nationality on their naturalization applications as Austrian, declaring themselves instead to be stateless. The total could well reach 20,000.

In the post-war years of settlement and gradual integration, the Jewish refugees from Austria had much more in common with their fellow refugees from Germany than with any other group, and these common elements of language, culture, heritage, everyday habits of life and religious observance (or the lack of it) drew the two groups together powerfully, as did their common fate as victims of Nazi persecution. Already before the war, Austrian refugees had come under the umbrella of organizations set up to deal with their German counterparts: Jewish refugees from Vienna were granted assistance by the Jewish Refugees Committee and looked, as did the German Jews, to the organizations based in Woburn House and Bloomsbury House, while the Society for the Protection of Science and Learning extended to Austrian scholars and scientists its programme for bringing over to Britain refugee academics from German universities. The earliest organizations set up by the refugees themselves, the Self-Aid of Refugees

(1938) and the Association of Jewish Refugees, founded in June 1941 and the most important and long-lived of all, likewise conceived of themselves as representing the interests of all refugees from the German-speaking lands (all Jewish refugees in the case of the AJR).

A key factor here is the self-image of the refugees from Austria, which can be said to be central to the development of their collective identity and to the evolution of their community. Arguably, the refugees from Austria who opted to stay in Britain after 1945 made a deliberate choice that reflected a significant change in their sense of their own identity and in the community to which they owed allegiance: almost all of them became British citizens and came to see themselves as British. Tellingly, the great majority of them did not opt for either of the clearly Jewish alternatives open to them, emigration to Palestine/Israel, or absorption into Anglo-Jewry, a community still primarily defined by its adherence to Jewish customs and values. Equally fundamental was their abandonment of their identity as Austrians, which had been largely forced on them by their treatment in post-Anschluss Austria and had been cemented by the post-war revelation of the destruction of the entire Jewish community in Austria in the Holocaust and the consequent disappearance of the emotional and cultural world in which the Jewish refugees had grown up.

A return to Austria was for many a journey to a familiar landscape now inhabited only by the ghosts of the past.[17] It soon became common knowledge among refugees that the welcome extended by Austrians to returning Jews was less than effusive and that the anti-Semitism that had flourished under the Nazis still lurked behind the Austrians' perception of themselves as victims (backed by the Moscow Declaration on Austrian independence issued by the Allies in 1943, which called Austria the first victim of Nazi aggression). It was particularly galling for victims of Nazi persecution to be greeted on return visits with descriptions of the sufferings undergone by Austrians that the Holocaust survivors had had the good fortune to escape. Arguably, most Jews from Austria no longer felt themselves properly to be Austrians after 1945, given that in the post-war years the Austrian state made little attempt to reintegrate them as Austrian citizens or to heal the wounds inflicted on them and their families in the Nazi years. They felt in effect that their expulsion from Austrian society had not been made good after 1945.

The high profile of many of the 'Remigranten' who did return should not disguise their small number. A considerable proportion were political activists, like those behind the Austrian Centre, or writers, journalists and theatre people, Hans Flesch-Brunningen and Otto Tausig for example, who returned to the country in whose language and culture they were most at home; some went back when their businesses were returned to them, some because they could not adapt to life in Britain. But they remained a small minority. In 1946, the *Zionist Review* reported that the Austrian Centre had registered 1,600 applications for return to Austria from Britain;[18] many would not have gone beyond applying, and some, like Ernst Flesch, stayed only briefly and came back to Britain again. As late as 1950, the AJR's journal reported that just 603 Austrian Jews had returned from Britain;[19] this was probably an underestimate, but even if one increases it by half, it still remains below a thousand.

However, many refugees felt an abiding attachment to Vienna, the city of their birth, to its culture, its beauty, its beguiling charm and easy-going way of life, to the romance of its spirit compared with the mundane greyness of daily life in London. The refugees were unwilling to be Austrians and unable to be English (as opposed to British by nationality), but could continue to think of themselves as Viennese in terms of their personal identity. Viennese culture was a key point here, both in the sense that the refugees continued to practise it in their reading, their appreciation of art and especially their love of music, and in the pride that they took in the outstanding contribution that Viennese Jews, a tiny group in a population of over fifty million, made to British culture. Their contribution in the musical field is so well-known that it needs no further recapitulation here, and the same applies in publishing, art history, psychiatry and psychology, and many other fields of art, science, culture, education and enterprise.

In a filmed interview Norbert Brainin of the Amadeus Quartet defined his identity as Viennese, not because he lived in Vienna or had any formal association with it, but because the spirit of his music was Viennese, and that, he said, putting his hand to his heart, he carried within him.[20] The spell of Vienna remained unbroken, as is evident from the loving nostalgia with which many refugees speak in interviews of the city of their childhood and youth. A romantic might say that if the spirit of Viennese Jewry survived anywhere, it survived in the post-war decades in the refugee heartlands of North-West London. In those years, the unmistakable flavour and style of Viennese life could be felt and heard along the Finchley Road, West End Lane and Haverstock Hill in North-West London: in the Blue Danube Club, where Peter Herz produced witty reviews in a Central European style with titles like *The Importance of Being Funny* and *Gentlemen Prefer Money*; in the Cosmo Restaurant, the famous refugee meeting-place, whose owners for many years were the Manheimer family from Vienna, and in other cafés (there was a Café Vienna), patisseries, restaurants, food shops and delicatessen; or in Libris bookshop, run by the Viennese bibliophile Dr Joseph Suschitzky.

It is true that in the early years organizations were created specifically to meet the needs of the refugees from Austria (leaving aside those like the Austrian Centre, which were not designed to last beyond the end of the war). There was the Jacob Ehrlich Society, founded in December 1941 to represent Austrian Jews and in particular to press for full compensation for the material, emotional and psychological losses that they had suffered. The Jacob Ehrlich Society, however, was soon absorbed into the Association of Jewish Refugees; indeed, its founder, Rudolf Bienenfeld, was also the sole Austrian on the founding Executive of the AJR. Other Austrians prominent in the early years of the AJR were Carl (Charles) Kapralik, another expert on restitution matters, and F. L. Brassloff.

Restitution was one of the very few areas where there was a clear separation between refugee Austrians and Germans, as they had to address their claims to different successor states on the territory of the former Reich. Even here, the Council of Jews from Austria, which concerned itself with restitution, was closely modelled on its German sister organization, the Council of Jews from Germany, created towards the end of the war by the organizations of the Jewish refugees in Britain, the USA and Palestine. The United Restitution Organisation, which was set up in 1948 by the Council of Jews from Germany to deal with restitution claims and which at first shared premises with the AJR in Fairfax Mansions, off Finchley Road, later had a separate Austrian Desk. Otherwise, the Jewish refugees from Austria set up no general representative organizations of their own after the war; an organization for ex-Berliners in Britain existed, and one for ex-Breslauers, but none for ex-Viennese, though Jews from Vienna living in Britain almost certainly outnumbered those from any other German-speaking city.

In general, the social development of the community of Jewish refugees from Austria closely paralleled that of the refugees from Germany. Both groups settled in large numbers in North-West London, though there was substantial settlement in other cities, especially Manchester and Glasgow, and in other parts of London, especially Stamford Hill and Stoke Newington, where the more Orthodox congregated. Many refugees, though by no means all, appear to have followed the pattern of resuming in Britain the process of assimilation that had been underway for some generations in Austria and Germany, after its brutal interruption in those countries by the onset of Nazism. The severing of the ties with the countries of birth probably accelerated the process of assimilation, as the mass adoption of British names in the post-war years testified.

The Jews of Vienna had long been noted for their assimilationist tendencies, probably because the Jewish community in Vienna was itself so new, having come into being only in the mid-nineteenth century, when Jews were permitted to reside in the imperial capital; many more German-Jewish families had been settled in their native areas for generations – even the Jewish community in Berlin was solidly established far earlier than that in Vienna. The extraordinarily rapid growth of Vienna's Jewish community in the period between 1867 and 1914, accompanied by a degree of economic success that propelled many Jews into the professional and commercial middle classes, along with a cultural and intellectual flowering of Europe-wide importance, reflected the restless dynamism of a largely secularized community, much of which had thrown off its traditional beliefs and practices and had opted headlong for assimilation into the modern, bourgeois world.

Arguably, the Jews from Vienna were in the vanguard also when it came to integrating into British society and building their lives here afresh. Jews from Austria were at least as eager as those from Germany to assert their right to choose their new homeland. They resisted any attempt to repatriate them to their native lands after the war, they took British citizenship, many also took British names, and few returned to Austria. Unfortunately, there are no precise figures on which to establish a comparison between German and Austrian Jews in these respects. I would speculate, from my own experience of refugees from Austria, that former Viennese Jews were rather more inclined than their German counterparts to abandon their ties with their former environment. This applies, for example, to the large numbers of them who did not join a synagogue or any other of the communal institutions so prominent in Jewish life – with the notable exception of the AJR, an organization that is studiously neutral in religious matters, but devoted to preserving the cultural heritage of Central Europe.

Mainly Jewish and preponderantly from Vienna, the refugees tended already to be middle-class, well educated and non-observant before emigration, a pattern that continued in Britain and that separated them from British Jews, who maintained traditional customs and were, at least on arrival, poor and lower-class. The difference in the areas of initial settlement, the East End of London in the case of the Jews from Tsarist Russia and the North-Western suburbs in that of the Jews fleeing Hitler, underlines the point. The occupational and professional structure of the Austrian-Jewish community also bears this out, with a considerable number engaged in business, trade and commerce, in the legal and medical professions, in education and the arts, science, media and culture, and with a low proportion in manual, unskilled and semi-skilled jobs. The refugees from Austria held firmly to their culture, proud of that part of the heritage that they had brought with them to enrich their adopted homeland. A distinctly Viennese brand of culture was discernible, from the refugees who thronged the Wigmore Hall to consumers of the products of firms like O. P. Chocolate Specialities (Manufacturers) Ltd., which styled itself 'Makers of the Original "Viennese Dessert"', of '"Pischinger Torten" to the original recipe', '"Mozart bon-bons" and Viennese wafer biscuit specialities', though it hailed from Merthyr Tydfil, Glamorgan.

The Viennese character also made itself felt in Britain. The announcement of the death of Mrs Margaret Bourne, wife of Dr Curt Bourne of Croydon, in the AJR's journal stated: 'She was a real Viennese, possessed of grace and charm, liked and respected everywhere.'[21] In 1969, the journal's obituary of the distinguished musicologist Hans Ferdinand Redlich quoted from *The Musical Times*: '[…] he was a kindly man, with a lively, Viennese sense of humour and a warm, open personality'.[22] The obituary of Arnold Lorand, who came from Vienna to Leeds in 1938 and died in February 1966, recalled that he and his wife had succeeded in creating a 'Miniature Vienna' in their home, although he was by profession an exporter of English cloth. It continued: 'Books, pictures, a collection of neatly framed old programmes of operas and concerts, of which he was particularly proud, some of them 50 years old, a piano, a violin, a 'cello and music stands for the quartet in which Mr Lorand played the violin until last year – all this bore witness to the atmosphere prevailing in his home.'[23]

But the refugees' adherence to Viennese culture was not matched by a continuing sense of Austrian identity. In the absence of this and also of any deep commitment to specifically Jewish practices and beliefs and any desire to integrate into Anglo-Jewry, the refugees from Austria chose instead to build their new lives within the broad framework of British society, as did those from Germany. This extended beyond the formal acquisition of British nationality, though it did not go so far as to enable them to feel fully English. On the whole, sources like their recorded testimony and memoirs or the journal of the AJR show that they experienced little hostility or open anti-Semitism, though most, especially those who arrived as adults, remained aware of an unspoken divide between themselves and the native British. With that reservation, they mostly perceived themselves as satisfactorily integrated and were proud of their new identity, the new lives that they had built and their adaptation to British society. They displayed a conditional willingness to adapt to and integrate into British society and appeared to feel that the British were on the whole reasonably well disposed towards them. Some scholars would dissent from these conclusions, but, significantly, the proportion of such dissenters is far higher among non-refugee academics than it was, and is, among the former refugees themselves.

Notes

[1]   Wolfgang Muchitsch, *Österreicher im Exil: Großbritannien 1938-1945. Eine Dokumentation* (Vienna: Österreichischer Bundesverlag, 1992), p. 8.

[2] The standard studies of British immigration policy are A. J. Sherman, *Island Refuge: Britain and Refugees from the Third Reich* (Ilford: Frank Cass, 1994; original edition London: Elek, 1973), and Bernard Wasserstein, *Britain and the Jews of Europe 1939-1945* (Oxford: Oxford University Press, 1979). Louise London, *Whitehall and the Jews, 1933-1948: British Immigration Policy, Jewish Refugees and the Holocaust* (Cambridge: Cambridge University Press, 2000) concentrates too exclusively on portraying British policy as illiberal and ungenerous to admit the possibility that the increase in refugee admissions after March 1938 was in any way due to a change in immigration policy and practice.

[3] G. E. R. Gedye, *Fallen Bastions: The Central European Tragedy* (London: Gollancz, 1939), pp. 300ff., 'Terror Unchained', and William L. Shirer, *The Rise and Fall of the Third Reich: A History of Nazi Germany* (New York: Crest Books, 1962; original edition New York: Simon and Schuster, 1960), p. 477.

[4] George Clare, *Last Waltz in Vienna: The Destruction of a Family 1842-1942* (London: Macmillan, 1981), pp. 195f. and 208f.

[5] See the interview with Hanne Norbert-Miller in the Oral History Collection of the Research Centre for German and Austrian Exile Studies, held at the Institute of Germanic & Romance Studies, University of London.

[6] See for example the interview in the same collection with Helga Reutter, where she relates how her husband secured an invitation to come and work in Britain, and that with Wilhelmine (Mimi) Glover, where she records how her cousin Artur Grünfeld, the father of the author of this article, used his business association with the Dunhill company to secure admission to Britain for himself and for several family members trapped in Vienna.

[7] The Passport Control Department of the Foreign Office issued a circular to Consuls and Passport Control Officers on 27 April 1938 containing instructions on the categories of people who should and should not be granted visas. See Sherman, *Island Refuge*, pp. 90f.

[8] See the interviews conducted by Anthony Grenville with Bina Wallach, 18 December 2000, and with Polly Zinram, 21 January 2001, in the possession of the author.

[9] See Anthony Grenville, 'The Integration of Aliens: The Early Years of the *Association of Jewish Refugees Information*, 1946-50', in *German-speaking Exiles in Great Britain: Yearbook of the Research Centre for German and Austrian Exile Studies*, 1 (1999), 1-23 (pp. 10f. and 17ff.). See also Richard Bolchover, *British Jewry and the Holocaust* (Cambridge: Cambridge University Press, 1993), and Anthony Grenville, 'Relations between the Jewish Refugees from Hitler and Anglo-Jewry', unpublished lecture delivered at the Wiener Library, London, 3 April 2001.

[10] Quoted in Georg Stefan Troller, 'Eine Art Venedig ohne Lagune', in *Ein Niemandsland, aber welch ein Rundblick!: Exilautoren über Nachkriegswien*, ed. by Ursula Seeber (Vienna: Picus, 1998), pp. 87-90 (p. 87).

[11] *Changing Countries: The Experience and Achievement of German-speaking Exiles from Hitler in Britain, from 1933 to Today*, ed. by Marian Malet and Anthony Grenville (London:

Libris, 2002), is a study based on 34 interviews with former refugees from Nazism who found refuge in Britain.

[12] See the filmed interview with Otto Deutsch conducted by Anthony Grenville as part of the project 'Refugee Voices: The Association of Jewish Refugees Audio-Visual Testimony Collection'.

[13] Wolfgang Muchitsch has produced two valuable volumes documenting the Austrian exile in Britain, *Österreicher im Exil* (see footnote 1) and *Mit Spaten, Waffen und Worten: Die Einbindung österreichischer Flüchtlinge in die britischen Kriegsanstrengungen 1939-1949* (Vienna: Europaverlag, 1992). The politics and political activities of exile are very fully covered in Helene Maimann, *Politik im Wartesaal: Österreichische Exilpolitik in Großbritannien 1938-1945* (Vienna/Cologne/Graz: Böhlau, 1975).

[14] Marietta Bearman, Charmian Brinson, Richard Dove, Anthony Grenville, Jennifer Taylor, *Wien – London hin und retour: Das Austrian Centre in London 1939 bis 1947*, translated by Miha Tavčar (Vienna: Czernin, 2004). The English version, *Out of Austria: The Austrian Centre in London, in World War II* (London: I. B. Tauris, 2007), is forthcoming.

[15] Marion Berghahn's *Continental Britons: German-Jewish Refugees from Nazi Germany* (Oxford: Berg, 1988), originally published as *German-Jewish Refugees in England: The Ambiguities of Assimilation* (London: Macmillan, 1984), the fullest published investigation of its subject in terms of the number of refugees surveyed, makes plain in its title that it excludes refugees from Austria.

[16] The registers, published annually by His Majesty's Stationery Office in London, are held at the National Archives at Kew.

[17] See the testimonies collected in *Ein Niemandsland, aber welch ein Rundblick!.*

[18] Quoted in *AJR Information*, the monthly journal of the Association of Jewish Refugees, May 1946, p. 3. The article added that 'the vast majority of Austrian Jews reject the idea of going back to a country which has murdered their families and where the poison of anti-Semitism is as virulent as ever'.

[19] *AJR Information*, September 1950, p. 3.

[20] Interview conducted by Bea Lewkowicz for the film *Continental Britons* that accompanied the exhibition of the same name held at the Jewish Museum, London, May - October 2002, to mark the sixtieth anniversary of the foundation of the Association of Jewish Refugees.

[21] *AJR Information*, December 1968, p. 10.

[22] *Ibid.*, February 1969, p. 10.

[23] *Ibid.*, April 1966, p. 13.

The Propagandists' Propagandist: Bruno Adler's 'Kurt und Willi' Dialogues as Expression of British Propaganda Objectives

Jennifer Taylor

Increasingly, scholars are stressing the control exerted on the BBC in wartime by Government censorship procedures. Adler's 'Kurt und Willi' radio feature, written while he was employed by the Political Intelligence Department of the Foreign Office under Richard Crossman, is examined from this perspective. This series ran from the late autumn of 1940 until the end of the war, so offering a unique insight into contemporary British propaganda priorities.

In the early summer of 1940 when the actress Annemarie Hase, the voice of 'Frau Wernicke', was introduced to Bruno Adler she was surprised that the author of this radio feature written in Berlin dialect was not himself a Berliner: 'zu meinem Erstaunen war [er] ein zarter, lebhafter [...] und sehr engagierter Mann im mittleren Alter, der einen unverfälschten süddeutschen Akzent […] sprach.'[1] Adler had been born an Austrian citizen, and it was with recent political developments in mind that, in August 1939, he first approached the BBC with a proposal for a programme on a Czech topic: 'I am a Sudetengerman [sic] Czech, and have been a well-known author in Germany and Czechoslovakia. One of my books describes an important event in Masaryk's life. I can also look back on knowing him personally.'[2] This rather lame attempt to sell himself obviously emanated from an outsider: it was evident the writer had just arrived in town, for the embossed Kent address on the headed notepaper was crossed out and a west London address inserted. Additionally, in directing the letter to 'News Bulletins for Abroad', he seemed unaware of the existence of the German Service, which by that time had been broadcasting for nearly a year. In the circumstances – attention had moved to Poland and Britain was bracing itself for war – it was hardly surprising that the BBC replied with a polite refusal: 'You will appreciate that at the present time we can make no definite arrangements for German talks. If we find we are wanting a talk of the type you suggest in September we will not hesitate to write to you.'[3] Yet just over a year later Adler was very much an insider, enjoying recognition as the author of a successful propaganda feature and being headhunted for the Political Intelligence Department of the Foreign Office (PID),[4] under whose auspices he wrote the 'Kurt und Willi'[5] radio feature series which ran until the end of the war.

Adler's work for the BBC began in the early summer of 1940[6] and by mid-July his popular 'Frau Wernicke' scenes were established in a weekly slot.[7] This voluble Berlin housewife whose apparent goodwill to the Nazi regime was in fact unremittingly subversive was ably interpreted by the exiled actress Annemarie Hase. Hase's skilful delivery of Adler's carefully crafted Berlin dialect proved a winning formula, and the series was immediately successful. It must be supposed that it was his authorship of this excellent propaganda tool which brought Adler to the attention of the British authorities.

By mid-November Adler was working for the German Section of the PID under Richard Crossman, in the 'country end' of Electra House (EH), that is, away from London and the blitz.[8] Among his duties was the security vetting of scripts submitted to the German Service. The BBC had been instrumental in his recruitment. In early October his commissioning editor Christina Gibson, head of German talks,[9] reported on the steps she had taken in this regard:

> As requested by the Planning Committee, I sounded Dr. Adler to find out what his reactions would be if he were invited by E. H. to live near them in the Country and co-operate in their work. [....] I have today given particulars concerning him and his wife to [...] the Political Intelligence Department of the Foreign Office.[10]

Adler's work for the PID is even now shrouded in the secrecy which, despite the Freedom of Information Act, still attends such matters. Similar secrecy surrounds the genesis and development of the 'Kurt und Willi' dialogues. Correspondence released to researchers contains few references to the scenes, but it can be established that the first broadcast was on 11 December 1940 and the second a week later,[11] although it would appear that regular weekly broadcasts did not start until the spring of the following year.[12]

It was Crossman's practice to issue a weekly policy directive to be observed by the German news programmes.[13] These guidelines also applied to German Features, a section founded in the autumn of 1940 under the German actor Walter Rilla, who was tasked with enlivening the treatment of current events, a requirement he solved by dramatization.[14] In the circumstances it was hardly surprising that Gibson did not hesitate to offer Adler quite detailed and very specific suggestions, as the following example from August 1940 illustrates:

> In spite of admitting, as it were accidentally, a vast amount of damage done by the RAF, Frau Wernicke should appear to be convinced that the war will be over very shortly. [...] I enclose some details of British air raids on Germany so that you may be able to quote a few actual places.[15]

Scripts which did not conform to current propaganda objectives were simply rejected.[16]

Although no such helpful references are available for the development of the 'Kurt und Willi' dialogues, the guiding hand of the propaganda directive can be inferred from their design and execution. Willi, who works in the Propaganda Ministry, inducts Kurt into the craft of news management. This concept provided a vehicle suitable for delivering approved propaganda themes[17] and the opportunity for judiciously leaking information.[18] This type of propaganda broadcast was aimed at the middle ground of ordinary Germans, perceived as honest and decent members of the middle and lower-middle classes, many of whom would be civilians. The arguments of psychological warfare most evident in these scenes are: an appeal to the German people over the heads of their leaders, discrediting Government and Party leaders, reasserting the values of common decency constantly subverted by the Nazi Party and the assertion that loyalty to Nazism could only result in death and the destruction of the whole nation.

'Frau Wernicke' and 'Adolf Hirnschal' by Robert Lucas, the third long-running radio propaganda series to emerge from the BBC German Service, were written from the perspective of the ordinary German – a housewife facing the privations of wartime Berlin and a private soldier enduring the horrors of life at the front. The 'Kurt und Willi' scenes, on the other hand, depicted current events from the point of view of those who manage the news. Willi Schimanski, an official in the Berlin Ministry of Propaganda, interprets the war news for the benefit of his interlocutor, Kurt Krüger, a schoolmaster. This scheme afforded the author the opportunity to expose the degree of subterfuge and obfuscation which attended the pronouncements of the German media. While 'Frau Wernicke' and 'Adolf Hirnschal' are dramatized monologues, the dialogue form of the 'Kurt und Willi' scenes made for a looser structure which is often dramatically less satisfying. However, the more leisurely delivery afforded by this design had certain advantages from a propagandist's point of view, since it enabled the insertion of detailed material which required the minimum of reworking. 'Kurt and Willi on German Bombing', broadcast on 9 March 1943 (the very month when the elite RAF squadron colloquially known as the 'Dam Busters' was being formed) is an extreme example of this approach. Parts of the scene read like the briefing paper on which it was presumably based. Willi launches into a long lecture on Goering's failure to equip the German air force with heavy bombers. Beginning with a reference to the International Air Exhibition in Zurich in 1937, he details the retooling necessary for such an undertaking, and points out the three-year lead time for aircraft production. Finally, he concludes by remarking that Goering had only adopted the 'elastischeren Prokuktionsmethoden' of the British and American manufacturers the previous spring. The wealth of detail and analysis of the manufacturing process contained in this scene would imply that the argument was addressed to the German Air Ministry and the political authorities rather than the civilian population which normally formed the target audience of these scenes. Indeed, it is possible to see the broadcast as a terrible warning to the German authorities, for the raids which destroyed the Ruhr Dams on 16 and 17 May and devastated Hamburg on 24 July and 2 August were carried out by the type of heavy bomber referred to in this scene.

Some aspects of the genesis of the series can be gleaned from the correspondence. Adler was conscious of the limitations of the 'Frau Wernicke' format. Certain topics (such as war guilt) were, he felt, not suitable for a female character or for the Berlin dialect in which the scenes were written. 'If certain political problems are to be dealt with I don't consider a woman to be the adequate speaker,' he wrote to Gibson at the end of August 1940, suggesting that male voices, in particular soldiers, would be a more appropriate vehicle for such sentiments.[19] At that time he himself had already contributed two soldiers' dialogues, and a further three were to be broadcast before November.[20] It was, then, unsurprising that he adapted this concept of a dialogue between two male characters once he arrived at Electra House, and it is entirely possible that the initiative came from his side. Kurt and Willi meet every week, originally in a café on the Potsdamer Platz; once the Berlin cafés had been bombed, in Kurt's flat. Their discussion of the war news exposes Willi's cynicism, and gives him the opportunity to explain some of the tricks involved in presenting war developments to the German public. For example, at a time when the RAF air raids were causing considerable collateral damage as a result of inaccurate aiming at military targets, Willi conceals the extent of the casualties by arranging for regional editions of the *Völkischer Beobachter* to be published, so that the larger national figures will remain unreported ('Kurt and Willi on German Home Morale', 18 June 1941). The cynical manipulative approach involved in this process offends Kurt, whose appreciation of current events is almost wholly naïve, and the scenes derive their dramatic effect from this contrast.

As time wore on, this initial conception of two characters, both of whom had questionable characteristics, proved dramatically untenable and modifications had to be made. Kurt was gradually allowed to develop positive traits to provide the foil to Willy's unprincipled cynicism. For example in 'Kurt and Willi on Soldiers and Shares' (20 August 1941) Kurt storms out of the café in righteous indignation when he learns that Willy is prepared to speculate with the lives of German front-line soldiers.

Subsequently, Kurt is shown as the defender of the interests of the young men sent to their deaths amid the slaughter on the eastern front. 'Mein Gott, mein Gott! – also immer neue Schlachten, immer weiter Blutvergiessen,' he objects, when Willi explains to him that the current strategy is to assume Stalingrad will not be taken until the early spring ('Kurt and Willi on Stalingrad and Time', 14 October 1942); 'Aber etwas muß doch getan werden! Sonst – was soll denn sonst aus unseren Jungs werden – in ihrem zweiten russischen Kriegswinter!' he remarks a few months later ('Kurt and Willi on the Russian Winter', 8 December 1942). For his part Willi derides these sentiments as misplaced humanitarianism. Finally, towards the end of the war, Kurt becomes the mouthpiece of the honest but misguided German people who had blindly followed their leaders, oblivious to the fact that the Nazis could promise only death and destruction, a theme which runs like a *leitmotif* through so much BBC output during the war years. Adler even introduces a Frau Wernicke-like figure as an embodiment of popular sentiment to summarize this perception. Frau Lutschek, Kurt's charwoman, is quoted as saying the V1 flying bomb should not be called a 'Vergeltungswaffe' but a 'Verdammungswaffe' ('Kurt and Willi on Fritzsche and Goebbels', 4 July 1944).

As over two hundred scripts were broadcast, it is not possible to consider the content of all the scenes in the series; the remarks that follow give a short survey from two closely-connected aspects – the theme of discrediting the Nazi leaders, and comments on the conduct of the campaign on the eastern front – the theatre of war which was to seal Hitler's fate.

Discrediting leaders

That Willi's character was conceived as venal from the outset is clear from the second broadcast. Willi, who of course has privileged access to enemy broadcasting, informs Kurt of BBC reports that German Party leaders are transferring assets abroad. He can confirm this allegation from personal experience: a friend of his already transferred his assets from Switzerland to Sweden.[21] This venality is maintained throughout the series. For example, at the time when German troops were advancing victoriously eastwards across Russia Willi receives insider information from the foreign press corps which enables him to make a killing on the stock exchange. However, profits can only be maintained at the expense of German reversals – too many victories will deflate the market. This situation provokes an outburst of righteous indignation from Kurt, who contrasts this 'dreckige Spekulation' with the fate of his former pupils: 'Fast jeden Tag höre ich, daß einer meiner alten Schüler auf dem Felde der Ehre gefallen ist, für Führer und Vaterland [...]' ('Kurt and Willi on Soldiers and Shares', 20 August 1941). Towards the end of the war when German military defeat seemed inevitable and escape the only option, Willi attempts to obtain some hard currency by selling an Italian art work he had doubtless acquired by nefarious means. In the face of Kurt's passionate plea for an end to the war:

> das Volk will Frieden, die Front will Frieden – nur die Führung will den Krieg den sie schon verloren hat ... und dieser Führung sollen wir Vertrauen schenken [...] obwohl sie uns nichts mehr geben kann als einen Schrecken ohne Ende.

Willi for once agrees – not because he is experiencing moral outrage at the death and destruction which surrounds him, but so that he can escape to Switzerland where the work is currently being exhibited and collect his cash ('Kurt and Willi on the Last Hope', 5 September 1944).

Willi's character served as a vehicle for delivering one of the major British propaganda themes – discrediting German leaders. The success of the German military campaign in the early months of the Russian offensive meant that the authors were faced with a near-impossible task. This difficulty was overcome by employing a technique borrowed from the popular press – that is, revealing the unedifying spectacle of internecine feuds between the Party and the military. For example, in an episode broadcast the day Smolensk was taken, it was claimed that reports of German progress in Russia had led to disagreements over the assessment of the strength of the Red Army. This had prompted a dispute between the Propaganda Ministry, the Supreme High Command (OKW) and Hitler's Headquarters (Führerhauptquartier) which, it is feared, would implicate the Führer himself: 'Ich vermute, das OKW beabsichtigt, die ganze Verantwortung auf die Schultern des Führers abzuwälzen, sodaß, wenn es schief geht, der Generalität nichts anhaben kann' ('Kurt and Willi on the Generals', 16 July 1941). This theme is continued in a broadcast on 6 August, shortly before Kiev fell to the Germans. This time the opposing parties are the War Ministry and the Propaganda Ministry; the point at issue is also an assessment of enemy capability – in this case an underestimate of the number of tanks available to the Russian forces. Willi remarks that the War Ministry is angry that an unfortunate officer has had to sacrifice his career over this matter 'nur um die Prestige des Führers zu wahren' ('Kurt and Willi on Hitler's Responsibility', 6 August 1941). Even a major turning point in the Allies' favour, the Japanese attack on Pearl Harbour in December 1941, which brought the United States into the war so vitiating the German attempts to maintain American neutrality, is trivialized and sensationalized in a similar manner. The event leads Willi to comment on the unstable alliances formed among the Nazi leaders: Goering supports the

OKW against Himmler and the SS, while the rumours in the popular press that the former is taking morphium have been planted not, as Kurt mistakenly thinks, by the 'Staatsfeind' but by Himmler himself ('Kurt and Willi on External Warfare', 10 December 1941).

Feuding, scurrilous gossip and financial speculation also characterize the depiction of the German generals themselves. 'Kurt and Willi's Assistant on the Sacking of von Bock', broadcast on 20 October 1942, refers to an event which took place earlier that summer, on 13 July. Von Bock was the latest in a long line of generals sacked because they could not support the strategy of Hitler's Eastern Campaign. But in this scene it is not the strategic argument which is to the fore, but the personal animosity that existed between Goering and von Bock, occasioned by an incident in 1935 when the latter had insulted Goering's fiancée. This, it is suggested, is the real reason for the sacking. In 'Kurt and Willi on the Honour of the German Generals', broadcast on 23 March 1943, contemporary material is eschewed altogether and the leaders are discredited by reference to historical material; firstly, by repeating the claim that the generals betrayed the state in 1918, then by outlining a financial scandal in which Hindenburg was implicated at the time of the Weimar Republic when his debts, incurred as a result of speculation, had to be defrayed by the German Government.

In the light of almost certain defeat, such devices of generalized condemnation were no longer necessary and the events were allowed to speak for themselves. 'Kurt and Willi on German Generals', broadcast on 11 July 1944, refers to a recent broadcast on Radio Moscow in which a certain General Bammler, who had surrendered to the Russians, justified his previous conduct by reference to superior orders. Willi comments in disgust:

> Die deutsche Generalität ... solange die Führung Erfolg hatte, haben sie auf die Partei geschworen. Kaum hat sich das Blatt gewendet, entdecken sie auf einmal, daß sie nur blinde Werkzeuge sind. [...] 'n deutscher General sei eigentlich nicht mehr als ein Aufseher, der nur dafür zu sorgen hat, daß die Befehle von oben aufgeführt werden, nur eine Marionette, und wenns dann schief geht, ein Sündenbock für die Führung.

However, the incontrovertible heroism of the 20th July Generals' revolt put the matter in a different perspective, although the tensions between the military and the Party remain. In 'Kurt and Willi on the Small Clique', broadcast five days after the abortive coup, Willi shares the assessment of the situation conveyed by Hitler in a broadcast to the nation in the early hours of 21 July, and condemns the assassination attempt as the work of an unrepresentative minority. Kurt, on the other hand, takes comfort from these signs of rebellion which he sees as signalling an end to the prolongation of war irrespective of the cost to the German people, and heralding a desire for peace. In a direct appeal to the German people over the heads of their leaders, a widely used technique in the BBC's propaganda output, he articulates his hopes of a popular uprising in pursuance of the aims of the conspirators: 'Wenn auch deutsche Stabsoffiziere keine Meister im Bombenwerfen sind – aufs Organisieren verstehen die sich […] sie werden diese Bewegung ins Volk tragen.' Willi's exasperated query, 'In diesem Kampf aufs Messer zwischen der Führung der Partei und der Führung der Wehrmacht, auf welcher Seite stehst du?' elicits the resounding affirmation, 'Auf der Seite des wahren Deutschland'.

In the end, as the Götterdämmerung approaches, the focus shifts back to Willi as an exemplar of an unscrupulous and corrupt leadership. For him the only hope of escape is through stratagems such as stealing the identity of an air-raid victim, although Kurt doubts that in Willi's case this would be possible: 'Bei Dir wirds leider nichts sein […] mit dem Untertauchen heute in so markanten Stellungen, da heißt eben mitgefangen, mitgehangen' ('Kurt and Willi on Home Morale', 14 March 1944). A few months later, with Allied troops rapidly approaching Germany, Willi is equally pessimistic: 'Meine Waffe ist das Wort. Daran kann man leider auch zugrundegehen' ('Kurt and Willi on Leaving the Ship', 12 September 1944).

Russian Campaign

As the remarks quoted above show, Willi is a working propagandist, his weapons the print and broadcast media. Nowhere is this more evident than in the way the Russian campaign is treated in this series. The depiction of events often lacks immediacy – topicality is often conspicuously absent and the arguments deployed tend to be a refutation of German propaganda claims rather than a reaction to the events themselves. Furthermore, Willi's reaction is filtered through the demands of news management and the propaganda slant of his Ministry. Thus events at the front are, for the most part, depicted from the perspective of their effect on the long-suffering German people, the target audience of these broadcasts. This indirect approach contrasts markedly with that of the Communist writer Friedrich Wolf who was writing similar dialogues at that time, but with a somewhat different aim. As an officer of the Red Army stationed at the front, Wolf addressed his pieces to the German troops directly, composing graphic descriptions of the privations they endured in an attempt to encourage desertion and defection.[22]

As Hitler's plans for an attack on Russia were known to the Foreign Office,[23] the event itself could be commented on immediately. 'Kurt and Willi on Russia' was broadcast on 25 June 1941, three days after the launch of Barbarossa. While Willi is preoccupied by the Führer's U-turn, the logistical difficulties of conquering the vast terrain, and the difficulties of persuading the German people to accept yet another postponement of the 'Endsieg', Kurt views the development from the perspective of its impact on Hitler's plans for the invasion of England: 'Der Führer hat erklärt, daß wir durch die russische Verschwörung gezwungen waren, so viele Soldaten an der Ostfront zu halten, daß wir gegen England den Entscheidungsschlag leider nicht führen konnten.' This point is elaborated in 'Russian Casualties and the Invasion of England', broadcast on 16 September, three days before the capture of Kiev: 'England kann man nicht mit Luftlandetruppen allein im Sturm nehmen', Willi remarks with reference to the capture of Crete, 'Die Invasion Englands ist vom Programm gestrichen'. A similar emphasis had characterized Adler's treatment of the invasion of that island which had taken place in May 1941 when German troops had suffered such severe casualties (approximately 4,000 dead and 2,000 wounded) that Hitler vowed never again to mount a major airborne operation against an enemy occupied territory.[24] Grete Fischer's 'The Dream of the Islands', a BBC feature broadcast on 7 June 1941,[25] emphasized the humanitarian aspect of this pyrrhic victory, stressing the unacceptably high loss of life, but in 'Kurt and Willi on Crete' (4 June 1941) Adler concentrated on the logistical and strategic implications of the situation. Counselling against over-optimistic reporting, Willi remarks: 'Die Folge ist, daß Leute wie du in Begeisterung geraten und die Invasion von England und den Endsieg noch in diesem Jahr erwarten.' Viewed with hindsight, this perspective seems strange. It could be argued that while the assertion that Sealion could finally be regarded as cancelled was undoubtedly of concern to Great Britain (which had not ruled out an invasion as late as the spring of 1941[26]) more appropriate material could have been found to address the concerns of the German civilian population, faced as they were with a new phase of the war which was likely to be costly in terms of materials and personnel. However, if the propaganda aim of these scenes is seen primarily as a taunt to the military and government authorities in Berlin in the context of Goebbels' well-documented obsession with Great Britain,[27] the logic of the authors' approach becomes evident.

Despite Willi's complaint at the opening stage of the Russian campaign that the military were not releasing details, 'die ganze Sache wird von der Bendlerstraße als rein militärische Natur angesehen' ('Kurt and Willi on German Home Morale', 18 June 1941), the guiding hand of the Propaganda Ministry on the broadcast and print media soon becomes apparent. Instead of offering a direct depiction of the privations suffered by the German troops at the front, Adler's approach was to demonstrate the manipulative techniques to which reports from the front were subjected before they could be presented to the German people. For example, in the spring of 1942, in the aftermath of the abortive attack on Moscow, Kurt refers to a recently screened newsreel which purported to show front-line action with the comment: 'Man hat den Eindruck, als ob das Ganze dort so 'ne Art Landpartei sei.' Willi enlightens Kurt on the ground rules for editing this type of film for public consumption: in order to maintain morale German corpses must on no account be shown and so these sequences were filmed behind German lines. Images of the genuine front-line battle 'sehn Greuelbildern verdammt ähnlich' and were therefore never released ('Kurt and Willi on News-Reels from Russia', 17 March 1942). Hitler's notorious refusal to consider the logistics involved in keeping a large number of troops in the field over the winter months, briefly referred to in the first winter of the campaign ('Kurt and Willi on Rostov and Libya', 3 December 1941) received a more detailed treatment the following year from the perspective of the manipulation of the print media. 'Kurt and Willi on the Russian Winter' (8 December 1942) exploits the dramatic possibilities of contrasting Willi's cynical obsession with news management to Kurt's righteous concern for the lives of his former pupils. Anticipating the need for a second winter campaign – Stalingrad, which the German press had confidently predicted would fall in September 1942 was still stubbornly holding out – Kurt mentions a detail in the photographs of troops on the eastern front which had appeared the previous year. The steel helmets they were wearing were not appropriate attire for the freezing conditions of Russia. Willi's reaction, that he will inform the appropriate Department not to print such pictures, results in the following indignant protest from Kurt:

> Zum Teufel mit der Bildstelle der Presseabteilung! Du tust ja als käme es grade nur auf die Bilder an, und nicht auf die Jungs. [....] Aber etwas muß doch getan werden. Sonst – was soll denn sonst aus unseren Jungs werden – in ihrem zweiten russischen Kriegswinter!

Even official government figures, it is asserted, were subject to manipulation. 'Kurt and Willi on Casualties in Russia', broadcast on 7 July 1942, illustrates this point with reference to the casualty figures issued by Hitler's headquarters on the occasion of the first anniversary of the campaign. At 272,000 dead, the count was so ludicrously low (a contemporary estimate put the number of casualties as high as 743,000 even before the end of the previous year[28]) that Kurt remarks contemptuously that none of the people he knows will believe the authorities: '[Glauben sie] wir können nicht sehen, wieviel von unsern Freunden und Nachbarn und Kollegen und Schülern tot sind?' Willi responds with the information that it had been a matter of debate where exactly to pitch the official casualty figures. Furthermore, in a technique still used today by spin doctors, the announcement had been timed to coincide with good news, the fall of Sevastopol and Rommel's successes in Africa which, it was hoped, would overshadow the negative impact of the casualty figures.

The fateful turning point in the Russian Campaign, the capitulation of Paulus's Sixth Army at Stalingrad on 2 February 1943 is reflected through the prism of Goebbels' presentation of the disaster to the German people, in particular, his demand that 'the whole of German propaganda must create a myth out of the heroism of Stalingrad which is to become one of the most treasured possessions in German history'.[29] In 'Kurt and Willi on the Nibelungen as Scapegoats', broadcast exactly one week later, Willi outlines the by now familiar bickering among officials, the tension between the Propaganda Ministry, where the feeling is that the bad news simply cannot be concealed, and the Supreme High Command, intent on preserving the reputation of their Commander-in-Chief who, the previous autumn, had categorically stated that Stalingrad would not become a second Verdun (a defeat which had cost Germany approximately a third of a million casualties). Willi relates how Goebbels himself solved the problem by deciding that the details of the surrender should not be concealed, but that the whole scenario should be lifted into the mythical sphere. This had the advantage of absolving Hitler himself from blame: 'Wenn uns zugestoßen ist, was [...] den ollen Nibelungen passierte, dann waren die Nornen […] die den Schicksalsfaden spinnen daran Schuld, und nicht der Führer.'

After the defeat at Stalingrad another army was constituted and given the name of the defeated army. This force, it was reported by the Russian High Command on 18 March 1944, had suffered a reverse in the Ukraine. 'Kurt and Willi on the Sixth German Army', broadcast on 21 March 1944, uses this episode which occurred barely a year after the surrender to comment on the historical continuity of defeat, and to imply an inexcusable inability to learn the lessons of history. Kurt remarks that a former pupil had died at Stalingrad and that his father, also a member of the Sixth Army, had died in the Ukraine. Willi cynically concludes: 'Es wird sich vielleicht noch ein munterer *Großvater* finden für die dritte sechste Armee.'

Subsequently, attention shifts inevitably to the Western Front – Aachen became the first town taken by the Allied invasion force in October 1944 and 'Kurt and Willi on the Symbol of Aachen' was broadcast on 17 October 1944. Throughout the war Willi had never discounted Western Europe as a force in the political equation, frequently arguing that such was the unrest of the occupied peoples that a large German military force was needed to keep the rebellious populace in check, thus depleting the number of troops available for deployment to the eastern front.[30] Unfortunately, space precludes following this topic in detail although, as we have seen, this aspect of the war was clearly of interest to those supplying the brief for these programmes.

This short survey has perhaps given a flavour of the riches to be mined from this vast store of contemporary comment on the Second World War. In considering these scenes as examples of propaganda, it is clear that on many occasions the comment was aimed at the German Government rather than at the overt target audience, the civilian population. Yet throwing light on the murky craft of news management and presentation was a courageous approach for the time, and it seems that the BBC was permitted to broadcast scenes depicting a questionable character like Willi precisely because as a foreigner he represented the enemy. It would take many years and the revolution of the satirical movement of the sixties before a British proponent of these dark arts was allowed on British radio in Anthony Jay's series 'Yes Minister'. It is an irony that would, I like to think, have pleased both fictional protagonists that in inventing Willi Schimanski an Austrian author created the prototype of Sir Humphrey Appleby.

Notes

Grateful thanks are due to the following for their help in the compilation of this article: Agatha Jahn, Michael St. Aubyn and the staff of the BBC Written Archives Centre, Caversham.

[1] Quoted after Uwe Naumann, 'Frau Wernicke im Ätherkrieg' in Bruno Adler, *Frau Wernicke* (Mannheim: Persona, 1990), p. 164.

[2] Bruno Adler (BA) to BBC Overseas News Editor, n. d. (recd. 28 August 1939), 'Dr. Bruno Adler, Talks File 1, 1940-1962', R. cont. 1, BBC Written Archives Centre (WAC), Caversham; unless otherwise stated subsequent correspondence is taken from this source.

[3] BBC Overseas News Editor to BA, 30 August 1939.

[4] Later subsumed into the Political Warfare Executive.

[5] When referring to the series as a whole I have used the German form to conform with customary usage in BBC feature series, e. g. 'Frau Wernicke'; where the title of the programme is given in English, I have used the English form; both forms are used indiscriminately in the original scripts.

[6] See Naumann, *op. cit.*, p. 163.

[7] See BA to BBC Finance Dept, 17 September 1940.

[8] See Christina Gibson (CG) to BA, 14 November 1940.

[9] Originally designated 'Women's Talks'.

[10] Memo, CG to Mr Dunkerley, 4 October 1940.

[11] See 'Overseas Programmes as Broadcast', December 1940, BBC WAC.

[12] I base this assumption on the absence of scripts for the early months of 1941 and the absence of entries for the corresponding period of the 'Overseas Programmes as Broadcast' lists.

[13] See Bernhard Wittek, *Der britische Ätherkrieg gegen das Dritte Reich* (Münster: Fahle, 1962), p. 55; Carl Brinitzer, *Hier spricht London* (Hamburg: Hoffmann und Campe, 1969), p. 143.

[14] Cf. Richard Dove, '"It tickles my Viennese humour": Feature Programmes in the BBC Austrian Service, 1943-1945', in *'Stimme der Wahrheit'. German-Language Broadcasting by the BBC: Yearbook of the Research Centre for German and Austrian Exile Studies,* ed. by Charmian Brinson and Richard Dove (Amsterdam/New York: 2003), pp. 57-71 (p. 60).

[15] CG to BA, 30 August 1940.

[16] See the present author's, 'Grete Fischer: "Outside Writer" for the BBC', in *'Stimme der Wahrheit',* pp. 43-55 (pp. 46-47); cf. also Richard Dove, '"Marching On": Karl Otten at the BBC' in *Keine Klage über England?,* ed. by Charmian Brinson and others (Munich: iudicium, 1998), pp. 39-47 (pp. 40; 45).

[17] Adler shared authorship of these scenes with the British writer Norman Cameron – the precise degree of collaboration remains to be established, see Uwe Naumann, 'Kampf auf Ätherwellen. Die deutschsprachigen Satiren der BBC im Zweiten Weltkrieg', in *Keine Klage über England?,* pp. 31-38 (pp. 34-35).

[18] That there was input from official sources is indicated by the frequently occurring attribution 'Script by E[lectra] H[ouse]'; cf. Brinitzer, *op. cit.,* p. 116.

[19] BA to CG, 28 August 1940.

[20] On 24 September, 3 October and 10 November; first two untitled, last entitled 'Austrian Soldiers in France'; see BA, Copyright 1, 1940-1950, R. cont 1, BBC WAC.

[21] See Wittek, *op. cit.,* pp. 179, 224.

[22] See the present author's 'Propaganda as an Art Form? Some Reflections on Friedrich Wolf's Work in the Soviet Union in 1942', *German Life and Letters,* 2 (1985), p. 138-54.

[23] See William L Shirer, *The Rise and Fall of the Third Reich* (London: Pan, 1972), p. 1009.

[24] See *The Oxford Companion to World War II,* ed. by I. C. B. Dear (Oxford: OUP, 2001), p. 215.

[25] See the present author's 'Grete Fischer', *loc. cit.,* pp. 49-50.

[26] See Richard Overy, *The Battle* (London: Penguin, 2000), p. 117.

[27] See Helmut Heiber, *Joseph Goebbels* (Munich: DTV, 1965), pp. 270-71.

[28] Quoted after Shirer, *op. cit.,* p. 1029.

[29] Quoted after Anthony Beevor, *Stalingrad* (London: Penguin, 1999), p. 399.

[30] For example, 'Kurt and Willi on Russia', 25 June 1941; 'Kurt and Willi on the Coming Eastern Offensive and European Resistance', 8 June 1942; 'Kurt and Willi on Dissension in the High Command', 22 September 1942; 'Kurt and Willi on the Russian Winter', 8 December 1942.

'Zum Emigranten habe ich kein Talent': Stefan Zweig's Exile in London

Tatiana Liani

Stefan Zweig, the Austrian-Jewish writer of literary biographies and psychological novellas, enjoyed in the 1930s a worldwide literary reputation: in fact he was considered one of the most popular authors in the world. In 1933 he decided to leave his country and settle in Britain, where he remained until 1940. This paper follows the course of Stefan Zweig's life in Britain and attempts to shed light on several surprising facts about his exile.

Stefan Zweig, the world-famous Austrian-Jewish writer of biographies and novellas, arrived in London on 20 October 1933. He initially intended to finish his biography of Erasmus there, but after a two-month visit to Austria, he settled in Britain for what turned out to be no less than seven years. The primary aim of this article is to follow the course of Zweig's life in his exile in Britain through his own words in his autobiography, diaries and letters. It will also attempt to clarify the reasons for his voluntary and premature decision to leave Austria as early as 1933 and the surprising choice of Britain, the only European country where his books were not successful, at a time when, according to PEN' s records, he was the most translated author in the world. This paper, finally, aims also to shed light on the way historical events transformed Zweig from an 'emigré' into a 'refugee' and then into an 'enemy alien', and on how this process affected him and his feelings towards his adopted country.

   Zweig's first acquaintance with Britain dates back to a short visit to London in 1904; by that time he had already realized that he wanted travelling to be a part of his life: between 1901 and 1911 he visited more than 15 countries all over the world. He was very eager to meet new people, see new places and learn something about other cultures 'from the inside': so, in 1906, when he arrived in London for the second time, he was determined to stay for at least three weeks. But he was soon disapointed; in a letter to Ellen Key he wrote:

> Ich lebe hier in London ein wenig unwillig, weil ich die Sonne sehr gern habe und den düsteren Himmel wie einen Bleiring ums Herz empfinde. Auch habe ich wenig Menschen, die mir hier nahe stehen: es sind zu viel Kühle, Besonnene hier und zu wenig Herzliche.[1]

Zweig thought it was impossible to obtain a good knowledge of the world, as he fervently desired, without knowing better the country that had influenced half of it. However he found it extremely difficult to get used to the 'British way of life':

> [I]ch hatte – wie wir Kontinentalen alle – wenig literarischen Kontakt jenseits des Kanals, und bei allen Breakfast-Gesprächen und small talks in unserer kleinen Pension über Hof und Rennen und Parties fühlte ich mich jämmerlich unzuständig. [...] In London mußte ich mühsam suchen, was in Paris einem überflutend entgegenkommt: Geselligkeit, Kameradschaft und Heiterkeit. Ich fand niemanden, um die Dinge zu diskutieren, die mir die wichtigsten waren. [...] Nirgends gelang es mir, mich einem Milieu, einem Kreis innerlich zu verbinden.[2]

It seems only natural that Zweig did not return to this (both literally and metaphorically) 'cold' country for the next 27 years, during which he travelled around the world. By the spring of 1933, after Hitler's accession to power in January and the burning of the Reichstag in February showed clearly that it was only a matter of time before the National Socialists seized complete control of Germany, Zweig, a renowned pacifist and a great upholder of European unity, wrote to his friend Romain Rolland:

> Soll ich besser bleiben? Soll ich gehen? Bleiben bedeutet: leiden. Bedroht werden. Gezwungen sein, zu schweigen. Wie ein Gefangener leben. Gehen heißt: die anderen zurücklassen, die durch ihre Arbeit nicht das Glück materieller Unabhängigkeit genießen, das Schiff als Kapitän als erster zu verlassen. Aber Redefreiheit haben. [...] Ich glaube, ich werde mich zum Bleiben entscheiden. Wie immer (Italien, Russland und jetzt Deutschland) tun die Emigranten denen, die bleiben, schrecklich unrecht.[3]

In the same month he wrote to his friend Frans Masereel: 'Ich habe die stärkste Abneigung, Emigrant zu werden'.[4] But only one month later, in May 1933, although fully protected from the Nazis by his Austrian citizenship, he changed his mind:

> Ich bin innerlich darauf eingestellt wegzugehen. Innerlich habe ich mich von meinem Haus, meiner Sammlung, meinen Büchern verabschiedet – sollen sie all das nehmen, ich schere mich einen Dreck darum, im Gegenteil, ich werde viel freier sein, sobald dieses gelebte Leben nicht mehr auf meinen Schultern lastet. Eine neue Art zu leben verjüngt.[5]

By that time Zweig was not only one of the most famous writers in the world, but also the close friend of many intellectuals, who were always welcome in his Salzburg villa: Romain Rolland, Arturo Toscanini, Maurice Ravel, Maxim Gorki, Paul Valéry and many others. It is not a coincidence that most of them were Frenchmen – Zweig was a great francophile, who had begun his literary career as the translator of Baudelaire and Verlaine into German.

However, one month later, determined to leave Austria and exploring his options, he rejected the idea of France, precisely because he would be constantly surrounded by friends and colleagues; he wrote to Rolland:

> Und nun unter uns: ich bin fast sicher, daß ich Salzburg im Herbst verlassen werde. Es ist unmöglich, in diesem Milieu des Hasses zu leben, zwei Schritte von der deutschen Grenze entfernt. Ich weiß nur noch nicht, wie ich mich einrichten soll. Ich hätte Rom vorgezogen, aber leider – die Politik! Ich würde mich nicht gerne in der Schweiz einrichten, vor allem nicht in der deutschen Schweiz. Und in der Nähe von Paris fürchte ich, zu sehr in das Marktgeschrei gezogen zu werden.[6]

And in the same month, his first mention of Britain, in a letter to Joseph Gregor, in which complained about his lack of concentration: 'Ich brauche Gegengewichte wie Musik, Menschen, und am meisten lockt mich Rom oder London, ich möchte nur nicht in eine Emigrantenecke.'[7]

Indeed, four months later he chose London to work on his biography of Erasmus; his rather unpleasant memories of the reserved Englishmen assured him that London would afford him the privacy and anonymity he so longed for in order to concentrate on his work. Although he acted as if his stay in London was just a business trip, deep inside he might have felt that he had taken the first step towards exile. Contrary to his habits, he rented a small flat (11 Portland Place) just a few days after his arrival, not wanting to stay in a hotel, and enjoyed what he had rejected decades earlier:

> Nach einigen Tagen fühlte ich mich in London unbeschreiblich wohl. Nicht daß sich London wesentlich geändert hatte. Aber ich selbst hatte mich verändert. Ich war dreißig Jahre älter geworden und nach den Kriegs- und Nachkriegsjahren die Spannung und Überspannung voll Sehnsucht, einmal wieder ganz still zu leben und nicht Politisches zu hören. [...] Hier konnte man atmen, denken und überlegen.[8]

Even though Vienna was a city famous for its culture, in a letter to Hans Carossa he seemed extremely impressed by the British capital: 'Ich bin in Carthago, der schiffstüchtigen Hauptstadt der Welt. Aber hier ist das Parthenon und Egypten, hier Rom und Teheran in den Museen, hundert Städte in einer, eine verwirrende Welt.'[9]

The British Museum became his refuge once again: according to his letters he worked there every day until 3 in the afternoon, and then continued with his work at home. He wrote to Rolland: 'Gesegnet sei das British Museum, die schönste Bibliothek der Welt, wo man die politische Dummheit nicht zu spüren bekommt und man sich noch konzentrieren kann.'[10] In the British Museum he became interested in the story of Mary Stuart; when he left London six weeks later, in December, he was determined to return for the Mary Stuart project. He remained in Vienna, where he found a new publishing house, only for two months and then returned to his London flat. He made great progress with his new biography, but he still saw his stay in Britain as temporary; he intended to settle back in Austria and then travel around the world. But when he returned to Salzburg, in February 1934, he had to face the reality of the rise of Austro-fascism: four policemen woke him up early in the morning and informed him they had orders to search his house for weapons. The order was absurd, as it was well-known that Zweig fanatically avoided any political involvement: nevertheless the policemen searched the house, found nothing and left. Zweig, deeply insulted and disturbed, began to sort his papers. Two days later he travelled to London, determined to abandon his home forever; from there he wrote to Rolland that he was determined to remain in London whatever happened in Austria. Shortly after, he informed the authorities in Salzburg that he no longer lived there.

Until February 1934, Zweig was just a celebrity visitor to Britain. With this official letter he changed into an emigrant. Although his friends were unable to understand this decision ('Lieber! Du bist kein Emigrant, mach Dich nicht freiwillig dazu!', Csokor wrote to him some months later[11]) and despite the painful break-up with his long-time publisher Kippenberg, Zweig was at last content with his life after a long period of time. In his autobiography he wrote that this time he saw Britain with new eyes: 'Anders sieht man eine Stadt, in der man entschlossen ist zu bleiben, als eine, die man nur als Gast betritt.'[12] Nevertheless he did not feel an emigrant,[13] as he still had his Austrian passport and the freedom to visit Austria or the rest of the world whenever he wished to. ('So wenig wie seinerzeit Sorrent fur Gorkij, bedeutete England in den ersten Jahren für mich ein Exil. Österreich bestand weiter, [...] ich konnte zu jeder Stunde heimkehren, ich war nicht verbannt, nicht geachtet.')[14] He did not have to grapple with the bureaucracy nor with the financial problems that plagued other emigrants, as international royalties and lecture tours ensured his financial independence. Irmgard Keun, who met Zweig in Ostende, reported in her memoirs *Wenn wir alle gut wären* about his special position among the emigrants:

> Damals in Ostende ist er sicher von vielen armen kleinen
> Emigranten glühend beneidet worden. Seine Bücher waren in
> allen Ländern bekannt, geachtet und viel gekauft. In allen
> Ländern war er mit den namenhaftesten Männern bekannt und
> befreundet. Für ihn gab es keine verschlossenen Grenzen, keine
> Paß- und Visumschwierigkeiten. Er konnte stets leben, wo er
> wollte und wie er wollte.[15]

And it seemed that this time he really was living where he wanted
to; in a letter to Erich Ebermayer he sounds rather enthusiastic about his
choice:

> Ich habe mich [in London] ungewöhnlich wohlgefühlt und bin
> Paris in weitem Bogen ausgewichen. Es ist für mich eine Wohltat,
> nichts von dem innerlich doch ganz leeren und wertlosen
> Geschwätz über die Zeitfragen zu hören. Dort sah ich wenige
> Menschen, aber die besten: Shaw, Wells, Schalom Asch, die
> Galerien und viel Musik und arbeitete viel in der Bibliothek.
> Auch Novellen beginnen wieder zu entstehen, und ich habe das
> Gefühl, ad personam die Krise überwunden zu haben.[16]

He now felt, for the first time in many years, free, free from his
possessions, from his wife, from his friends and his literary circle in Austria,
free in a country where he could work quietly and escape the war sirens that
were to be heard across the rest of Europe. He always had contradictory
needs: he longed for human contact, for stimulating discussions with old and
new friends, and at the same time he yearned for solitude, for a peaceful
haven where he could dedicate himself to his work. This is why he had left
Vienna for Salzburg, why he left Austria for Britain, why he would later
leave London for Bath. But for the time being, London was his new home
and he would remain in a state of euphoria for the next two years. In a letter
to Joseph Roth in May he expressed vividly his 'Glück': 'Ich sage mir jeden
Morgen ein Dankgebet, daß ich frei, daß ich in England bin. Denken Sie sich
mein Glück, ich fühlte mich in einer solchen Irrsinnzeit stark genug, noch
andere moralisch aufzurichten'[17] and two months later he wrote to Richard
Strauss: 'Ich habe mich seit Jahren an keinem Ort besser gefühlt.'[18]

There was also a new woman in his life, his young secretary, Lotte
Altmann, who admired him greatly and gave him back his self-confidence,
which seemed to have suffered from his wife, Friderike's, independence and
her 'stubborn' decision to remain in Salzburg. As if to strengthen his belief
that he did the right thing in choosing London, his biography *Maria Stuart*,
which was published in 1935, finally earned him the success in his adopted
country which he had long enjoyed in the rest of the world. Not only did it
become a best seller in Britain, where the critics praised it, but by the end of

1936 it had become an international best-seller, having been published in more than 15 languages.

   Although his connections in the country remained limited[19] he developed a great respect for the English. In a letter to Rolland he wrote about their 'tiefes Gespür für Gerechtigkeit'[20] and in his autobiography he fondly mentioned their 'Loyalität', their 'Ehrlichkeit', their 'tiefe Kraft' and their 'Gutgläubigkeit'.[21] In 1935 Zweig travelled to the United States, where journalists attempted in vain to force him to make a statement against Hitler. His 'passive' attitude towards the events in Germany was criticized by many fellow-exiles. Nevertheless he still remained optimistic; on board the S. S. Manhattan he wrote to Hermann Hesse, once more mentioning the word 'Glück': '[M]ein Haus in Salzburg [...] ist mir nicht recht Heimat mehr, zum Emigranten habe ich kein Talent, so lebe ich jetzt beinahe studentisch, bald da, bald dort und spüre es beinahe als ein Glück, aus diesem sichern Behagen herausgestossen zu sein'.[22] Not even the ban of the Strauss opera *Die schweigsame Frau* for which he had written the libretto was able to ruin his mood, as he seemed to have expected the Nazis' reaction.

   After America, Zweig continued to travel, spending some time in Austria and in Switzerland, from where he wrote to Lotte about London:

> Ich verstehe es eigentlich selbst nicht, wie es mir mit dieser Stadt ergangen ist. Zuerst ließ sie mich gleichgültig [...]. Aber je mehr ich mich einlebte, [...] desto mehr entdeckte ich mir, ich liebte ihre Formen, ihre besondere Atmosphäre [...] und ich säße lieber dort als hier unter den schönsten Bergen.[23]

   After his return to London, he began searching for a new, bigger flat and he found it at 49 Hallam Street, where he moved in March 1936. He was now working on a new project, the biography of Sebastian Castellio, and once more dividing his time between the British Museum and his own study. In the spring he decided to accept the invitation to the international PEN – Club Congress and travel to South America in August. He enjoyed a royal reception in Rio and although he disliked public appearances, he made an exception and gave several lectures. This trip helped lift his spirits, after a quite difficult time when the burden of Salzburg and Friderike depressed him more and more. Back in Britain, he continued to live relatively withdrawn, and although he managed to build a relatively close relationship with his English publishers, Newman and Desmond Flower, his closest friends in London were fellow-exiles, such as Max Hermann-Neiße, Victor Fleischer and Robert Neumann. The days of euphoria were now gone: his book *Castellio gegen Calvin*, caused controversies even among the emigrants, and he himself was disappointed by his new publishing house in Austria and his

English translators Eden and Cedar Paul. His political pessimism deepened, as the situation in Germany deteriorated and the thought of his threatened friends oppressed him. His depression haunted him increasingly and he seemed tired of Britain; in April he wrote to Gisella Selden-Goth that he felt very strongly that '[der] Kanal England viel mehr vom Kontinent abtrennt, als die eine Stunde Wasser es vermuten ließe. Im letzten verstehen sie nichts von unseren Wünschen oder Sorgen und zum Gutteil deshalb, weil sie es nicht verstehen wollen'.[24]

The year 1937 was one of growing resignation for Zweig; the psychological pressures of exile, the estrangement, the constant insecurity, the loss of his cultural environment seemed unbearable: 'Die letzten vier Jahre zählen mir wie vierzig und haben mich innerlich um so viel älter gemacht', he wrote to Friderike.[25] In the beginning of the year he travelled to Italy, but not even his beloved country seemed to soothe him, as desperate letters from old acquaintances asking for his help reached him even there: 'es ist mir schrecklich, dieses Nein-Sagen und sich noch entschuldigen müssen.'[26] His friend Richard Friedenthal remembered a meeting during this time: 'Der kräftige Mann in der Mitte der Fünfziger, der noch kaum ein graues Haar aufwies, wirkte wie gebrochen.'[27] Although he published three new books with Reichner, and almost finished his first novel *Ungeduld des Herzens*, this year's letters were full of negative descriptions of his situation, such as 'tragisch', 'unerfreulich', 'schwer', 'Qual', 'erschöpft'.[28]

For a long time he had been pressuring his wife, Friderike, to sell their Salzburg villa, and when this happened in May, he took the first legal steps towards their separation. His indecisiveness caused great pain not only to his wife and to Lotte, but to himself too – he longed to break free from the chains of the past, but at the same time he felt like a tree losing its roots; in a letter to Friderike he acknowledges how much exile had changed him:

> Ich bin nicht mehr derselbe, ein menschenscheuer, ganz in sich zurückgezogener Mensch geworden, den eigentlich nur mehr die Arbeit freut. Du siehst, von wie viel ich Abschied genommen habe und ich weiß auch, daß es an mir liegt, wenn es um mich stiller und leerer wird; jener Schlag von Deutschland her hat uns alle tiefer getroffen als Du vermutest, und alles Festliche, Vergnügliche ist mir gespentisch fremd geworden[29].

The painful separation from his companion of 25 years, in addition to his increasing pessimism about the future, led him to one of the most intense crises of his life; he wrote to Joseph Roth: 'Dieses Jahr 37 ist ein schlimmes für mich, alles faßt mich mit Teufelsklauen an, die halbe Haut ist abgeschunden, und die Nerven liegen bloß […]' and he adds: '[F]ür unsereinen wäre es das Klügste, in Shanghai oder Madrid sich von einer

Gasbombe   auslöschen   zu   lassen   und   damit   vielleicht   einen
Lebensfreudigeren zu retten.'[30]

Even before Hitler's invasion of Austria, Zweig felt oppressed by
the optimism and naiveté of the English and by Chamberlain's policy of
'appeasement', and this only led to further isolation: 'Je mehr die politische
Spannung sich verschärfte, um so mehr zog ich mich darum von Gesprächen
zurück und von jeder öffentlichen Aktion.'[31] His withdrawn life in Britain
suited him, but at the same time disappointed him. He felt completely cut
off, as he had no access to publicity; in his autobiography he wrote:
'England ist das einzige Land der alten Welt, in dem ich nie einen Artikel
zeitgebundener Art in einer Zeitung veröffentlichte, nie im Radio
gesprochen, nie mich an einer öffentlichen Diskussion beteiligt habe.'[32]

At the end of 1936 Zweig travelled to Vienna and saw his mother for
what turned out to be the last time. Three months later Austria's annexation
to Germany was completed. With Austria's *Anschluss* the period of Zweig's
'Halbexil', as he called it,[33] came to an end, and the even bitterer period of
'Exil' began. Austria's annexation meant not only the loss of his home
country and the confiscation of his property, but also the loss of his last
chance to be read in his own language. In contrast to some of his fellow
exiles, like Robert Neumann or Hilde Spiel, he felt unable to write in
English: 'Da wir unsern "Markt" verloren haben, unser Publikum uns
gestohlen worden ist, materiell nur der englische Markt gilt, müßte man
versuchen, sich dem angelsächsischen Geschmack bewußt anzupassen, was
ich nicht kann, und Sie wahrscheinlich ebenso wenig,'[34] we read in a letter to
Rene Schickele, while to Lavinia Mazzucchetti he wrote that he had 'ein
Gefühl, als schriebe ich Deutsch ins Leere'.[35] The realization that he had lost
the reading public, with whom he shared a common language and cultural
heritage, and his linguistic isolation, deepened his despair and his frustration.

The fall of Austria also meant that Zweig's Jewish friends and
relatives in Vienna were lost – he was overwhelmed by terrible feelings,
among them feelings of guilt for being safe in London: 'Diese Tage, da
täglich die Hilfeschreie aus der Heimat gellten, da man nächste Freunde
verschleppt, gefoltert und erniedrigt wußte und für jeden hilflos zitterte, den
man liebte, gehören für mich zu den furchtbarsten meines Lebens.'[36] The
death of his mother in Vienna came as a relief; in the meantime he turned his
home at Hallam Street into a 'Wohlfahrtsbüro',[37] and tried to help and
support as many Austrians as he could. The devastated people he had to
confront and the realization of how limited the help he could offer, made
him even more dejected.

In addition to all this, he had to face problems of his own as well:
Austria's Anschluss deprived him of his nationality and his Austrian

passport, he was now 'staatenlos'. He always had an aversion to bureaucracy, but waiting for hours in lines to beg for a British 'Fremdenpapier', undermined his self-esteem and made him feel deprived of his dignity: '[I]ch, der einstige Kosmopolit, [habe] heute unablässig das Gefühl, als müßte ich jetzt für jeden Atemzug Luft besonders danken, den ich einem fremden Volke wegtrinke.'[38] His self-confidence was shattered:

> Über Nacht war ich abermals eine Stufe hinuntergeglitten. Gestern noch ausländischer Gast und gewissermaßen Gentleman, der hier sein internationales Einkommen verausgabte und seine Steuern bezahlte, war ich Emigrant geworden, ein "Refugee". Ich war in eine mindere, wenn auch nicht unehrenhafte Kategorie hinabgedrückt.[39]

The publication of his new biography, *Magellan*, was overshadowed by his official divorce from Friderike, and his application for British naturalization,[40] which he could not receive for another year. His feelings towards Britain seemed to have altered significantly, although his respect for it remained: in August he wrote to Felix Braun 'Ich leide sehr unter England, weil es uninspirativ ist, ermüdend, entschwindend, unsinnlich und ganz in Sport und Gleichgiltigkeit vernarrt – aber ich bin doch dankbar, hier sein zu dürfen'[41] and two months later to Lavinia Mazzucchetti: 'Ich weiß nicht warum, aber seit der allerletzten Zeit ist mir England nicht mehr das, was es gewesen ist, und ich bedaure fast, daß ich nicht auch gleich in den anderen Weltteil hinübergesprungen bin.'[42] At the end of the year he left for the USA for a lecture tour in 30 cities. Two months later he wrote to Gisella Selden-Goth from San Francisco that he planned to return to Europe on 3 March 1939, 'wahrscheinlich der größte Unsinn, den ich begehen kann'.[43]

Immediately after his return to London, the news that the Germans had invaded Prague exacerbated his depression. As politics intruded on his life, his defeatism increased, and he seemed tired of helping other people: 'Gewiss, es rechtfertigt im ganzen meine Existenz und ihre bisherige Haltung, daß soviele Leute sich an mich wenden, aber dieses Vertrauen ist zur Zeit eine Höllenpein; es verätzt mir wie Vitriol die Seele'.[44] The letters of this period are full of complaints and self-pity; in June he wrote to Albert Einstein: 'Täglich ist mein Morgengebet: Herr, mache mich egoistisch und siehe zu, daß ich meinen Tag nicht ausschließlich an andere Menschen verliere'.[45] Wishing to avoid the crowd and concentrate at last on his work he chose to leave London in July and seek a peaceful asylum in the beautiful little town of Bath, an 'Ersatz–Salzburg'.[46] He rented a room at Lansdown Lodge with Lotte and began to work on his 'Big Balzac', as he called the extensive biography he thought would be the pinnacle of his work. The summer was extremely sunny, Zweig spent a great deal of time outdoors hiking and for a brief period he seemed happy. His happiness though would not last long: on 1 September Germany invaded Poland, two days later Great Britain declared war on Germany.

Zweig began to keep a daily diary again, a 'war diary', this time in English:

> 1 September 1939 [S]uddenly one clerk, hastily passing says that Germany has started war on Poland this morning. And now we have a unique opportunity to admire the nerves of the English. [...] The whole town is not at all changed. Nobody hurries or seems excited, everything goes smoothly and quietly.[47]

On 3 September, with Britain's declaration of war on Germany, Zweig reflected:

> Now begins another life for me, being no more free and independent. I regret only to have no opportunity to write as I am unable to do it in English and have nobody here to rectify my mistakes and to give more colour to what I want to say; that's what oppresses me most, that I am so imprisoned in a language, which I cannot use.[48]

One day later he and Lotte were branded 'enemy aliens'; they were denied the status of a 'friendly enemy alien' and received 'Grade B', which meant 'exempt from internment, but subject to restrictions': 'Wieder war ich eine Stufe herabgefallen, seit einer Stunde nicht bloss der Fremde mehr in diesem Land, sondern ein "enemy alien", ein feindlicher Ausländer; gewaltsam verbannt an eine Stelle, an der mein pochendes Herz nicht stand.'[49] Nevertheless he expressed his hope that they would be granted their naturalization soon as 'there are certain indications to it'.[50] On the 6 September he married Lotte in order to protect her, and he concluded negotiations to buy a house in Bath – he was determined to leave London which was for him 'verdorben, seit es mit Wiener und Prager Gespenstern überfüllt ist',[51] and settle in the country, where he could work undisturbed. As he always tended to avoid fanatically any political involvement and preferred to withdraw into the privacy of his work, he had been extremely productive during his exile years: from 1934 to 1939 he had published seven books.

He spent the following days speculating about the war and finding consolation in the beauty of nature until, on the 14th, he was informed that his naturalization would take time; he was frustrated, and felt resentful towards Britain; in his diary he noted:

> I will try now to get out of here, to France, to Sweden or
> wherever else. This state of things, to have to report to the police
> if one wants to go somewhere for a day is really a shame in my
> age and in my position. I must finish with my modesty and seek to
> avoid such humiliations.[52]

He would feel this 'shame' even more ten days later, when he had difficulty
getting permission to visit London for Sigmund Freud's funeral:

> I will of course go to the funeral. But I feel again my isolation in
> this country – I have no newspaper to write a few words, no
> opportunity to let say something and this after six years in
> Britain. In such moments and in such alone I regret not to have
> gone to another country – but now I have no more choice, I have
> to stay where I am.[53]

His self-respect suffered from this feeling that he was completely 'nutzlos',[54]
in contrast to his friends in France or in other neutral countries who actively
contributed to anti-Nazi propaganda. On 17 October, the day the 'real' war
began with German bombers near Edinburgh, we read his last entry in his
diary: 'Day of depression'.[55]

Despite his reservations, his novel *Ungeduld des Herzens* became a
great success in Britain – which made him feel more intensely how unfair his
treatment by the British authorities was. He had long been feeling like an
enemy in the country, perceived his situation as 'gefährlich'[56] and
'bedrohlich'[57] and started taking precautions; his fear impelled him to a
peculiar self-censorship; he asked his American publisher Ben Huebsch to
change some words in the English edition of his essay *Charles Dickens*:
instead of 'British hypocrisy' he asked him to use the term 'British
conscience', instead of 'for us Germans' the term 'us Continentals' etc.[58] He
also started asking his British acquaintances to speak on his behalf, but he
would not receive his British naturalization until 12 March 1940.

His former wife, Friderike, who managed to escape to France,
sensed his deep depression and organized some lectures for him in Paris,
where he travelled immediately after his British naturalization. He stayed in
his beloved city for three weeks and spoke in a packed theatre on 'Das Wien
von gestern', a prelude to the autobiography he had decided to write;
immediately after his return to Bath he wrote to Max Herrmann-Neiße:

> Die Stadt heiter und sorglos, interessiert in Theater und Kunst,
> ich selbst, der Verschollene, war auf einmal wieder ein Autor und
> las vor 1.600 Leuten im Theater und dann mehrmals im Radio
> [...], ich sah Freunde und speiste und trank vortrefflich – man
> *vergass* für einen Augenblick das Grauen.[59]

But once back in Britain, he fell back into depression at the news of the invasion of Belgium and Holland, events which went far beyond his worst predictions. The loss of four of his friends – Roth, Toller, Freud and Schickele – in one year, the thousands of refugees who fled into the country really took their toll on him. He now considered it his duty to remain in Britain, seeing the abandonment of Europe as an 'intellectual treason'.[60] In May he started keeping a new 'Notebook war 1940' for a month; as the Germans forces marched and occupied his beloved Europe, he wrote constantly about his dark feelings concerning the future. He saw the fall of France as inevitable and was frightened about his future in a post-war Britain:

> Ich leide schwer unter meiner vorausdenkenden Phantasie; ich sehe jetzt schon in zuckenden Umrissen die Nachkriegsepoche hier in England mit ihrer ausbrechenden Erbitterung, die sich – abermals – gegen uns kehren wird, sei es in der einen Form als Ausländer oder der anderen als Juden.[61]

Again he started thinking about leaving the country, about settling in America, as he was very pessimistic about Britain's future, but remarked many times that he was too old, too tired to begin a new life elsewhere: 'Und doch, ich habe – ist es Trägheit, Mut oder Treue – keine rechte Lust zu fliehen.'[62] Nevertheless, some days after the tragic news of the fall of Paris he departed for a lecture tour in South America via New York. He was determined to return to Bath where he left valuable manuscripts and all his papers on Balzac; to Max Herrmann-Neiße he wrote that he hoped to be back in the autumn 'denn bleiben kann und will ich dort nicht. Solange es Europa gibt (es wird immer kleiner), möchte ich mich daran ankrallen',[63] and to Thomas Mann: 'Ich bin eigentlich entschlossen, nach England zurückzukehren [...]. Ist es in England halbwegs möglich trotz deutscher Sprachzugehörigkeit und jüdischer Belastung zu leben [...], so werde ich es tun.'[64] This is his last mention of his intention to return to Europe. The flood of European emigrants that overwhelmed New York (among them Friderike Zweig) and some lecture invitations led him to Brazil, where he felt blessed by the beauty of its nature and the warmth of its people. It is there that he wrote *Schachnovelle* and *Die Welt von gestern*, which are today considered his finest works.

As it became clear that a return to Britain would be extremely dangerous, if not impossible – 'Eine Rückfahrt nach England, die ich erhofft hatte, ist in diesem Augenblick technisch unmöglich, denn auf Monate hinaus sind keine Schiffsplätze zu bekommen'[65] – he settled in Petropolis, a quiet Brazilian town, where he seemed to find peace for a while: in

November 1941 he wrote to Ben Huebsch: 'Wir denken keinesfalls an Rückkehr. Ich habe selten in meinem Leben so angenehm verschollen gelebt.'[66] Three months later the burden of exile seemed too heavy to carry;[67] in the farewell 'Declaracao' he left before commiting suicide together with his wife, he wrote: 'Ich grüße alle meine Freunde! Mögen sie die Morgenröte noch sehen nach der langen Nacht! Ich, allzu Ungeduldiger, gehe Ihnen voraus.'[68]

'Keiner unter allen Emigranten war weniger Emigrant als dieser wirkliche Weltbürger, der in den Ländern des Exils zu Hause war, ehe es noch ein Exil gab',[69] wrote Franz Werfel of Zweig. And it is truly ironic that he seemed to possess all the prerequisities of a successful life in exile: he had travelled widely, spoke five languages, had many friends and contacts all over the world and he was extremely wealthy. But the fear that Hitler would win the war, the prospect of many more years in exile, his feelings of rootlessness, of estrangement from his native language, were devastating: his roots ran deep in Austrian culture and as he wrote to Max Herrmann-Neiße: 'alte Bäume verdorren, wenn man sie umpflanzt'.[70]

Notes

[1] Stefan Zweig, *Briefe 1897-1914* (Frankfurt: Fischer, 1995), p. 117.

[2] Stefan Zweig, *Die Welt von gestern* (Frankfurt: Fischer, 2000), pp. 184-85.

[3] Stefan Zweig, *Briefe 1932-1942* (Frankfurt: Fischer, 2005), p. 416.

[4] Stefan Zweig, *Briefe an Freunde* (Frankfurt: Fischer, 1978), p. 227.

[5] Zweig to Romain Rolland, *Briefe 1932-1942,* p. 426.

[6] *Ibid*, p. 432.

[7] Cited by Donald Prater, *Das Leben eines Ungeduldigen* (Munich/Vienna: Hanser, 1982), p. 298. Zweig described as 'Emigrantenecken' the four most popular destinations for German emigrants, Holland, France, Czechoslovakia and especially Switzerland, the country which already harboured Alfred Döblin, Emil Ludwig and Erich Maria Remarque.

[8] *Die Welt von gestern*, p. 431.

[9] *Briefe an Freunde*, p. 239.

[10] *Briefe 1932-1942*, p. 467.

[11] *Das Leben eines Ungeduldigen*, p. 314.

[12] *Die Welt von gestern*, p. 441.

[13] His voluntary exile clearly differentiates Zweig from the Germans who left their country to escape imprisonment or even death. The majority of them rejected the term 'Emigranten' (a term used by the Nazis), and considered themselves 'Exilanten', as they had not left their homeland voluntarily (see B. Brecht's poem 'Über die Bezeichnung Emigranten').

[14] *Die Welt von gestern*, p. 441.

[15] Irmgard Keun, 'Stefan Zweig, der Emigrant', in *Der große Europäer Stefan Zweig*, ed. by Hanns Arens (Frankfurt: Fischer, 1981) pp. 99-100 (p. 100).

[16] *Briefe 1932-1942*, p. 244.

[17] *Briefe an Freunde*, p. 247.

[18] *Das Leben eines Ungeduldigen*, p. 315.

[19] Zweig knew H. G.Wells and George Bernard Shaw and he met occasionally with John Drinkwater, Joseph Leftwich and Hugh Walpole, but none of them counted among his intimates.

[20] *Briefe 1932-1942*, p. 479.

[21] *Die Welt von gestern*, pp. 443-44, 467.

[22] *Briefe an Freunde*, p. 264.

[23] Cited by Donald Prater, *Das Leben eines Ungeduldigen*, p. 337. This letter is part of Zweig's 'Nachlass' in London.

[24] *Briefe 1932-1942*, p. 160.

[25] *Das Leben eines Ungeduldigen*, p. 355.

[26] Stefan Zweig – Friderike Zweig, *Ein Briefwechsel* (Bern: Scherz, 1951), p.306.

[27] *Das Leben eines Ungeduldigen*, p. 356.

[28] *Briefe an Freunde*, pp. 281, 283.

[29] *Ein Briefwechsel*, p. 313.

[30] *Briefe an Freunde*, p. 284.

[31] *Die Welt von gestern*, p. 444.

[32] *Ibid.*

[33] *Ibid*, p. 443.

[34] *Briefe an Freunde*, p. 289.

[35] *Das Leben eines Ungeduldigen*, p. 366.

[36] *Die Welt von gestern*, p. 459.

[37] See: *Das Leben eines Ungeduldigen*, p. 367.

[38] *Die Welt von gestern*, p. 468.

[39] *Ibid*, p. 462.

[40] The urgent need to apply for British naturalization, being now stateless, must have been another blow to Zweig's self-esteem, as only a few months earlier he wrote to Rolland that he did not even think of becoming an English citizen, as he did not like London at all (see: Romain Rolland-Stefan Zweig, *Briefwechsel 1910-1940 II* (Berlin: Rütten & Loening, 1987), pp. 677-78).

[41] *Briefe 1932-1942*, p. 230.

[42] *Ibid*, p. 235.

[43] *Das Leben eines Ungeduldigen*, p. 373.

[44] Letter to Felix Braun, *Briefe 1932-1942*, p. 254.

[45] *Das Leben eines Ungeduldigen*, p. 376.

[46] *Briefe 1932-1942*, p. 248.

[47] Stefan Zweig, *Tagebücher* (Frankfurt: Fischer 1984), p. 415.

[48] *Ibid*, p. 418.

[49] *Die Welt von gestern*, p. 491.

[50] *Tagebücher*, p. 420.

[51] *Briefe 1932-1942*, p. 257.

[52] *Tagebücher*, p. 425.

[53] *Ibid*, p. 429.

[54] Letter to Felix Braun, *Briefe an Freunde*, p. 304.

[55] *Tagebücher*, p. 431.

[56] Letter to Felix Braun, *Briefe an Freunde*, p. 307.

[57] Letter to Felix Braun, *ibid*, p. 310.

[58] *Briefe 1932-1942*, p. 246.

[59] *Briefe an Freunde*, p. 312.

[60] Zweig to Hermann Kesten; cited by Richard Dove in his excellent study *Journey of no return. Five German-speaking literary exiles in Britain, 1933-1945* (London: Libris, 2000), p. 187.

[61] *Tagebücher*, p. 456-57.

[62] *Ibid*, p. 460.

[63] *Briefe an Freunde*, p. 314.

[64] *Ibid*, p. 318.

[65] Letter to Richard Friedenthal, *ibid*, p. 325.

[66] *Briefe 1932-1942*, p. 324.

[67] See: Rosi Cohen, 'Emigration: a contribution factor to Stefan Zweig's suicide', in *The World of Yesterday's Humanist Today*, ed. by Marion Sonnenfeld (New York: State University of New York Press, 1983), pp. 254-61.

[68] *Briefe 1932-1942*, p. 345.

[69] Franz Werfel, 'Stefan Zweigs Tod' in *Der große Europäer Stefan Zweig,* pp. 148-155 (p. 150).

[70] *Briefe an Freunde*, p. 314.

Exil, Judentum und Sprache in ausgewählten Nachlass-Aufzeichnungen von Elias Canetti

Anne Peiter

Anhand unveröffentlichter Nachlassaufzeichnungen, die in der Züricher Zentralbibliothek aufbewahrt werden, zeige ich das ambivalente Verhältnis, das Elias Canetti zum Exil unterhielt. Auf der einen Seite betrachtete er den Verlust einer deutschsprachigen Umgebung als Chance, die sein paradoxes Verhältnis zum Judentum festige; auf der anderen Seite zieht sich die Angst vor einer Einschränkung des erzählerischen Atems durch seine Notizen.

„Ich habe eine unüberwindliche Scheu davor, mich mit der Zeit zu befassen, an deren zermürbenden Nachwirkungen meine Frau gestorben ist."[1] Mit diesen Worten lehnte Canetti im Jahre 1970 die Bitte Victor Suchys ab, sich an einer Veranstaltung über die „Psychologie des Exils" zu beteiligen. In Anbetracht der Erfahrungen, die Canetti in seinem posthum veröffentlichten Buch *Party im Blitz*, das seine „englischen Jahre" zum Gegenstand hat, beschreibt, ist diese Aussage überraschend. Zwar kommen hier der Hunger und die Abhängigkeit zur Sprache, unter denen das Ehepaar Canetti nach seiner Evakuierung aus London im Haushalt eines geizigen Pfarrers litt, doch ist der Gestus dieses erst Anfang der 90er Jahre entstandenen Manuskripts von einem gewissen Stolz geprägt: dem Stolz, wie die englische Bevölkerung den deutschen Bomben getrotzt und den Mut zum Widerstand nicht verloren zu haben. Wenn man hingegen ein Bild von den inneren Konflikten gewinnen möchte, die Elias Canettis Schreiben im Exil offenbar nicht weniger als das seiner Frau begleiteten, muss man sich in seinem Nachlass umtun.[2] Die Materialien, die ich im Folgenden vorstellen möchte, sind, sofern nicht ausdrücklich auf die Buchtitel hingewiesen wird, sämtlich unveröffentlicht. Vorauszuschicken ist, dass Canetti eine sehr strenge Auswahl vornahm, als er die Publikation seiner *Aufzeichnungen* vorbereitete. Diese hatten seine jahrzehntelange Arbeit an der „poetischen Anthropologie" *Masse und Macht* begleitet und galten ihm als Ventil, um bei aller Konzentration auf das Hauptwerk nicht der Erstarrung zu verfallen. Wenn ich im Folgenden eine Auswahl aus *den* Aufzeichnungen vorstelle, die Canetti in seinen Büchern *nicht* berücksichtigt hat, verfolge ich die Absicht, die Bedeutung zu zeigen, die das Thema des Exils für Canetti quer durch die Jahrzehnte gehabt hat. Zwar finden sich auch in der *Provinz des Menschen* mehrfach Reflexionen zum Exil, doch sind viele unveröffentlichten Zitate insofern neuartig, als eine starke Ambivalenz aus ihnen spricht.

Obwohl Canetti die Notizen, die den Schreibprozess an anderen Büchern begleiteten, einheitlich als *Aufzeichnungen* bezeichnet hat, sind sie formal sehr unterschiedlich. Sie umfassen sowohl Aphorismen im engeren Sinne, als auch Ideenskizzen, die durch ihre Nähe zu Canettis Konzeption des „dramatischen Grundeinfalls" zum Kern eines Theaterstückes hätten werden können, als auch längere Reflexionen zu zentralen Themen des canettischen Werkes wie Tod, Verwandlung und Massenpsychologie. Charakteristisch für die unveröffentlichten Aufzeichnungen ist, dass sie dem leichtfertigen Behagen entgegenwirken, mit dem viele Leser der Autobiographie Canettis Eintreten für die deutsche Sprache Beifall spendeten, ohne sich den schmerzlichen Prozess bewusst zu machen, dem sich seine Haltung verdankt.

Elias Canetti, 1905 in Bulgarien als Sohn spaniolischsprachiger Eltern geboren, siedelte im Jahr 1911 mit seiner Familie nach Manchester über, wo das Englische zu seiner Hauptsprache wurde. Der Wechsel des 8jährigen, polyglott aufwachsenden Kindes zum Deutschen ist oft kommentiert worden. In meinem Kontext ist allein die Tatsache von Bedeutung, dass Canetti Wien in dem Bewusstsein verließ, dass er, der durch die Übersetzung von Büchern Upton Sinclairs seine Kenntnisse frisch gehalten hatte, in England nicht mit den sprachlichen Barrieren konfrontiert sein würde, die viele andere Emigranten zu fürchten hatten. Vor dem Hintergrund dieser privilegierten Situation interessiert mich die Frage, wie die Emigration und der Verlust einer deutschsprachigen Umgebung Canettis Sicht auf das Judentum beeinflusst haben und wie diese sich wiederum in seinem Werk niederschlägt. Dabei werde ich zeigen, dass das Festhalten am Deutschen sich einem paradoxen Blick auf die Möglichkeiten jüdischer Existenz nach der Shoah verdankt und für Canetti ebensowenig eine Selbstverständlichkeit darstellt wie für andere deutschsprachige, jüdische Exilautoren.

Im Juli 1929 denkt Canetti ausgerechnet während eines *Berlin*aufenthaltes über sein Verhältnis zur *Schweiz* nach. Als Junge habe er „jede Äußerung dieses Volkes abgöttisch geliebt",[3] gesteht er. Ein starkes Gefühl von Zugehörigkeit und Identifizierung – die nicht zuletzt eine Übernahme des Schweizerdeutschen bewirkte – treten hervor. Doch im darauffolgenden Satz wird deutlich, dass sich Canetti nicht einfach an eine der Heimaten seiner Jugend erinnert, sondern dass er in Auseinandersetzung ist mit dem antisemitischen Stereotyp des wandernden, heimatlosen Juden: „Vielleicht wird man mir Mangel an Heimatgefühl zum Vorwurf machen. Das verdien ich nicht. Ich gebe zu, *dass* ich kein Vaterland habe, mein Vater schon war entwurzelt und hatte nichts von einem Türken an sich. Aber jedes Land noch, in das ich kam, begann ich bald zu lieben, der starke Geschmack

der Erde schlägt einem überall entgegen.“[4] Der Versuch, Vaterlandsliebe
und heimatliche Zugehörigkeit zusammenzudenken, hat beim 24jährigen
Canetti insofern einen defensiven Klang, als dass er mit dem Hinweis auf
den „starken *Geruch* der Erde" noch auf das Vokabular derer zu reagieren
scheint, die Karl Kraus als antisemitische „Blubostándige", d. h. als
Ideologen des Blut-und-Boden-Mythos gegeißelt hatte. Mit der Flucht aus
Wien im November 1938 entwickelt Canetti jedoch ein Verhältnis zum
Judentum, das immer klarer und selbstbewusster den Kosmopolitismus
betont, der wesentlichen Anteil an der Geschichte der Juden habe. Die
eigene Vertreibung gewinnt daher schrittweise positive Züge. Am 15.
August 1939, kein ganzes Jahr nach seiner Ankunft in London, notiert
Canetti:

> Es ist ein außerordentliches Glück, aus einer langsam sich
> abzeichnenden Heimatbahn herausgeschleudert zu werden. Ich
> war fast ein Bauer, jetzt bin ich wieder Zigeuner, o die triefende
> feuchte trockene immer wechselnde Planke unter meinen Wegen,
> fremde Laute, fremde Polizei und der Himmel rot von Raketen![5]

Zwar spielt Canetti auf die Unsicherheit und Bedrohung an, die seinen
späten Weg ins Exil kennzeichneten – nur eine Planke hat ihm, der wie ein
Schiffbrüchiger das rettende Ufer zu erreichen suchte, Halt geboten –, doch
ist zugleich klar, dass die fremde Sprache und vielleicht sogar auch die
fremde Polizei als Schutz vor den Gewalttaten erlebt werden, die mit SA und
Gestapo in Österreich Einzug gehalten hatten.

Am gleichen Tag, an dem Canetti das Herausgeschleudertwerden
aus dem Gewohnten als Chance bezeichnet, denkt er jedoch auch darüber
nach, was es bedeutet, als Schreibender nicht länger von der Muttersprache
umgeben zu sein: „Wie verlernt man eine Sprache? (das wäre auf das
Genaueste, in jeder Phase, zu untersuchen, und den allmählichen Verlusten
wäre überallhin nachzuspüren).“[6] Dass Canetti schreibt, er wolle ihnen
„überallhin" nachspüren, *folgen*, heißt implizit, dass auch die zunehmende
sprachliche Unsicherheit neue Wege ins Unbekannte zu öffnen vermag.
Zugleich sieht er sich jedoch vor dem Problem, dass mit den Zweifeln das
Schreiben in eine Krise geraten kann: „Ich beginne um mein Deutsch zu
fürchten; es trocknet langsam aus, es hat keine Luft; werde ich wenn ich
Glück habe, nun schon in der Mitte meines Lebens, noch in einer andern
Sprache so voll atmen dürfen?“[7] Diese Aufzeichnung vom Juli/August 1941
zeigt, dass Canetti – wie seine Frau[8] – durchaus die Möglichkeit erwog, in
einer anderen Sprache als der deutschen zu schreiben. Vor kurzem ist ein
Text mit dem Titel „Proust, Kafka, Joyce" wiederentdeckt worden, den
Canetti im Jahre 1948 in englischer Sprache verfasste und vortrug.[9] Dennoch

scheint ihn der Atem, der mit der neuen Sprache in ihn einging, um sodann wieder, neu und in Worte verwandelt, aus ihm herauszugehen, nicht wirklich befriedigt zu haben. Am 16. Juli 1942 prognostiziert er wiederum den Wechsel hin zu einer anderen sprachlichen Luft: „Ich werde einmal englische oder spanische oder gar slawische Gedichte schreiben; die deutschen habe ich erwürgt."[10] Wenn man bedenkt, dass Canetti am Tag zuvor in Vorwegnahme des bekannten adornoschen Verdikts den Gedanken festhält „Die Sprache, in der man zu ernst geworden ist, erlaubt einem kein Gedicht",[11] muss die Präferenz für das Englische, Spaniolische oder Slawische als unmittelbare Konsequenz der sich immer deutlicher abzeichnenden, tödlichen Ausgrenzung der jüdischen Bevölkerung im von deutschen Truppen besetzten Europa interpretiert werden. Zwar beginnt Canetti ab 1942, sogenannte *Aufzeichnungs*-Hefte in deutscher Sprache zu führen, denen er – wie schon erwähnt – eine Ventilfunktion für die immer wieder stockende Arbeit an *Masse und Macht* zuspricht, doch tritt das Gedichteschreiben in der Tat weitgehend zurück. So ist es nur konsequent, dass Canetti den alltäglichen Umgang mit dem Englischen, das sein Deutsch mitstrukturiert, quantitativ zu steigern wünscht: „Ein kleines Land, in dem die streitenden Sprachen der Welt schon immer zu Hause sind, also eine Schweiz mit noch englischen, spanischen und russischen Kantonen wäre das ideale Refugium des Geistes", notiert er am 22. März 1941.[12] An dieser Stelle wird deutlich, dass Canetti trotz aller politischen Abgrenzungsversuche weiterhin unter dem Einfluss von Karl Kraus steht. Sprache und Sache, Wort und Wirklichkeit als unmittelbar zusammengehörig betrachtend, ist er offenbar der Überzeugung, dass die Opposition von Sprachen den kriegerischen Fanatismus der europäischen Nationalstaaten verstärkt. Wenn der Exilierte sein Refugium inmitten mehrerer, gleichberechtigter Sprachen sieht und die Zugehörigeit zu ihnen allen als Utopie des Friedens präsentiert, wertet er den Verlust der deutschsprachigen Umgebung erneut als positiv. Deutsch in einer englischen Umwelt zu schreiben, heißt, die sprachlich definierte Kategorisierung von Freund und Feind und damit auch den Krieg selbst zu unterlaufen.

1943 wird in der *Provinz des Menschen*, d. h. in einem der großen Aufzeichnungsbände, hingegen betont, besonders der Dramatiker leide unter dem fehlenden Kontakt zur Muttersprache. Er sei „nach mehr als einer Richtung hin ernsthaft geschwächt. Aus seiner sprachlichen Luft entfernt, entbehrt er die vertraute Nahrung der Namen. Er mochte früher die Namen, die er täglich hörte, gar nicht beachten; doch sie beachteten ihn und riefen ihn rund und sicher."[13] Ähnlich wie in seiner Rede zu Brochs 50. Geburtstag[14] unterscheidet Canetti unterschiedliche Atemräume. Während die sprachliche Heimat es dem Dramatiker erlaubt, sich finden zu lassen,

d. h. die umgebenden Namen einfach nur einzuatmen, ringt er im Exil nach Atem, holt er mühsam Luft, um neue Worte zu formen. Die Häufigkeit, mit der die *Aufzeichnungen* um das Thema des Atems kreisen, verdeutlichen den Einfluss des Weltkriegsdramas *Die letzten Tage der Menschheit*, in dem Karl Kraus die historische Zäsur, die mit den Giftgasangriffen des Ersten Weltkriegs markiert wurde, klar benennt. Jetzt, im Jahre 1943, wirken Canettis Reflexionen über Luft und Exil, Atem und Sprache ihrerseits unheimlich, weil mit den Gaskammern die Vielfalt der Atemräume erstickt und die Namen der Juden massenhaft ausgelöscht werden. Das feinnervige Empfinden, erneut werde Macht durch die Beschneidung des Atmens demonstriert, stellt jedoch nur eine Schicht in Canettis Aufzeichnungen dar. In einer Nachlass-Aufzeichnung kommt auch die Konsequenz zur Sprache, die sich aus der Abwesenheit vertrauter Namen und Orte ergibt:

> Die warmen Landkarten von Wien; vertraute Namen; begonnene oder für später aufgehobene Wege; Häuser als winzige Striche, kompakt und noch nicht zerstört; verschwundene Bäche, Weinberge, Beethovens Gang; Dörfer noch in der Stadt, ein Name wie Nussdorf, und Heiligenstadt daneben.[15]

Namen bezeichnen hier Räume, die durch ihre Ferne eine fast mythische Dimension bekommen. Nach Hans Blumenberg sind Namen, die stets das erste gewesen seien, zugleich auch das letzte, das noch da sei, wenn die einzelnen Geschichten bereits vergessen seien.[16] Namen gewinnen also in dem Maße an Bedeutung, in dem die Erinnerung an die Orte von einst undeutlich wird. Dass der Autor, der mit dem Roman *Die Blendung* nach Alban Berg ein „Epos des Hasses" geschaffen hatte, nun zunehmend die Schönheiten der deutschen Sprache in den Vordergrund zu stellen beginnt, ist für ihn selbst überraschend:

> Manche Worte des Deutschen werden mir jetzt schön und schöner. Ich sage ruhig „Sehnsucht". Ich dehne das Wort, ich lasse es nochmals vorübergleiten, wenn es, viel zu rasch, zu Ende gegangen. Es gibt vieles im Deutschen, das so schön ist wie Sehnsucht und ich beginne es langsam zu wissen. Ein Schamgefühl hat mir das Schöne versagt, solange ich es von grellen und hässlichen, von triefenden, kleinen, von vollen, von jedermanns Lippen hören konnte. Nun sind sie verstummt, es ist zu weit, nicht einmal ihr Chor erreicht mich.[17]

Auf der einen Seite zeigt das Wort „Sehnsucht", dass für Canetti die Integration nicht so leicht war, wie angesichts seiner Vielsprachigkeit oft angenommen wurde. Auf der anderen Seite macht er klar, dass die Ferne der willfährigen, österreichischen Jedermanns als Glück erlebt wird. Die

Schönheiten der deutschen Sprache hatten nur darum keinen Widerhall finden können, weil die Sprache missbraucht und auf die blinde Zustimmung von Sprechchören reduziert worden war.

   Das Exil vermittelt, weil der Vertriebene sich hier als individueller, vom alltäglichen Sprachgebrauch gelöster Sprecher erfahren muss und darf, das Gefühl der *Verantwortung* für diese Sprache. Wenn Canetti 1945 in der *Provinz des Menschen* schreibt, er sei den Deutschen ihre Sprache schuldig, denn er habe sie sauber gehalten, bewahrt er ähnlich wie Kraus die Hoffnung, die Sprache habe Anteil an der Beendigung und Verhinderung von Gewalt.

> Damals schien es ihm noch von keiner tieferen Bedeutung, daß er in dieser deutschen Sprache dachte und schrieb. In einer anderen Sprache hätte er dasselbe gefunden, der Zufall hatte ihm diese ausgesucht. [...] Heute, mit dem Zusammenbruch in Deutschland, hat sich das alles für ihn geändert. Die Leute dort werden sehr bald nach ihrer Sprache suchen, die man ihnen gestohlen und verunstaltet hat. Wer immer sie rein gehalten hat, in den Jahren des schärfsten Wahns, wird damit herausrücken müssen. Es ist wahr, er lebt weiter für alle, und er wird immer allein leben müssen, sich selber als höchster Instanz verantwortlich: aber er ist jetzt den Deutschen ihre Sprache schuldig; er hat sie sauber gehalten, aber er muß jetzt damit auch herausrücken, mit Liebe und Dank, mit Zins und Zinseszinsen.[18]

Canetti betrachtet sich hier als Autor, der – trotz oder sogar wegen des Genozids am europäischen Judentum – im ethischen Sinne „Sprachpflege" betrieben hat. Eine Sprache zu bewahren, heißt für Canetti, dass sie sich nicht verengen darf, sondern Luftaustausch mit dem Menschlichen überhaupt pflegen muss. Es ist mehr als ein Bonmot, wenn Canetti noch 1959 behauptet: „Zuhause fühle ich mich, wenn ich mit dem Bleistift in der Hand deutsche Wörter niederschreibe und alles um mich herum spricht Englisch."[19]

   In diesem Heimatbegriff gibt Canetti seiner Auffassung vom Wesen des Judentums Ausdruck. Jude-Sein heißt für ihn, das Exil als weltbürgerliches Versprechen aufzufassen. Schon 1943 kann er daher das vielzitierte Bekenntnis ablegen: „Die Sprache meines Geistes wird die deutsche bleiben, und zwar weil ich Jude bin. Was von dem auf jede Weise verheerten Land übrig bleibt, will ich als Jude in mir hüten. Auch *ihr* Schicksal ist meines, aber ich bringe noch ein allgemein menschliches Erbteil mit."[20] Das Festhalten an der deutschen Muttersprache darf also nicht dahingehend interpretiert werden, Canetti trage der Ermordung des europäischen Judentums nicht ausreichend Rechnung. Vielmehr geht es ihm darum, sich den Ohnmächtigen, den Opfern auf *allen*, d. h. auch auf deutscher Seite zuzuwenden. Ähnlich wie in *Masse und Macht* hebt Canetti mit dem Hinweis auf das „allgemein menschliche Erbteil" die Weite seiner Identität als Jude hervor. In seinem wissenschaftlichen Hauptwerk hatte es geheißen:

> Kein Volk ist schwieriger zu begreifen als die Juden. Sie sind über die ganze bewohnte Erde verbreitet, ihr Stammland war ihnen verloren. [...] Narren mögen überall von ihrer Gleichheit fabeln. Wer sie kennt, wird eher der Meinung sein, daß es unter ihnen viel mehr verschiedene Typen gibt als unter jedem anderen Volk. Die Variationsbreite der Juden in Wesen und Erscheinung gehört zum erstaunlichsten, das einem unterkommen kann. Die populäre Sage, daß es unter ihnen die besten wie die schlechtesten Menschen gibt, drückt die Tatsache auf naive Weise aus. Sie sind anders als die andern. Aber in Wirklichkeit sind sie, wenn man so sagen könnte, untereinander am meisten anders.[21]

Was es bedeutet, Jude zu sein, entzieht sich also jeder einsträngigen Definition. Canettis Hinweis auf die Vielfalt des Judentums muss als Plädoyer für die Vielfalt von kulturellen, gesellschaftlichen und religiösen Praktiken im allgemeinen verstanden werden. Wenn er sich als Autor sprachlich durch die Entscheidung für das Deutsche scheinbar begrenzt, will er in Wirklichkeit die menschlichen Werte, die in Exil und Diaspora gefunden werden können, in eben diese Sprache wieder hineintragen. Canettis Weigerung, sich nur als Jude zu betrachten, seine Abgrenzung von Freunden, die nach der Shoah ihr Judentum ganz ins Zentrum ihrer Identität stellten, erklärt sich aus seiner Überzeugung, die Welt und ganz besonders die Jedermanns der deutschen Sprache seien auf einen Autor wie ihn angewiesen, für den, deutschsprachig zu sein, gar nicht zu trennen war von Vielsprachigkeit und Kosmopolitismus. Gegen die Beseitigung der vielfältigen, kulturellen Quellen jüdischer Identität steht daher in der *Provinz des Menschen* der Aphorismus: „Es gibt eine Klagemauer der Menschheit, und an dieser stehe ich."[22]

Canetti scheint in seinen Aufzeichnungsbänden sehr selektiv verfahren zu sein: Zweifel an der Entscheidung, das Deutsche müsse seine Sprache bleiben, werden kaum thematisiert. Auch Hassgefühle gegenüber Deutschen und Österreichern tauchen nicht auf. Der Hass stünde nämlich im Widerspruch zu dem Versuch, in *Masse und Macht* das zu überwinden, was Canetti als Fehler der üblichen Geschichtsschreibung betrachtet: Diese halte durch den verehrenden Gestus ihrer Namens-Mythologie nicht nur die Erinnerung an Gewalthaber wach, die die „Nachfolger" implizit zu Nachahmung und Überbietung ermutigten, sondern perpetuiere durch die Festschreibung hasserfüllter Erinnerungen auch die immer gleichen Konflikte. Wenn Canetti sich darauf konzentriert, die utopischen Ideen in

den Vordergrund zu stellen, die er aus seiner jüdischen Identität herleitet,
versucht er der Dialektik von Gewalt und Gegengewalt entgegenzuwirken.

Wie schwer Canetti das Festhalten an der deutschen Sprache
mitunter geworden sein muss, geht jedoch aus einigen unveröffentlichten
Reisenotizen aus dem Züricher Nachlass hervor. Sie sind zwischen dem
31.8. und dem 20.9.1953 entstanden und gelten Erfahrungen, die Canetti bei
seiner ersten Rückkehr nach Wien machte:

> Meine erste Nacht in Wien. Bin ich wirklich an den Folter-Ort
> geraten? Und wer ist in diesem Zimmer, in dem ich schlafen
> konnte, gemartert worden? Die Rede des Portiers. Die
> unheimliche Freundlichkeit des Hausdieners. „Flüsterpropaganda"
> der Engländer – wogegen?[23]

Der Autor der *Blendung* scheint hier einen Vergleich zu ziehen zwischen der
Figur des Benedikt Pfaff, in deren sadistischer, von Frauen- und Judenhass
getragener Brutalität und Banalität sich die Wiener Atmosphäre Anfang der
30er Jahre verdichtete, und seinen realen Brüdern, den nur äußerlich
entnazifizierten Portiers der 50er Jahre. Nichts hat sich an der Realität, die
das Erstlingswerk beschrieb, geändert, scheint Canetti aus der Sprache der
letzteren zu schließen. Die Anstrengungen, die für den Satz nötig gewesen
waren „Die Sprache meines Geistes wird die deutsche bleiben, und zwar
weil ich Jude bin", erweisen sich als vergeblich. Canetti klagt:

> Ich ertrage die Sprache nicht mehr, die Sprache der Wiener. Jede
> Abweichung von seinem Klang des Deutschen ist mir verhasst.
> [...] jetzt bin ich in Wien und es kostet mich grosse Überwindung
> zu *hören*. Die Laute dieser Menschen erscheinen mir als die
> Verlegenheit selbst. Ich habe nie gewusst, dass ich die Wiener
> hasse, jetzt aber bin ich daraufgekommen. Ich hoffe, dass es kein
> *historischer* Groll ist, den ich plötzlich fühle, ich dachte, ich bin
> ohne alle Rachegedanken zurück, – aber was bedeutet diese tiefe
> Abneigung, dieser Widerwille, die Ohren zu öffnen, dieser
> Abscheu vor jeder alten Wendung, dieses Entsetzen über die
> Brutalität, die man hinterm Schleim der Oberfläche spürt? Ich
> denke mit Heimweh und Bewunderung an die Ruhe der Engländer,
> ihre Zurückhaltung, ihre Unlust davor, den Mund überhaupt zu
> öffnen.

Canetti macht klar, dass er die Menschen, die die gleiche Sprache wie er zu
sprechen scheinen, in Wirklichkeit als fremd wahrnimmt. Die Fremdsprache
Englisch hingegen wird als vertraut, ja als Heimat eingestuft, weil die
Vorsicht und Bewusstheit ihrer Verwender das Gefühl der Zugehörigkeit
dauerhaft zu sichern vermögen. Interessant daran ist, dass Canetti, der als
Student durch die kraussschen Vorlesungen und durch ausgiebige Besuche in

Wiener Cafés und Nachtbars das Hören gelernt und sein Konzept der
„akustischen Maske" im Kontakt mit der Vielfalt *dialektaler* Färbungen
entwickelt hatte, nun die Mündlichkeit nicht länger ertragen kann. Das Exil
scheint eine Verschiebung hin zur deutschen Schriftsprache zu bewirken.
Die Reise führt zu der Erkenntnis, dass der Optimismus einer Aufzeichnung,
die Canetti im August 1939, d. h. noch vor Kriegsbeginn, niederschrieb, nun
nicht mehr gerechtfertigt ist. Damals hatte er geschrieben:

> Durch eine andre Sprache wird mir das Alte wieder neu. Schal
> waren die deutschen Worte; ihre politische Verwertung hatte sie
> entleert; die Dialekte, gewiss, waren nicht umzubringen; aber wer
> brachte ein geschriebenes Wort über Herz?[25]

Jetzt hat sich die Situation umgekehrt. Den Dialekten ist nicht mehr zu
trauen. Wenn überhaupt noch auf etwas gesetzt werden kann, dann auf die
schriftliche Überlieferung früherer Zeiten.

Vor dem Hintergrund des ungeheuren Lesestoffes, mit dem sich
Canetti bei der Arbeit an *Masse und Macht* auseinandersetzte, möchte ich
mit einer letzten Frage schließen. Könnte es nicht sein, dass dieses 1960
erschienene Buch den sprachlichen Abschied von den frühen,
dialektgefärbten Theaterstücken bezeichnet und die Reinigung des
Deutschen durch die Rückbesinnung auf die eminent jüdische Tradition des
Lesens in Angriff genommen werden soll? Die selbstkritische Frage, ob es
wirklich kein historischer Groll sei, den er gegen die Wiener empfinde, ist
ein Beweis für Canettis Bemühen, über die eigene Zeit hinweg, bis in ferne
Vergangenheiten hinein, nach Material für eine Bekämpfung der Macht zu
suchen. Ein Rückfall ins Historische läge vor, wenn Shoah und Vertreibung
zur Ausblendung der Opfer anderer Epochen und Räume führen würden.
Aus der Ermordung des europäischen Judentums ergibt sich für Canetti ein
Paradox. In dem Maße, in dem sich in dem Namen „Auschwitz" jüdisches
Leid verdichtet, bezeichnet er etwas, was die ganze Menschheit angeht.
Wenn man aber das Allgemeine, das im Singulären steckt, wirklich ernst
nimmt, folgt aus der nationalsozialistischen Vernichtungsmaschinerie die
Notwendigkeit, vom Leid *anderer* Völker zu lesen und zu berichten. Die
Zitate, die *Masse und Macht* „eingeschöpft" sind, sind daher immer beides:
nah und fern zugleich. Das Buch spricht von Afrikanern und Indern,
Australiern und Eskimos – immer aber verschränken sich verschiedene
Deutungsmöglichkeiten: Auf der einen Seite sind die Opfer einem ganz
bestimmten Land in einer ganz bestimmten Zeit zugehörig. Auf der anderen
Seite legt Canetti jedoch so wenig Wert auf eine chronologische und
räumliche Einordnung, dass dann doch auch die europäische Geschichte des
Zweiten Weltkriegs entlang dieser nur scheinbar fremden Ereignisse erzählt

werden kann. So wie Canetti im Exil das Gefühl bekam, im Kontakt mit dem Englischen wichtigere Entdeckungen im Deutschen zu machen als in Wien, so spricht aus *Masse und Macht* der Gedanke, aus den Dokumenten von Völkern, die mit der Geschichte Europas nichts zu tun haben, lasse sich über die Shoah mehr lernen als bei der „direkten" Beschäftigung mit ihr.

Die Forschung hat den anthropologisch-philosophischen Essay oft auf das Vorhaben reduziert, universale Machtmechanismen und die biologischen „Ursprünge" der Gewalt aufzudecken. Ich meine hingegen, dass Canettis Exilbegriff dazu geführt hat, dass *Masse und Macht* sich als sehr viel widersprüchlicheres Buch darstellt. Wenn nämlich aus Canettis Sicht auf das Judentum die Abkehr von einem einsträngigen Heimat-Begriff folgt, ist der Rückgriff auf das Ferne, Unvertraute immer auch einer positiven Verfremdung des Eigenen verpflichtet. Anders gesagt: In der Geschichte der afrikanischen Xosas oder des Sultans von Delhi liegen Vertrautes und Unvertrautes ebenso nah beisammen wie Jüdisches und Nicht-Jüdisches in Canettis Ideal jüdischer Diaspora. *Masse und Macht* zu lesen, heißt, dass im Fremden plötzlich die eigene Geschichte aufleuchtet, dass zugleich aber durch die Unvertrautheit der Materialien der Schrecken, der von Deutschland ausging, als vollkommen absurd und unbegreiflich erlebt wird. Eben darin liegen die Hoffnungen, von denen Canetti gesagt hatte, er habe sie in *Masse und Macht* versteckt. Das Judentum bildet eines der Fundamente dieser Hoffnungen, denn sein Kosmopolitismus verbürgt das, was Canetti als „Verwandlung" in andere Menschen bezeichnet hat. Gemeint ist mit diesem schillernden Begriff nicht nur die Fähigkeit zur Empathie, sondern auch die Bereitschaft, in der Begegnung mit dem Fremden sich selbst und die eigene Geschichte zu entdecken.[26]

Fast könnte man sagen, auch im Formalen spiegele sich Canettis Verhältnis zum Judentum. So wie sich die Bedeutung seiner Aphorismen und Aufzeichnungen immer auch durch die Leerstellen konstituiert, die jeweils den Raum zwischen ihnen bilden, setzt Canetti in *Masse und Macht* die unterschiedlichsten Erzählungen nebeneinander, ohne ihre Verbundenheit kenntlich zu machen oder zu erklären. Dadurch ist die Leserschaft dazu aufgefordert, eine Einheit zu stiften und doch die Selbstständigkeit der unterschiedlichen Erzählelemente anzuerkennen. Wenn aber auch für die jüdische Diaspora die Vielfalt charakteristisch ist und nicht die Einheitlichkeit, eine positiv konnotierte Offenheit und Hybridität und nicht eine eindeutige sprachliche, kulturelle und religiöse Zugehörigkeit, macht Canetti in seinem Hauptwerk mit seinem Exilbegriff Ernst: Vielstimmigkeit und kosmopolitisches Interesse am Fremden, Bereitschaft zur „Verwandlung" ins Unbekannte und damit eine Offenheit, die eigene Identität als wandelbare zu erfahren.

Anmerkungen

[1] Elias Canetti an Victor Suchy vom 20.9.1970. Nachlass Elias Canetti 1000. Weiter heißt es: „Es gibt Dinge, über die man soviel zu sagen hätte, dass man am besten schweigt."

[2] Den größten Teil dieses Nachlasses sowie seine Bibliothek hat Canetti 1994 der Zentralbibliothek Zürich vermacht, wo er seitdem auch aufbewahrt wird. Der Nachlass enthält die Tagebücher und die Korrespondenz des Autors; beide sind bis zum Jahre 2024 gesperrt. Hingegen sind seit Sommer 2002 die Vorarbeiten zu seinen Werken, seine äußerst umfangreichen Hefte mit „Aufzeichnungen" sowie Materialsammlungen, die u.a. dem Buch *Masse und Macht* zugrundeliegen, zugänglich. Mit einer ersten Auswertung des noch kaum erschlossenen Nachlasses hat Sven Hanuschek begonnen, dessen Biographie über Elias Canetti viele interessante Materialien zu Leben und Werk enthält. Vgl. Sven Hanuschek, *Elias Canetti. Biographie* (München, Wien: Hanser 2005).

[3] Nachlass Elias Canetti 2.

[4] *Ibid.*

[5] *Ibid*, 5 a.

[6] *Ibid.* Die Aufzeichnung stammt ebenfalls vom 15.8.1939.

[7] *Ibid.*

[8] Es scheint ein Romanmanuskript in englischer Sprache gegeben zu haben, das leider verschollen ist. Bekannt ist hingegen eine in englischer Sprache veröffentliche Erzählung, der Veza Calderon-Canetti den Titel „Air raid" gab. Vgl. Veza Calderon-Canetti, „Air Raid", in *Der Fund* (München: dtv 2001), S.190-93. Vgl. auch das Nachwort von Angelika Schedel in *ibid.*, S. 309-26, besonders S. 322, wo es heißt: „Im Nachlaß fand[ ] sich [...] eine englischsprachige Fassung von Air Raid – die offenbar unter dem Mädchennamen Venetia Calderon angeboten werden sollte. Sie wurde[ ] in diesem Band nicht aufgenommen, beleg[t] jedoch, wie sehr sich Veza Canetti um Veröffentlichungen bemüht hat." *Ibid.* Zu Veza Calderon-Canettis Werk vgl. die Ausführungen in meiner Doktorarbeit *Komik und Gewalt. Die literarische Verarbeitung der Weltkriege und der Shoah in den Werken von Karl Kraus, Veza Calderon-Canetti, Elias Canetti und Victor Klemperer*, deren Veröffentlichung im Böhlau-Verlag in Vorbereitung ist.

[9] Elias Canetti, *Aufsätze, Reden, Gespräche* (München, Wien: Hanser, 2005), S. 9-48. Der Vortrag wurde in der Bryanston Summer School gehalten. Das Manuskript befindet sich im Besitz des Marie-Louise von Motesiczky Charitable Trust, London.

[10] Nachlass Elias Canetti 6.

[11] *Ibid.* Die Aufzeichnung stammt vom 15.7.1942.

[12] *Ibid.* 5 a.

[13] Elias Canetti, *Die Provinz des Menschen* (Frankfurt/M.: Fischer-Taschenbuch, 2003), S. 57; künftig zitiert als: Canetti, *Provinz*.

[14] Elias Canetti, „Hermann Broch" in *Das Gewissen der Worte* (Frankfurt/M. Fischer-Taschenbuch: 1998), S. 11-24. Canetti schreibt hier, Broch sei mit etwas begabt, „was ich nur als Atemgedächtnis zu bezeichnen vermag. [...] Ja, ist eine Dichtung, die aus der

Atemerfahrung gestaltet, überhaupt denkbar? Und welches sind die Mittel, deren sie sich im Medium des Werkes bedient? Darauf wäre vor allem zu antworten, daß die Vielfalt unserer Welt zum guten Teil auch aus der Vielfalt unserer Atemräume besteht. Der Raum, in dem Sie hier sitzen, in ganz bestimmter Anordnung, fast völlig von der Umwelt abgeschlossen, die Art, in der sich Ihr Atem vermischt, zu einer Ihnen allen gemeinsamen Luft, und dann mit meinen Worten zusammenstößt, die Geräusche, die Sie stören, und die Stille, in die diese Geräusche wieder zurückfallen, Ihre unterdrückten Bewegungen, Abwehr oder Zustimmung, das alles ist, vom Standpunkt des Atmenden aus, eine ganz einmalige, unwiederholbare, in sich ruhende und wohlabgegrenzte Situation. Aber gehen Sie dann ein paar Schritte weiter und Sie finden die völlig andere Situation eines anderen Atemraumes". (*Ibid.*, S. 20-21.)

[15] Nachlass Elias Canetti 7. Die Aufzeichnung datiert aus der Zeit zwischen dem 1.8. und dem 31.12.1943.

[16] Hans Blumenberg, *Arbeit am Mythos* (Frankfurt/M.: Suhrkamp, 1996), S. 51.

[17] Nachlass Elias Canetti 5 a. Die Aufzeichnung datiert wohl vom 1.1.1940.

[18] Canetti, *Provinz*, S. 88-89.

[19] Canetti, *Provinz*, S. 242.

[20] *Ibid.*, S. 74.

[21] Elias Canetti, *Masse und Macht*, Frankfurt/M.: Fischer-Taschenbuch 2001, S. 208.

[22] Canetti, *Provinz*, S. 306.

[23] Nachlass Elias Canetti 57.

[25] Nachlass Elias Canetti 5 a.

[26] Wie sich die sog. „seitliche Methode" von *Masse und Macht* u.a. auch auf eine ambivalente Komik stützt, zeigt mein Aufsatz „,Man lacht, *anstatt* es zu essen.' Canettis Analyse des Lachens in *Masse und Macht*", der 2007 in einem von Gerald Stieg herausgegebenen Band der Zeitschrift *Austriaca* über Elias Canetti erscheinen wird.

Exil der Wiener Medizin in Großbritannien

Renate Feikes

Nach dem März 1938 waren in Österreich ca. 3.500 Ärzte durch die NS-Gesetze gefährdet, von denen ca. 3.000 ins Ausland flüchten konnten, die meisten davon in die USA und nach Großbritannien. Bereits 1939 waren ca. 1.200 deutsche und österreichische Ärzte in Großbritannien, von denen allerdings nur 200 praktizieren durften; 50 österreichische Mediziner waren dabei, sich zu qualifizieren. 1941 gab die Regierung die Anweisung, die Anstellung in Spitälern und Kliniken auch ohne englische Qualifikation zu ermöglichen. Das Medical Directory von 1945 zeigt, dass sich 243 österreichische Ärzte in London befanden.

Zu Beginn möchte ich einen kurzen Überblick über die Situation der Mediziner in Österreich nach dem „Anschluss" Österreichs an das Deutsche Reich bieten. Nach dem März 1938 begann die systematische Verdrängung der jüdischen bzw. politisch nicht opportunen Ärzte.

Die ersten Maßnahmen erfolgten im Bereich der Universitäten bereits im März 1938; die jüdischen Hochschullehrer sollten so rasch wie möglich von den Universitäten entfernt werden. Die ersten Entlassungen erfolgten an der medizinischen Fakultät der Universität Wien bereits Ende April. Insgesamt wurden (ausgehend von 309 Hochschulassistenten und 43 Emeriti[1]) – rund 160 Hochschullehrer Opfer der rassischen Verfolgungsmaßnahmen.[2] Dieser Vorgang war binnen eines Jahres abgeschlossen. Rektor Knoll schrieb bereits für das Studienjahr 1938/39 zum Geleit:

> Unsere Universität wurde vor allem rasch und gründlich von all jenen Professoren und Dozenten befreit, die als Lehrer an einer nationalsozialistischen Hochschule nicht geeignet waren.[3]

Natürlich betrafen die NS-Maßnahmen auch die jüdischen Medizinstudenten und bereits im November 1938 konnte die Universität Wien für „judenfrei" erklärt werden.

Die Ausschaltung der jüdischen Ärzte ging jedoch auch in den Spitälern rasch vor sich – die meisten verloren bereits im März 1938 ihre Anstellung. Mit dem 1. Juli 1938 waren die Kassenzulassungen der niedergelassenen praktischen und Fachärzte ungültig. Endgültig aus dem Berufsleben verdrängt wurden die jüdischen Mediziner mit dem 1. Oktober 1938. Ab diesem Zeitpunkt war es ihnen untersagt, sich Arzt zu nennen; sie durften unter keinen Umständen Patienten behandeln. Nur im Spital der

Israelitischen Kultusgemeinde in Wien waren noch jüdische Mediziner beschäftigt. Für die Behandlung der jüdischen Bevölkerung wurden 372 sogenannte jüdische Krankenbehandler zugelassen.

In den Akten der Israelitischen Kultusgemeine (IKG) Wien findet man eine monatliche an die Gestapo gerichtete Liste von Oktober 1938 bis Oktober 1942. In diesen Listen wurde der jeweils aktuelle Stand der Krankenbehandler veröffentlicht und genau festgehalten, wer ausgewandert oder gestorben war und ab 1941 wird auch angegeben, wer deportiert wurde. Die IKG forderte daher 1940 die ständige Ergänzung der Krankenbehandler aus dem Stande der nicht zugelassenen praktischen und Fachärzte. Leider ist nicht überprüfbar, inwieweit dieser Forderung nachgegeben wurde.

Nach der Definition der Nationalsozialisten waren somit 3.200 Ärzte (von 4.900) in Wien in ihrer Existenz gefährdet, denn diese galten nach den Nürnberger Rassegesetzen als Juden oder „Judenstämmlinge". Das ab diesem Zeitpunkt geltende Berufsverbot wird in der Deutsch-Österreichischen Ärztezeitung so kommentiert:

> Wie befreiend wird sich die Tat unseres Führers erweisen, durch die er den Juden die Ausübung des ärztlichen Berufes verbot! [...] Vom 1.Oktober aber des Jahres ab ist kein deutschblütiger Mensch der Gefahr mehr ausgesetzt, von jüdischen Ärzten an Körper und Seele vergiftet zu werden, es gibt von da ab keinen jüdischen Arzt auf deutschem Boden mehr.[4]

Nach dem März 1938 waren in Österreich ca. 3.500 Ärzte gefährdet, von denen sich wahrscheinlich 3.000 ins Ausland retten konnten.[5] Natürlich galten auch für die Mediziner dieselben Emigrationsbedingungen wie für alle anderen Flüchtlinge. Andererseits konnten viele Mediziner sich auf internationale Kontakte und Netzwerke stützen, da das medizinische Wien in den 20er und 30er Jahren des 20. Jahrhunderts weltweit bekannt war.

In der Auswanderungsabteilung der IKG Wien wurde eine eigene Ärzteberatung eingerichtet, welche sich mit Fürsorge, der Versendung von Fragebögen bezüglich der Auswanderung etc. befasste. Leider gibt es keine Möglichkeiten festzustellen, wieviele dieser Fragebögen ausgefüllt wurden, da die Akten nicht in Wien aufbewahrt werden und derzeit nicht alle in Kopie vorliegen.

Die Ärzteberatung war auch durch bürokratische Hindernisse aller Art in ihrer Tätigkeit behindert. Die Emigrationsmöglichkeiten der Ärzte beschränkten sich hauptsächlich auf einige wenige Länder; die meisten Ärzte flüchteten in die USA und nach Großbritannien. Ich möchte nun einen kurzen Überblick über die Voraussetzungen geben, die sich den österreichischen Medizinern in Bezug auf das Exilland Großbritannien boten. (Ausführliche Informationen über das medizinische Exil in den Vereinigten Staaten bietet meine Dissertation.[6])

Emigration nach Großbritannien

Theoretisch benötigte man bis 1938 zur Einreise nach Großbritannien nur einen Reisepass; die Entscheidung darüber, ob ein Flüchtling einreisen durfte oder nicht, oblag jedoch dem Ermessen der Einwanderungsbeamten in den britischen Ankunftshäfen. Das wichtigste Kriterium für deren Entscheidung war eine ausreichende finanzielle Sicherstellung der Einreisewilligen.

Nach dem „Anschluss" Österreichs 1938 an das Deutsche Reich stieg die Zahl der Flüchtlinge in Großbritannien drastisch an; als Reaktion darauf wurde im April 1938 ein Visasystem für Einreisende mit deutschen und österreichischen Reisepässen eingeführt.[7] Die neuen Vorschriften galten ab dem 2. Mai 1938 für Inhaber österreichischer Pässe und ab dem 21. Mai 1938 für Inhaber deutscher Reisepässe.[8]

Entscheidendes Kriterium für die Visumausstellung war der „Wert oder Unwert des Antragstellers für das Vereinigte Königreich".[9] Als Konsequenz erhielten renommierte Persönlichkeiten aus Wissenschaft, Kunst und Forschung oder Industrielle ohne Probleme Visa, während kleine Gewerbetreibende, Handwerker, aber auch Juristen und Ärzte von vornherein davon ausgenommen waren.[10] Diese erhielten ein Visum nur dann, wenn sie nachweisen konnte, dass sie sich in unmittelbarer Gefahr befanden oder in Großbritannien über einen finanziellen Bürgen verfügten (häufig übernahmen britische Flüchtlingsorganisationen diese Aufgabe). Jeder Bewerber musste klarlegen, ob er eine Emigration anstrebe oder nur einen – zeitlich begrenzten – Besuch in Großbritannien plane:[11]

> Those who should not be refused visas without reference to London include leading persons in science, medicine or research; artists, architects, and designers of sufficient standing to maintain themselves by private commissions and industrialists who planned to transfer well-established businesses to Great Britain. Visas could be granted on the spot to 'distinguished persons, i. e. those of *international* repute in the field of science, medicine, research or art' – provided there was evidence that the applicant would be assured of the hospitality of friends or colleagues in Great Britain.[12]

Noch im August 1938 berichteten britische Flüchtlingsorganisationen, dass die Situation in Wien immer schlechter und chaotischer werde, alles war käuflich – angefangen vom Ticket bis zum lateinamerikanischen Pass – es gab sogar Evidenz, dass man auch gefälschte britische Visa kaufen konnte.

Mit der Einrichtung der Zentralstelle für jüdische Auswanderung in Wien unter der Leitung Eichmanns, die darauf ausgelegt war, dass möglichst viele Menschen so rasch wie möglich das Land verließen und das ohne ihren Besitz mitzunehmen, verschlechterte sich die Situation zusehends. Es gab auch viele Klagen der potentiellen Emigranten, die sich besonders auf Langsamkeit und Gleichgültigkeit der Beamten bezogen. Zuzuschreiben war dies sicherlich zu einem Teil der völligen Überlastung der zuständigen Ämter. Die Ausländerabteilung des Home Office klagte über den enormen Arbeitsaufwand im britischen Konsulat in Wien und den meist sehr schlechten Allgemeinzustand der Visumbewerber. So schreibt das Britische Generalkonsulat, seine Angestellten verteidigend:

> Considering the immense numbers of persons dealt with daily and the very trying nature of the duties involved in such dealings, the number of complaints is infinitesimal [...] Kendrick (the Passport Officer) tells me that his staff are so overwrought that they will burst into tears at the slightest provocation and every means must be found of easing their burden. The same applies to my own staff [...] In order to conduct the work of the Passport Office as applicants desire, we should need a staff of 40 people and a building like the Albert Hall – but why should we incur such a burden?[13]

Zwischen März 1938 und Jänner 1939 wurden 13.500 Visa in Wien ausgestellt (34.000 in Berlin).[14] Pro Tag wurden 100 Visa ausgestellt, 200 Leute interviewt.[15] Vor allem die „Reichskristallnacht" vom 9. zum 10. November 1938 löste eine weitere Flüchtlingswelle aus. Unter dem Druck der Öffentlichkeit lockerte die britische Regierung ihre Einreisebestimmungen.[16] Vor allem Flüchtlinge, die weiteremigrieren wollten, wurden aufgenommen.

Zusätzliches Personal wurde den Konsulaten zugewiesen und das Prozedere der Antragstellung vereinfacht; den freiwilligen Flüchtlingsorganisationen war es nun erlaubt, Personen zur Emigration auszuwählen.[17] So erstellten die Organisationen in Berlin, Wien, Prag etc. Namenslisten, die sie an das Home Office schickten; diese ersetzten zum Großteil die individuellen Visaanträge. Das Home Office setzte voraus, dass die Organisationen für den Lebensunterhalt der ausgesuchten Personen aufkommen würden.[18]

Der Kriegsausbruch Anfang September 1939 jedoch bedeutete eine Wende in der Politik; alle an „feindliche" Ausländer ausgestellten Visa verloren ihre Gültigkeit. Das Home Office war der Meinung, dass bereits mehr als genug Flüchtlinge im Land waren; das Resultat war, dass die Weiterreise beschleunigt wurde.

Über das tatsächliche Ausmaß der Gesamtemigration aus Österreich bzw. der Einwanderung nach Großbritannien liegen keine präzisen Angaben vor; die einzelnen Angaben schwanken beträchtlich. So waren zum Beispiel die Zahlen des Home Office vor Kriegsbeginn immer untertrieben, wie Sherman schreibt:

> Another fact important in assessing the overall record of the British Government on refugee issues is that the official statistics on admission of refugees to the United Kingdom, whether for settlement or transmigration, were consistently under-reported throughout the pre-war period. The Home Office, the Jewish community, and the many refugee organizations all had an interest in minimizing these numbers, especially as war and the plausible fear of German invasion approached; and even now, accurate statistics are hard to obtain.[19]

Die Angaben über die Gesamtzahl der Emigranten sind unterschiedlich; bis 1939 standen keine amtlichen Daten zur Verfügung, da das Home Office zwischen Flüchtlingen und anderen Einreisenden keinen Unterschied machte. Bis Kriegsbeginn waren etwa 40.000 jüdische Flüchtlinge (Angaben des Council for German Jewry) aus Deutschland, Österreich und der Tschechoslowakei in Großbritannien eingetroffen.[20]

Man darf auch nicht außer Acht lassen, dass die britischen Konsulate in Deutschland und Österreich über 50.000 Visa ausstellten (ohne Bericht nach London); die jeweiligen Antragsteller benutzten diese jedoch nicht sofort, um nach Großbritannien zu kommen:

> It should moreover be recalled that British consular officials in Germany and Austria issued without reference to London well over 50.000 visas to refugees who did not ultimately take them up for admission to the United Kingdom.[21]

Diese Visa waren von den Konsularbeamten freigiebig ausgegeben worden, um Flüchtlinge, die auf ihre Einreisegenehmigung nach Amerika u. s. w. warteten, vor der Gestapo zu schützen oder ihre Entlassung aus Konzentrationslagern zu erreichen.[22] Diese Großzügigkeit der britischen Beamten, die dem Home Office und Foreign Office bekannt war, aber nie publik gemacht wurde, steht in Kontrast zur rigiden Verwaltung der amerikanischen Konsularbeamten.

Es gab keine Organisation, die wirklich alle Flüchtlinge genau verzeichnete. Vor allem gelangten viele Österreicher mit deutschen Reisepapieren nach Großbritannien und wurden dadurch in den offiziellen Statistiken als „Germans" geführt.[23] Laut Herbert Rosenkranz befanden sich Ende Februar 1939 bereits 3.340 männliche und 2.446 weibliche österreichische Flüchtlinge in Großbritannien.[24] Zuverlässige Angaben über das tatsächliche Ausmaß der österreichischen Emigration nach Großbritannien liegen nicht vor. Während des Krieges sprachen die britischen Behörden von rund 15.000 Österreichern, wobei jedoch, wie schon erwähnt, ein Teil als Deutsche registriert war. Die österreichischen Exilorganisationen sprachen von 16.000.[25]

Gemäß den Angaben der IKG und der Reichsvereinigung der Juden Deutschlands in einem Bericht an das Reichssicherheitshauptamt vom 11. November 1941, die die statistische Grundlage für die Wannsee-Konferenz bildeten, sind bei einem Gesamtstand von 206.000 österreichischen Juden (2. Mai 1938) vom 2. Mai 1938 bis 31. Oktober 1941 insgesamt 146.816 österreichische Juden aus der „Ostmark" ausgewandert, davon 27.293 nach Großbritannien.[26] Die jüdischen Vertriebenen dürften rund 90% der Gesamtemigration gebildet haben. In den Jahren 1939 – 1940 erreichte die Emigration ihren Höhepunkt; bis November 1941 hatten 30.850 Juden in Großbritannien Zuflucht gesucht,[27] das heißt, dass Großbritannien mehr österreichische Flüchtlinge aufgenommen hatte als die USA.

Die Flüchtlinge waren primär von der Vermittlertätigkeit und den finanziellen Leistungen der zahlreichen privaten Hilfsorganisationen abhängig. Die meisten davon wurden nach 1933 in der britischen Tradition der zivilen Selbsthilfe sowohl von jüdischen und christlichen Kreisen als auch von der Arbeiterbewegung ins Leben gerufen.[28]

Besonders sind die Leistungen der IKG Wien hervorzuheben, bei der sich Zehntausende Auswanderungswillige registrieren ließen. Andere Organisationen in Wien waren: die Gildemeester-Auswanderungshilfsaktion, die Wiener Zentrale der Quäker und die Gesellschaft der Freunde (Society of Friends); letztere bearbeitete zwischen März 1938 und Kriegsausbruch 11.000 Bewerbungen, wobei 4.500 Personen die Ausreise nach Großbritannien bewilligt wurde.[29] Die Anträge der IKG und der Gesellschaft der Freunde wurden an die zuständigen Hilfsorganisationen in Großbritannien weitergeleitet, das Jewish Refugees Committee bzw. the Society of Friends German Emergency Committee, die diese an das Home Office weitergaben.

Vor allem nach dem Novemberpogrom übernahm London eine zentrale Rolle. Die größeren Hilfsorganisationen hatten dort ihren Sitz – für jüdische Flüchtlinge das Jewish Refugees Committee und der Council for German Jewry (ab 1940 Central Council for Jewish Refugees), für Christen das International Christian Committee for German Refugees. Auf Initiative des Home Office wurden diese Hilfsorganisationen im April 1938 im Dachverband des Central Coordinating Committee for Refugees, das im ehemaligen Plaza Hotel in der Bloomsbury Street untergebracht wurde, zusammengeführt, damit alle Hilfsorganisationen sich auch tatsächlich unter einem Dach befanden.

Bis Kriegsbeginn war es die primäre Aufgabe dieser Organisationen, die nötigen finanziellen Mittel aufzutreiben, um die Flüchtlinge aus dem Deutschen Reich herauszubekommen.

Ärzteemigration

Nur wenige Österreicher waren bereits vor 1938 emigriert. 17 führende Mediziner unterschrieben einen Brief, der im *British Medical Journal* vom 26.3.1938 erschien, in dem ihr Mitgefühl für die österreichischen Kollegen zum Ausdruck kam.[30] In der medizinischen Zeitschrift *The Lancet* äußerte man jedoch Bedenken: „the profession is so overcrowded that no refugees could be absorbed."[31]

Nach einem Treffen mit Vertretern des Home Office und Repräsentanten verschiedener Colleges wurde jedoch beschlossen, dass nur eine begrenzte Anzahl von Flüchtlingen zugelassen werden könne und „that any such admissions must be the subject of careful selection".[32] Ein Komitee hatte 50 österreichische Ärzte und 40 Zahnärzte ausgewählt, denen es gestattet wurde, sich zu qualifizieren.

Die Befürchtungen der Berufsgruppen äußerten sich besonders bei den Medizinern, so hatte die British Medical Association sich geweigert, einer Zulassung von mehr als der sehr limitierten Zahl von Flüchtlingsärzten, zuzustimmen:

> The British Medical Association adamantly refused to agree to the admission of more than a very limited number of the refugee doctors, some of world-wide repute, streaming out of Vienna, and set up a committee to advise the Home Secretary on the conditions under which such refugees were henceforth to be allowed into Great Britain.

> That committee was able later to report to the meeting of the British Medical Association that it had achieved a 'severe limitation on the admission of refugees'; each individual applicant would have to undergo very careful scrutiny and would be obliged to undertake at least two years of clinical study before admission to practice.[33]

Die britische Ärztekammer weigerte sich sehr lange, österreichische Ärzte aufzunehmen. Arrivierte Mediziner hatten es etwas einfacher, in Großbritannien zu bleiben. Viele Österreicher blieben nicht in England, sondern gingen weiter in die USA.[34] Louise London schreibt, dass vor

Kriegsausbruch von 1.000 österreichischen Ärzten nur 50 zugelassen wurden.[35]

Der Kriegsausbruch vergrößerte den Druck auf Universitäten und Flüchtlinge. 1941 gab die Regierung die Anweisung, die Anstellung in Spitälern und Kliniken auch ohne englische Qualifikation zu ermöglichen. Noch 1938/39 war die britische Ärztegewerkschaft dagegen aufgetreten, eine übergroße Zahl von Flüchtlingen aufzunehmen; von jedem Arzt wurde eine Prüfung und ein zweijähriges Praktikum gefordert, bevor er zur Prüfung zugelassen wurde.[36]

In Bezug auf Zahnärzte gab es einen wesentlichen Unterschied: wie Paul Weindling schreibt:

> With dentistry one was dealing with what in Austria was a postgraduate medical specialism, whereas in Britain it was regarded as a low-grade profession which still retained the aura of a craft skill.[37]

Die Haltung der „British Dental Association" manifestierte sich in Ablehnung der möglichen Immigranten, „who despite their often superior academic qualifications were stigmatised as untrained in ‚national methods', ‚traditions' and ‚language'".[38] Österreichische Zahnärzte waren frustriert, da das Niveau in Großbritannien niedriger war, die meisten Dozenten und Universitätsassistenten aus Wien keine Möglichkeit fanden, akademisch tätig zu werden und die Mitgliedschaft bei der British Dental Association unmöglich blieb für Personen ohne britische Staatsbürgerschaft.[39]

Die wohl wichtigste Rolle in Hinblick auf das wissenschaftliche Exil spielte die Society for the Protection of Science and Learning (SPSL), die ursprünglich 1933 als „Academic Assistance Council" gegründet worden war, um Wissenschaftlern, die nach 1933 in Deutschland aus ihren Universitätsanstellungen entlassen wurden, zu helfen. In der Geschichte der SPSL, die 1959 veröffentlicht wurde,[40] heißt es, dass 418 österreichische Wissenschaftler um Hilfe baten. Die Situation wurde auch für die SPSL mit Kriegsbeginn immer schwieriger und vor allem mit dem Beginn der Internierungen. Die SPSL setzte sich verstärkt für die internierten Wissenschaftler ein, die Akten belegen die oft sehr umfangreiche Korrespondenz. Ende 1940 waren praktisch alle akademischen Flüchtlinge aus der Internierung entlassen worden.

Abgesehen von einer wissenschaftlichen Tätigkeit gab es für Ärzte, die sich niederlassen wollten, enorme Schwierigkeiten:

> „Temporary Registration" für Ärzte mit ausländischen Ausbildungen war eine Maßnahme aus 1941. Zuerst war „friendly

aliens" - Flüchtlingen nur die Arbeit im Krankenhaus gestattet, später durften sie auch Patienten zu Hause behandeln.[41]

In der „Foreign List" des „Medical Register" 1945 waren 243 österreichische Ärzte verzeichnet, von denen 101 in London wohnten und der Rest in Provinzen in England und Wales.[42] Die „Austrian Medical Association in Great Britain" wurde 1941 von Markus Hajek gegründet. 1945 hatte die Vereinigung 180 Mitglieder.[43] 1942 organisierten sich österreichische Mediziner in der Association of Austrian Doctors in Great Britain, unter dem Vorsitz des Pathologen Friedrich Silberstein (nach 1945 des Neurologen Max Schacherl). Diese Organisation konnte rund 180 Mitglieder verzeichnen. 1945 befanden sich ca. 3.000 europäische Ärzte und Zahnärzte in Großbritannien, 12% davon aus Österreich.[44] Der Medizinhistoriker Max Neuburger berichtet bereits 1943 über die Kontakte zwischen britischer und österreichischer Medizin in den 20er und 30er Jahren.[45]

Je näher das Kriegsende rückte, desto eindringlicher wurden die Aufforderungen des „Free Austrian Movement" (FAM) an die jüdischen Flüchtlinge, wieder nach Österreich zurückzukehren.[46] Der österreichische Ärztekammerpräsident Hans Karmel stellte 1946 fest, dass nur 50 Ärzte und 40 Zahnärzte das britische Diplom erworben haben und registriert sind.[47] Zu den emigrierten Medizinern zählten die Universitätsprofessoren Hugo Frey, Markus Hajek, Stephan Jellinek, Edmund Nobel, Max Neuburger, Julius Popper, Max Schacherl, Friedrich Silberstein und Walter Zweig sowie die Dozenten Alexander Cemach, Karl Eislinger, Ernst Freund und Eugen Pollak.[48] Das renommierte Forschungslabor der Pearson Stiftung konnte durch dessen Leiter Ernst Freund und seine Mitarbeiter von Wien nach London verlegt werden. Da der Großteil der österreichischen Ärzte in Großbritannien nur „temporary registered" war, d. h. nur für die Dauer des Krieges praktizieren durfte, erstrebte die Organisation die Rückkehr der Ärzte nach Österreich.[49]

Rückkehr nach Österreich

Die Angaben über die Remigrationsbewegung sind äußerst ungenau. So schätzte Alfred Sternfeld 1990 die Zahl der heute in Österreich lebenden Juden, die bereits vor 1938 gelebt hatten und nach 1945 zurückgekehrt sind, auf etwa 3.500.[50] Die österreichischen Exilorganisationen in Großbritannien, vor allem das FAM und das Austrian Centre, setzten sich vehement für die Rückkehr nach Österreich ein. Die politisch aktiven Flüchtlinge wollten meistens in die Heimat zurückkehren.[51] Die Exilorganisationen umwarben mit Kriegsende immer eindringlicher die Masse der jüdischen Flüchtlinge; in

Broschüren stellte man den jüdischen Österreichern ein Leben ohne
Verfolgung in der Heimat in Aussicht – allerdings noch ohne eine
Vorstellung vom wahren Ausmaß des Holocaust zu haben. Das FAM führte
einen Spezialisten- bzw. Berufskataster, in dem über 2.500 Österreicher aus
Großbritannien und anderen Exilländern verzeichnet waren, von denen sich
70% für eine Rückkehr und 10% dagegen aussprachen, 20% waren
unentschlossen.[52] Gottfried Ellmauer stellte fest:

> Eine nicht unbeträchtliche Zahl von Emigranten, die nach 1945
> wieder in ihre alte Heimat zurückkehren wollte, wurde oft von der
> politischen und wirtschaftlichen und gesellschaftlichen Realität
> abgeschreckt.[53]

Peter Eppel beschreibt, warum viele im Exil lebenden Österreicher den
Verbleib in der Emigration der Rückkehr nach Österreich vorzogen. Er sieht
die bestimmende Motivation der nicht erfolgten Remigration im familiären
und sozialen Umfeld der Vertriebenen. Man wollte die bereits assimilierte
nächste Generation nicht entwurzeln und das bereits aufgebaute soziale
Umfeld nicht zurücklassen; man wollte berufliche Positionen nicht wieder
aufgeben; es bestand eine gewisse Dankbarkeit und Wertschätzung dem
Immigrationsland gegenüber; die Erinnerungen an das erlittene Unrecht und
Leid waren mit der berechtigten Angst verbunden, bei einer Rückkehr erneut
auf Ablehnung zu stoßen.[54] Die angeführten Faktoren tragen dazu bei, die
„Unterstellung", dass der Großteil der Vertriebenen wieder nach Österreich
zurückkehren wollte, zu korrigieren, und gelten selbstverständlich auch für
die nach Großbritannien emigrierten österreichischen Mediziner. Nach 1945
war weder von seiten der Regierung noch – und das erscheint mir bedeutend
– von der Ärztekammer an die Emigranten herangetreten worden, nach
Österreich zurückzukehren.

Die Stimmung nach 1945 lässt sich mit „Rückkehr unerwünscht"
beschreiben. Die Zahl der Remigranten sank mit der Distanz zum
Heimatland, wobei den politisch aktiven Ärzten eher die Rückkehr gelang.
1945 kamen kurz nach Kriegsende viele Mediziner zurück, oft mit Hilfe der
Roten Armee, als Offiziere der Britischen Armee oder aus Jugoslawien. Die
Remigration wurde aber im Laufe der Zeit immer schwieriger.

In Bezug auf die vertriebenen Mediziner ist die Haltung der
Ärztekammer, die ursprünglich – zumindest offiziell – den Heimkehrern
positiv gegenüberstand,[55] zu erwähnen. Diese änderte sich rasch immer mehr
ins Negative.[56] Die Ärztekammer hat also – im Gegensatz zu ihrer
verkündeten Hilfsbereitschaft – de facto andere Prioritäten gesetzt, wenn
auch noch zu Beginn des Jahres 1946 der damalige Präsident der
Ärztekammer, Dr. Hans Karmel, verkündet hatte:

Alle zur Rückkehr Entschlossenen wollen der Heimat ihre
Leistungskraft beim Aufbau zur Verfügung stellen und rechnen
damit, daß die wirtschaftlichen Verhältnisse nicht die rosigsten
sein werden. Sicherlich wird der österreichische Staat alles tun,
um seine auch im Ausland treuen Söhne zu fördern, nicht
vergessend, daß es auch österreichische Ärzte waren, die in
Rundfunk und Presse für die Selbständigkeit Österreichs
erfolgreich aufgetreten sind. Die Österreicher und die Wiener
Ärzteschaft werden die heimkehrenden Kollegen, die sie im
Ausland so würdig vertreten haben, kameradschaftlich
unterstützen, soweit es in ihren Kräften stehen wird.[57]

Bereits ein halbes Jahr später sah die Situation schon anders aus; in
einem Artikel, der mit „Übersicht zur ärztlichen Situation in Wien"
überschrieben ist, heißt es:

1. Die emigrierten Kollegen sind unvergessen. Breite Schichten
    der Bevölkerung haben ihnen während der ganzen Jahre
    nachgetrauert und sie vermißt.

2. Die jüdische Klientel existiert nicht mehr. Sie ist durch
    Auswanderung und Mord eliminiert worden.

3. Der Wohnungsmangel ist ungeheuer. Ich habe zwar jetzt
    schon begonnen, organisatorisch gewisse Vorbereitungen zu
    treffen, um heimkehrende Kollegen unterzubringen. Ein
    wirklicher Erfolg ist aber nicht zu erwarten, es wird in jedem
    einzelnen Fall Schwierigkeiten genug geben. Die
    heimkehrende Kollegen können sich aber unbedingt darauf
    verlassen, daß die Wiener Ärztekammer alles für sie tun
    wird, was in ihrer Macht steht.

4. Leitende Stellen sind fast ausnahmslos neu besetzt worden.
    Nur in ganz vereinzelten Fällen kann damit gerechnet
    werden, daß eine solche Stelle – Chefarztposten, Primariat –
    für heimkehrende Ärzte in Betracht kommt.

[...] Zusammenfassend ist zu sagen: Die Leitung der Wiener
Ärzte, die Wiener Ärztekammer, in welche die wirtschaftliche
Organisation aufgegangen ist, so daß es nur mehr eine
gleichzeitig organisatorische und wirtschaftliche Standes-
vertretung gibt, ist vom besten Willen beseelt. Sie wird
heimkehrende Emigranten herzlichst aufnehmen und für sie tun,
was nur irgendwie möglich ist. Eben diese Möglichkeiten sind
aber durch die allgemeine Situation relativ klein, und der
Existenzkampf wird sowohl für die hiergebliebenen als auch für
die heimkehrenden Ärzte ohne Zweifel sehr hart werden. Es kann
daher den im Ausland tätigen Ärzten nur dringend geraten
werden, die in den Jahren der Emigration errungene Position
weiter zu behalten. Nur dann, wenn ein weiteres Verbleiben im

Gastlande aus wirtschaftlichen Gründen unmöglich sein oder werden sollte, wäre die Heimkehr in Betracht zu ziehen.

Eine Zusammenfassung dieses Artikels sandte der damals amtierende Ärztekammer-Präsident Alexander Hartwich nach London und New York, in der Hoffnung, dass sie „die meisten österreichischen Kollegen in England und den USA erreichen werde".[58]

Für mich sind zwei Dinge signifikant: erstens, die Ärztekammer fand es anscheinend selbstverständlich, dass nur wenige NS-Ärzte ausgeschieden sind, denn dieser Faktor wird auch sonst in den Publikationen kaum erwähnt; und zweitens, sie bietet zwar als Institutionen ihre Hilfe an, verweist aber zugleich die Emigranten in ihre Emigrationsländer und fordert sie auf, dort zu bleiben. Es ist also wie auf anderen Gebieten der Wissenschaft – die Angst vor drohender Konkurrenz war wahrscheinlich der Hauptgrund, warum man sich nicht mehr für die Emigranten eingesetzt hat.

Anmerkungen

Der vorliegende Artikel ist Teil einer weitläufigen Arbeit, die noch nicht abgeschlossen ist, und insofern als „Work in Progress" aufzufassen ist. Die Autorin hat eine Datenbank erstellt, die insgesamt 2.893 Ärzte erfasst, von denen 280 nach GB emigriert sind.

[1] Michael Hubenstorf, „Medizinische Fakultät 1938-45", in *Willfährige Wissenschaft*, Hrsg. Gernot Heiß/Siegfried Mattl/Sebastian Meissl/Edith Saurer/Karl Stuhlpfarrer, Österreichische Texte zur Gesellschaftskritik (Wien: Verlag für Gesellschaftskritik, 1989), Band 43, S. 238.

[2] Ebenda, und Judith Merinsky, „Die Auswirkungen der Annexion Österreichs auf die Medizinische Fakultät der Fakultät der Universität Wien im Jahre 1938" (Diss., Wien, 1980).

[3] Brigitte Lichtenberger-Fenz, „Österreichische Universitäten und Hochschulen" in *Willfährige Wissenschaft*, S. 3-15 (S. 5).

[4] Dr. Ramm, „Sechs Monate ärztliche Aufbauarbeit in der Ostmark", in *Deutsch-österreichische Ärztezeitung*, Jg. 1, Nr. 13, 1. Oktober 1938, S. 219.

[5] Michael Hubenstorf, „Vertriebene Medizin – Finale des Niedergangs der Wiener Medizinischen Schule", in V*etriebene Vernunft: Emigration und Exil der österreichischen Wissenschaft*, Hrsg. Friedrich Stadler (Wien: Jugend und Volk, 1987/1988), Bd. 2, S. 766-93 (S. 781).

[6] Renate Feikes, „Emigration Wiener (Jüdischer) Ärzte nach 1938 in die USA, speziell nach New York" (Diss., Wien, 1999).

[7] Ebenda, S. 56.

[8] Louise London, „British Immigration Control Procedures and Jewish Refugees 1933-1939", in *Second Chance, Two Centuries of German-speaking Jews in the United Kingdom*, Hrsg. Werner E. Mosse (Tübingen: Mohr, 1991), S. 485-517 (S. 504).

[9] *Österreicher im Exil: Großbritannien 1938-1945: Eine Dokumentation,* Hrsg. Wolfgang Muchitsch (Wien: Österreichischer Bundesverlag, 1992), S. 5.

[10] Johann Lettner, „Aspekte der österreichischen jüdischen Emigration in England 1936-45" (Diss., Salzburg, 1972), S. 9.

[11] Ebenda, S. 8.

[12] A.J. Sherman, *Island Refuge. Britain and Refugees from the Third Reich 1933-39,* 2. Auflage (Newbury Park: Cass, 1994), S. 91.

[13] Ebenda, S. 134.

[14] Louise London, *Whitehall and the Jews 1933-1948. British Immigration Policy and the Holocaust* (Cambridge: Cambridge University Press, 2000), S. 134.

[15] Ebenda, S. 135.

[16] Muchitsch, *Österreicher im Exil,* S. 6.

[17] London, „British Immigration Control Procedures" in *Second Chance,* S. 506.

[18] Ebenda.

[19] Sherman, *Island Refuge,* Vorwort zur 2. Auflage, S. 7.

[20] Waltraud Strickhausen, „Großbritannien", in *Handbuch der deutschsprachigen Emigration 1933-45,* Hrsg. Claus-Dieter Krohn, Patrik von zur Mühlen, Gerhard Paul, Lutz Winckler, (Darmstadt: Primus Verlag, 1998), S. 251-70 (S. 254).

[21] Ebenda.

[22] Ebenda.

[23] Muchitsch, *Österreicher im Exil,* S. 7.

[24] Herbert Rosenkranz, *Verfolgung und Selbstbehauptung. Die Juden in Österreich 1938-45* (Wien: Herold Verlag, 1978), S. 188.

[25] Muchitsch, *Österreicher im Exil,* S. 8.

[26] Vgl. Hugo Gold, *Geschichte der Juden in Wien. Ein Gedenkbuch.* (Tel Aviv: Olamenu House, 1966), S. 133; Erika Weinzierl, *Zu wenig Gerechte. Österreicher und Judenverfolgung 1938-45,* 3. Auflage (Graz: Verlag Styria, 1986), S. 52; Rosenkranz, *Verfolgung und Selbstbehauptung,* S. 270.

[27] Rosenkranz, *Verfolgung und Selbstbehaupung,* S. 270.

[28] Ebenda.

[29] Muchitsch, *Österreicher im Exil,* S. 9.

[30] Paul Weindling, „Austrian Medical Refugees in Great Britain: from marginal aliens to established professionals", *Wiener Klinische Wochenschrift,* 110 (1998) 158-61 (S. 159).

[31] Paul Weindling, „The Contribution of Central European Jews to Medical Science and Practice in Britain in the 1930s-1950s", in *Second Chance,* S. 243-54 (S. 249).

[32] Ebenda.

[33] Sherman, *Island Refugee,* S. 124.

[34] Ebenda.

[35] London, *Whitehall and the Jews,* S. 131.

[36] Helene Maimann, „Zur Politik der österreichischen Emigranten in Großbritannien 1938 – 45 " (Diss., Wien, 1973), S. 10.

[37] Weindling, „The Contribution ...", S. 249.

[38] Ebenda.

[39] Ebenda.

[40] Lord Beveridge, *A Defence of Free Learning*, (London/New York City/Toronto: Oxford University Press, 1959), S. 31.

[41] Weindling, „Austrian Medical Refugees...", S. 159.

[42] Weindling, „The Contribution ...", S. 253.

[43] Weindling, „Austrian Medical Refugees...", S. 159.

[44] Ebenda, S. 158.

[45] Ebenda.

[46] Maimann, „Politik", S. 363.

[47] Hans Karmel, „Kunde von den emigrierten Ärzten Österreichs", in *Österreichische Ärztezeitung*, 4 (Jänner 1946), S. 6.

[48] Vgl. Michael Hubenstorf, „Österreichische Ärzteemigration 1934-45. Zwischen neuem Tätigkeitsgebiet und organisierten Rückkehrplänen", in *Bericht Wissenschaftsgeschichte*, Nr. 7, 1984, S. 85 ff.; ders., „Österreichische Ärzte-Emigration, in *Vertriebene Vernunft*, Hrsg. Friedrich Stadler (Wien/München: Jugend & Volk, 1988), Bd.1, S. 359-415 (S. 359 ff.).

[49] Vgl. *Austrian Medical Bulletin*, Oktober-November 1945, 33, DÖW Bibliothek 3016/39a etc, S. 377.

[50] Alfred Sternfeld, *Betrifft: Österreich* (Wien: Böhlau Verlag, 1990).

[51] Helene Maimann, *Politik im Wartesaal* (Wien: Böhlau Verlag, 1975), S. 210

[52] Eva Kolmer, *Das Austrian Centre. 7 Jahre österreichischer Gemeinschaftsarbeit*, (London: Austrian Centre, 1946); 31 DÖW Bibliothek 3038.

[53] Gottfried Ellmauer, „Rückkehr unerwünscht? Remigration nach Österreich nach 1945", Diplomarbeit (Wien, 1992), S. 23.

[54] Peter Eppel, „Österreicher in der Emigration und im Exil 1938–45" in *Vertriebene Vernunft*, Band 2, S. 69-81 (S. 77).

[55] Ebenda, S. 35.

[56] *Österreichische Ärztezeitung*, Nr. 4, Jänner 1946, S. 11.

[57] Ellmauer, „Rückkehr unerwünscht", S. 35.

[58] Ebenda.

Enduring Exile? Or passing acquaintance? Images of Britain in the Work of Georg Kreisler

Colin Beaven

Georg Kreisler, best known for his German cabaret songs, fled from anti-Semitic persecution in his native Vienna in 1938, aged 16. After exile in Hollywood, he returned to Europe as a conscript in the US army. His brief acquaintance with wartime Britain is investigated here, along with its possible significance for the novel *Der Schattenspringer* (published in 1996, and set in the UK). It emerges that the image of Britain encountered in his reminiscences is consistent with the context he required for the novel, in which tensions between the artist and society, and between integrity and justice are explored.

In the course of transatlantic peregrinations necessitated by National Socialism, Georg Kreisler spent time in the UK during 1944.[1] Kreisler, best known for his career as a cabaret artist who is scurrilous and illustrious in equal measure, was born in Vienna in 1922, whence, being Jewish, he fled with his family to Hollywood in 1938. Six years later, after an interlude that afforded him a memorable introduction to the sunny hedonism and precarious glamour of life in California, Kreisler was back in Europe as a US conscript, and was for some months stationed near Yeovil awaiting transportation to France.[2]

While his sojourn in Britain was brief and enforced, it is of interest for three main reasons. First, it encourages reflection about the diversity encountered within manifestations of exile, and above all the difference between incidental exile during provisional residence, and lengthier exile in a replacement domicile. A version of exile that is transitory will, one assumes, generate a different response to a given location than circumstances that are more lasting. Kreisler has almost always lived in multiple exile: pre-war as a native Austrian in the US, post-war as an American citizen in Austria, Germany or Switzerland, more metaphorically as a Jew in Vienna or an artist in society. While in the UK he was exiled from both native language and culture on the one hand, and his adopted American refuge on the other. Second, the variations on exile in Kreisler's personal life and artistic output are an intriguing blend of the conventional, the unique, and the apparently representative, with portentous hints of significance and universality. Making a case study of his experience is likely to give an unexpected twist to our understanding of exile in general. Third, it is striking that the UK, after playing such a fleeting role in the story of Kreisler's life, re-emerged as the primary setting of his 1996 novel *Der Schattenspringer*, a work which explores the extent to which the artist and refugee relate successfully to the society they inhabit. Quite apart from all this, Kreisler, engaged at the time of writing on the score of his second opera, simply deserves to be better known, on the strength of his extraordinary curriculum vitae and artistic work. This article will consider some salient features of both from the perspective of what is known of the wartime British episode and what can be deduced about its significance.

Kreisler's biography, which appeared in September 2005 and relies largely on his own narrations, has of course provided welcome detail, including reference to a second trip to the UK in 1979 in order to commission costumes for a cabaret evening that he was preparing.[3] A 320-page biography is in fact somewhat unexpected from a man who admits that he has 'shied away' from writing about his life,[4] and whose relationship with reminiscence almost seems marked by the same love-hate duality that governs his sentiments towards Vienna and the United States. Kreisler included a 14-page autobiography in a (326-page) collection of aphoristic and impressionistic texts that appeared in 1986;[5] then, in a text called 'Meine Memoiren', which appeared in a similar collection in 2001, he concluded that he would not complete his memoirs, having discovered while in the process of trying to write them that 'ich war kein Thema für mich'.[6] This seemed a disappointing yet unequivocal verdict on the autobiography that had previously been reported as nearing completion and scheduled for publication in 2000.[7] Surprisingly, therefore, in the following year he published 'eine Erinnerung', not intended simply to recount his life story, but to set in context the text and contested genesis of his highly successful 'Eine-Frau-Musical', *Heute Abend: Lola Blau*.[8] The title adopted for his biography (*Georg Kreisler gibt es nicht*) is consistent with this ambivalence, and with an oeuvre that often draws inspiration from past events, but invariably focuses on the present and future, with a creative imperative taking precedence over the (mere) compilation of chronicles.

Kreisler owed his own and his family's escape from Nazi Austria largely to his cousin, Walter Reisch. Having been active as a screenwriter in Vienna in the 1930s, Reisch was already a success in Hollywood, contributing in his later career to screenplays for films such as *Titanic*, *Niagara*, and *Journey to the Centre of the Earth*, and he was able to supply the three members of the Kreisler family (Georg being an only child) with the affidavit that the US authorities required. Along with a chance of survival, the link with Reisch gave Kreisler access to Hollywood circles, and subsequent commentators the opportunity to indulge in extensive exile-related name-dropping. As a picaresque prelude to such social elevation,

Kreisler whiled away part of his journey across the Atlantic playing chess with another son of Austrian Jewish émigrés: the racketeer Bugsy Siegel,[9] then a pioneer mobster on America's West Coast, who was rescued from a stricken yacht off Costa Rica by the captain of the ship in which Kreisler was travelling.[10] Once in Los Angeles Kreisler's contacts included Marlene Dietrich, Billy Wilder, Bruno Walter[11] and Arnold Schoenberg, who indicated in a letter that he was willing to teach Kreisler but was in the event prevented from doing so.[12] This was not exile Ovid-style, spent in a black mood on the Black Sea, where the rupture in the relationship with home was a keenly felt wound; Kreisler thought the site of his exile 'paradiesisch'.[13] After a Vienna in which, as a Jewish family in 1938, 'wir zitterten uns von Stunde zu Stunde durch',[14] he was transported to and by the spectacle of orange and avocado trees growing on the street and sixteen year-old girls wearing make-up.[15] The relentless hours of piano practice imposed by his father as part of Kreisler's education in Vienna provided the family with contacts and an income of sorts, and he soon found himself, in an attack of madness, as he later put it,[16] married to Philine Hollaender, the daughter of Friedrich. After the war yet more luminaries made cameo appearances; Kreisler worked with Charlie Chaplin and Hanns Eisler to produce music for the film *Monsieur Verdoux*.[17]

Kreisler was conscripted into the American army and acquired American citizenship, which he retains to this day, having felt disinclined to reapply for Austrian citizenship, given that he discovered that it was not automatically restored to refugees such as him at the end of the war.[18] It was thus, as a GI preparing for invasion, that he encountered wartime Britain, a country that struck him as unprepossessing – understandably, perhaps, after life in California – and to which he devoted just five words in the autobiographical sketch he published in 1986: 'klein und arm war England'.[19] Even this is less caustic than the description reserved on the same page for France: 'schmutzig und verlogen Frankreich'.

Kreisler, as a German speaker, was attached to US Army Military Intelligence; like 13,000 or so other GIs between 1942 and 1945,[20] he underwent training in intelligence gathering techniques at Camp Ritchie in Maryland[21] and is said to have served in the same unit as Stefan Heym.[22] Unlike Heym, who was also one of the so-called 'Ritchie Boys', he devoted his time and energy where possible to the talent he had discovered for the production of military entertainments rather than the conduct of warfare. He ended the war at Wiesbaden, and, in the guise of interpreter came across a number of senior Nazis in the aftermath: Goering, Streicher, and Kaltenbrunner.[23]

Back in the US, Kreisler embarked on a career as an author (writing, like Heym, in English) and peripatetic bar entertainer. In the latter capacity he again came close to Bugsy Siegel; the commotion caused by Siegel's assassination on 20 June 1947 interrupted Kreisler's performance nearby.[24] By another quirk of chance, both had in the interim and on separate occasions encountered Hermann Goering.[25] Once he left California for New York Kreisler was dogged by professional setbacks and hardships unmitigated by the glamour of pre-war Hollywood; only when he eventually secured a fixed appointment at the Monkey Bar at the Elysee Hotel on East 54th Street in New York, performing to the likes of Tennessee Williams and Joe DiMaggio,[26] was he able to begin a return to solvency. In 1955 he decided to try his luck back in Europe. He quickly became successful as a cabaret artist in Vienna, starting an association with Gerhard Bronner and Helmut Qualtinger that in the case of the former ('mein sehr ehemaliger Kollege'[27]) was quick to sour irremediably; after three years he moved to Munich, and thence to Berlin, Salzburg and Basel, still his place of residence. Kreisler's nomadic curriculum vitae has accompanied hostile or unfavourable responses to his ethnic background and a consistently contentious creative output; the extent to which the three components of this distinctive blend are causally interrelated is an intriguing line of enquiry, and while the equation remains ultimately irresolvable, it reinforces the earlier claim here that a study of Kreisler gives a twist to our understanding of exile. His own analysis is this: 'Ich habe kein Heimatland, aus dem einfachen Grund, weil mich kein Land akzeptiert.'[28]

Given the panorama of his adventures and experiences, and the breadth of a career that has generated in Kreisler's own estimation a tally of songs between 500 and 1000,[29] alongside musicals, novels, an opera and miscellaneous other writings, the English episode in his story could scarcely seem less significant. Yet Marcel Prawy bears unexpected testimony to the contrary. Prawy, eleven years Kreisler's senior, was a wartime friend, and while Kreisler provides a reminiscence of memorably unheated opera performances they attended together in Paris,[30] Prawy has spoken of their joint escapades in the Worcestershire village of Broadway and the military entertainments they produced. The fulsome accolades that Prawy has bestowed on Kreisler's work from this time command authority, since they emanate from a man who went on to become Dramaturg at the Wiener Volksoper and later Chefdramaturg of the Wiener Staatsoper.[31] He was a lifelong friend of Leonard Bernstein – *West Side Story* being one of the musicals that Prawy introduced to Viennese audiences.[32] Prawy, in a tribute to Kreisler broadcast to mark the latter's 80th birthday, comments as follows:

> Ich habe kostbare Erinnerungen an die Jugend von Georg Kreisler
> ... [wir waren] zuerst stationiert in einem Dorf in England, das
> hieß Broadway, in der Nähe von Shakespeares Geburtsort
> Stratford-on-Avon, und dann waren wir in einem Vorort von
> Paris, Le Vésinet. Und unser gemeinsamer Beitrag zum
> Kriegsgeschehen, Kreisler und Prawy, war, dass wir Shows
> gemacht haben für die Soldaten, gewöhnlich ich den ersten Teil,
> der zweite Teil, immer besser als ich, war der Georg Kreisler.
> Aber ich hatte wichtige Arbeiten bei der Show zu erfüllen [...]
> nicht nur ein bisserl Klavier spielen [...] Ich musste Damen
> organisieren [...] Meine schönste seriöse Erinnerung an Georg
> Kreisler sind seine frühen Lieder – leider sind sie verloren, er hat
> sie nicht aufgeschrieben, er hat sie schon vergessen [...] Er
> behauptet immer, der einzige, der sie noch ein bisserl kennt, ist
> der Prawy. Mein Lieblingslied in dem Show, [wo] der spätere
> schwarze Humor von Georg Kreisler herausleuchtete, hieß
> 'Censored', auf deutsch 'zensoriert'. Das Lied war ein Brief. Ein
> Soldat schreibt an seine Braut – also ich fantasiere jetzt – Liebe
> Mary, Unterschrift usw., Dein Jo. Und dieser Brief passiert
> verschiedene Zensurstellen, und jeder Zensor streicht ein Wort,
> ändert ein Wort, [...] kurz und gut, wenn das Mädchen den Brief
> des Bräutigams bekommt, ist der Inhalt das Gegenteil von dem,
> was der Junge ursprünglich geschrieben hatte. Also ich betrachte
> es als eine wunderschöne Erinnerung, dass ich irgendwie an der
> Wiege der großen Karriere von Georg Kreisler stehen durfte.[33]

Comparable comments made by Prof. Tom Schlesinger underline the difficulty of reconstructing events at that time precisely. Schlesinger, whose later academic career as a political scientist took him to Plymouth, New Hampshire, arrived in the US as a Jewish refugee from Germany in 1940 and was trained as a 'Ritchie Boy' before being stationed at Broadway at 'Headquarters Military Intelligence, European Theater of Operations'.[34] (The exact location was probably Russell House[35] near the village hall.) Schlesinger writes the following recollection:

> While stationed in Broadway in Spring, 1944, I attended a
> wonderful performance of a raucous Broadway-style musical
> comedy. It totally spoofed and satirized the training activities so
> thoroughly that one had to be an insider, i.e. have been privy to
> the activities to get most of the humor, and supposedly no one
> outside the military was permitted to attend the performances. I
> learned from a friend that the show was even presented once at
> Fort Slocum, NY, during the few weeks when several hundred of
> us were held there awaiting our turn to board ship for England,
> i.e. to Broadway. My point is, of course, that the show was
> apparently written and produced by Georg Kreisler.[36]

But when Schlesinger sought confirmation of the episode from Kreisler himself the outcome was unexpected:

> Unfortunately [...] he could not help me much, except to mystify me considerably. He did write a musical for the troops, but it had nothing to do with the intelligence training. As I did not hallucinate having watched such a musical and laughed myself silly, and ever since quoted a line from it, there was some talented person other than Kreisler who perhaps was inspired by him.[37]

Despite this uncertainty, it is clear that Kreisler's musical for the troops, entitled *Out of This World*, was a great success; having initially presented it in Yeovil, where the base consisted chiefly of large numbers of tents, of which one was home to Kreisler and twenty of his comrades,[38] he obtained permission to take it on tour for a month, visiting American bases across England. He has also spoken of periods spent in Broadway, in Devizes, and near Salisbury.[39] It is unclear whether it was to one of these locations that he was diverted when, accustomed to spending time absent without leave from the base in Yeovil in the company of his English girlfriend, Kreisler almost came unstuck because his name appeared on the list for the next transfer to France and he was due to collect the equipment he needed for the journey. Through a ruse and judicious use of contacts he avoided punishment, and was on parade present and correct when it was time for departure, only to discover that the journey was in fact the prelude to a further four-week stay in camp: 'Mit dem Zug geht es 50 Kilometer zu einem neuen Standort.'[40]

While the extent of Kreisler's acquaintance with the Cotswolds is sketchy, Prawy's testimony suggests the irony that Worcestershire's version of Broadway brought him greater theatrical success than New York's, where the closest he came to the stage was a three-month contract as an (inactive) understudy to Otto Klemperer's son Wilhelm in the role of crazed Polish pianist.[41] Despite the setbacks, one can safely assume that when Schlesinger refers to the genre of 'raucous Broadway-style musical comedy' he does not suggest that it had its roots in a sleepy rural English village.

Other 'Ritchie Boys' have glossed over their life at 'Headquarters Military Intelligence, European Theater of Operations' in a similar manner. Alfred G. Meyer, a refugee from Bielefeld, found himself stationed at Broadway before being sent across the channel by a somewhat circuitous route akin to Kreisler's:

> To sit in Broadway, Worcestershire, for three months while exciting battles were being fought in France was very frustrating [...] Once I had some official business at the Field Interrogation Division near Southampton. FID, it was joked, really was an abbreviation for 'francs into dollar' because so many German

> prisoners came with large sums of money in their pockets which their interrogators took from them [...]
>
> In August of 1944, I spent a couple of weeks in London to attend some courses given by British Military Intelligence. This was the period of the famous buzz bomb blitz [...] In September, I at last received orders to go to the Continent and to report to Military Intelligence Service, ETO, for assignment to a combat unit. A short but stormy journey in the hole [*sic*] of a steamer carrying frozen sides of beef to France took me from Southampton to Normandy. From the ship we were loaded into landing craft, and from them we waded ashore at Omaha Beach.[42]

Kreisler also visited London in 1944 in order to procure costumes for a stage entertainment.[43] In his interview with Alfred Biolek he recalls Londoners' reaction to attacks by V1s in 1944; he describes sitting in a London bus and, following the example set by other passengers, lying down when the noise of an approaching V1 was heard. 'Alle haben sich hingelegt, man ist wieder aufgestanden und hat weitergemacht.'[44]

One further example of life at Broadway is the account given by Hans Vogel, who describes his progress from Military Intelligence Training Centre at Camp Ritchie in these words:

> Upon completion of training at MITC, we were furloughed to go home and say our good-byes. After our return we were shipped overseas to an Intelligence personnel pool based in Broadway, England. I spent 10 days of extra training at the Order of Battle school in London. On my return to Broadway, IPW Team 98 (Interrogation of Prisoners of War) was formed and attached to the 94th Infantry Division, which was preparing to cross the English Channel for France in early September 1944.[45]

For all his exposure to Cotswold idylls and the resumption of the London blitz, it would seem unlikely that England had much impact on Kreisler, however. While he distances himself whenever possible from the notion of 'Heimat', as illustrated in the title of the song 'Zu Hause ist der Tod',[46] the three countries to which he claims he feels attachment lie predictably elsewhere: 'Ich fühle mich drei Ländern verpflichtet [...]: Österreich, [...] Amerika, [...] und Israel'.[47] In his brief autobiography he states his feelings about America thus: 'Ich habe es noch immer lieb, obwohl ich es nicht leiden kann.'[48]

As for his songs, they contain two minor references to the UK: in the song 'In Deutschland', he plays with a string of national stereotypes in order to challenge the assumptions he anticipates finding among the German-speaking audience for whom the song is intended, and in the process juxtaposes negative images of Germany against relatively positive ones of other countries. In this panorama Britain is cast as quaintly feudal:

> Der Spanier liebt die Pose.   Der Deutsche Schritt und Tritt.
> 'Voilà!' sagt der Franzose.   'Und ob!' sagt der Herr Schmidt.
> Der Russe schluckt den Tadel. Der Deutsche spricht von Schmach.
> Der Brite liebt den Adel.   Der Deutsche weint ihm nach.[49]

A similar approach is used in the song 'Der Paule', about a North German seaman whose career as a licentious brute comes to an end only when he ventures to the UK, unaware that he will be called to account there and brought to justice for his unspeakable offences:

> Das war der Paule, er musste hangen,
> Weil er nach England ging, bei uns wär's nie passiert.
> Wär er doch bloß nicht dorthin gegangen,
> Wo man bis heute die Justiz noch respektiert.
>
> Denn was ein Brite für asozial hält,
> Das macht ein Deutscher, der sich stark fühlt, immer zu
> Drum bleibt auch Paule ein Nationalheld.
> Ein Mann wie ich und – du?[50]

As with the previous example, the use of a positive British, in fact English, stereotype in a song designed for German consumption simply meets the narrative need for a tongue-in-cheek change of scene in the fable, and furnishes a two-dimensional backcloth that contrasts with Paule's Cuxhaven origins. It is the negative insinuations that satirize German values, implying brutalism and disregard for the law, and seeking to make the audience question its own social attitudes, that are the theme in the foreground. While a rather rosy image of British justice is simply a device to reinforce this, and not to be overestimated, it remains for all that undeniably complimentary, and may appear to shed light on the choice of the UK as the chief setting for a novel cast as a detective story that Kreisler published in 1996: *Der Schattenspringer*.[51] Is the link between location and theme pure coincidence, is Kreisler simply exploiting a traditional German fondness for British detective fiction in general, or is there more to it?

Der Schattenspringer, analysed in more detail and at greater length elsewhere,[52] is a deceptively slight piece imbued with the experience of exile and reflections thereupon. The hero, John Greenway, is in fact Hans Grünberg, who has fled from Nazi anti-Semitism in his native Hamburg to become an author in southern England with the sort of literary success in the medium of English to which Kreisler aspired in the US. England in this respect contrasts with Germany as a libertarian refuge from a brutalized birthplace. The comfortable equilibrium in Greenway's émigré life is disrupted by the death in suspicious circumstances of his wife Peggy. The first of the novel's three parts thus becomes a traditional detective story in which the inevitable police inspector, Connally, happens to be an old friend of Greenway's, and succeeds in casting enough doubt on Greenway's conviction to secure his release. While the police never discover the true cause of Peggy Greenway's death, the narrator's revelations at the end of part one suffice to confirm that Greenway was not involved.

In some respects the English location is clearly skin-deep. The British judicial system acquires an unaccustomed continental import in the shape of an 'Untersuchungsrichterin', Helen Twyne by name, her diary being a key source of sagacity in the narrative. Connally, meanwhile, given the spelling of his name, sounds as if he would be more at home in New York than the New Forest. 'Connollys' and 'Connellys' are copious in the London phone book, while 'Connallys' are absent; in Brooklyn all three spellings are common. Greenway's house is situated in the town of Bottsville, a name more likely to evoke South Dakota than the South of England. The larger centre of civilization near Bottsville is Watts, a name redolent of urban America and 1965 riots in Los Angeles. Contrast this rather cavalier approach to plausibility with the opening lines of *Die Tote von Beverly Hills*, a short detective novel by Curt Goetz published in 1951:

> Dort oben in den Hügeln um Hollywood, wo ein gewundener, halb überwucherter Fußpfad, mehr von Schlangen als von Menschen begangen, zwischen Briarcrest Lane und Mulholland Drive eine wenig bekannte Verbindung herstellt, ging ich mit Winnetou, meinem englischen Setter, und starrte in die untergehende Sonne Kaliforniens [...] In diese Sonne, die dein europäisches Blut verdünnt, deine Energien einschläfert und deine Sinne aufpeitscht.[53]

Goetz, who was born in Mainz in 1888, and already a successful actor and author when he emigrated to California in 1939, appears to be admixing so much of the *couleur locale* that he absorbed during exile that the reader might half expect Bugsy Siegel to burst out of the undergrowth in the very next paragraph. In fact, though, the corpse of the title herself turns out to be an exile from the Third Reich; the narrative turns out to be as much an imported European erotic as an exported American exotic, and has much more in common with Kreisler's story than the opening lines suggest.

In both stories the narrator is an exile from continental Europe in an Anglophone world (in Kreisler's story the role of the narrator is concealed until the end), and both feature passionate relationships between a younger woman and an older man (Greenway and Sherry in Kreisler's story; Dr

Maning, alias Steiniger, and Lu Sostlova in Goetz's story). Both stories, moreover, have cyclical plots that allow progressively clearer and more amplified reiteration of a central theme – the theme in both cases being the ways in which passion and art can complement each other to generate a route to self-discovery and/or self-fulfilment. Kreisler's story is cyclical in several respects: Greenway is linked with two deaths in identical circumstances, that of his wife, and of his lover Marge; he has sexual relationships with Marge and her daughter Sherry in turn; the end of the story is a striking and abrupt reprise of the beginning. In the case of Goetz's story, meanwhile, Lu Sostlova is a Lolita figure who, having first ensnared the opera singer Olaf Swendka and inspired him to heights of musical achievement before his mysterious death, then brings the examining magistrate investigating Swendka's sexual misdemeanours under her spell in his turn; her relationship with the latter first occurs in Europe, and is itself then resurrected in America when the two characters meet there as exiles.

Such comparative reflections prompt an incidental reference to a parallel between the novel by Goetz and Kreisler's widely performed musical *Heute Abend: Lola Blau*. In the latter the naive Viennese actress Lola Blau flees anti-Semitism initially via Basel, ultimately achieving success in the US as 'ein amerikanischer Sex-Star [...] wobei sie selbst das Leben eines Sex-Stars nicht genießt'[54] before returning to Europe to seek the fulfilment that eludes her through reunion with her former lover. In *Die Tote von Beverly Hills* Lu Sostlova, having travelled from Basel to the States and incidentally married an archaeologist from Prague on the liner en route, writes in her journal in December 1941: 'Ich bin sehr nervös in letzter Zeit. Aber nicht wegen Pearl Harbour. Ich weiß nicht, was los ist mit mir [...] Ich glaube, ich habe Heimweh nach Europa.'[55] Lu then experiences not a return to Europe but the return of Europe in the shape of her former lovers.

Beside such similarities, there are also instructive differences between these two apparently innocuous detective stories. Goetz bestows a chatty and witty veneer of playful entertainment on a story, with its underlying obsession, violence, and hints of perversion. Kreisler, who peppers his cabaret oeuvre with gags and barbs aplenty, restricts himself to moments of sardonic humour in his predominantly sombre tale. This emerges from the ways in which the texts treat cross-cultural encounter – a source of humour in the story by Goetz, but of xenophobic prejudice with Kreisler. Goetz, resident in Switzerland from 1933-1939,[56] casts himself as narrator in his own story, and exploits his provenance in explaining to the Los Angeles police department why he is such a good shot: 'Dort schießen wir alle wie Wilhelm Tell.'[57] The sheriff then introduces Goetz to the detective with the words, 'Das ist Mr Goetz – Curt –, der die Leiche gefunden hat und der schießt wie Bill Tell'.[58] Kreisler's character Greenway, however, encounters a different attitude from the detective Connally who, despite being the exile's friend, regards him as irredeemably foreign; Connally, in response to his wife, who shows her presupposition of Greenway's guilt by asking how he could have done such a thing, replies 'Deutsch bleibt deutsch'.[59]

Different attitudes to the police are a particularly revealing point of contrast between the two stories. Not only does Goetz provide his Columbo-style detective Ben Blunt (played by the cabaret artist Wolfgang Neuss in the 1964 film of the story) with a mischievous and creative streak: 'Wir Detektive haben auch unseren künstlerischen Ehrgeiz, weißt du das?';[60] in Dr Maning he creates a character who starts off as a (continental) European 'Untersuchungsrichter' of the sternest and most authoritarian kind, but whom sexual obsession transforms into a sculptor with enough creativity to be described as 'einer der wenigen Emigranten, [...] die in diesem Lande Karriere gemacht haben'.[61] By contrast Kreisler's story claims that policemen and artists are irreconcilably separated by their differing outlook on the world, as indicated in a diary entry made by Helen Twyne, a magistrate who seems to carry authorial authority:

> Polizisten glauben tatsächlich, dass die Welt nur aus Polizisten und deren Feinden besteht, daher ist die einzige Wahrheit, die sie akzeptieren, ihre eigene [...] Maler kommen der Wahrheit wesentlich näher als Polizisten [...] Wenn im Fernsehen ein gutes Theaterstück läuft, schaltet ein Polizist automatisch um, und zwar nicht, [...] weil er das Stück nicht versteht, sondern im Gegenteil, weil er es nur allzu gut versteht. Er versteht genau, dass es ihn und seine Wahrheit in Frage stellt.[62]

While the forces of law and order that Goetz depicts in California seem to enjoy the titillating process of unearthing latent sexual obsessions and violent emotional enslavements, Kreisler's loftier English counterparts interrogate the very nature of artistic endeavour, and postulate a difference between the human laws that are intended to uphold justice and the natural laws that determine artists' responsibilities. In subscribing to this distinction Helen Twyne, the investigating magistrate, is blunt in her verdict on inauthentic artists who shirk them:

> Die meisten Menschen, die wir für Künstler halten oder die von den Medien als Künstler gepriesen werden, sind keine. Sie befriedigen lediglich den Zeitgeschmack, was zwar seine Berechtigung, aber nichts mit Kunst zu tun hat.[63]

She would probably have little time for a work such as *Die Tote von Beverly Hills*, with its author's avowed intention to disprove his wife's claim that he was incapable of writing an erotic novel.[64] Strictures such as Twyne's clearly imply immutable criteria for the identification of art that succeeds in approaching universal truth; to meet them, Greenway must by the end of the novel 'jump over his shadow' – transcend the twin personae of imperfectly assimilated English immigrant in part one, and German Jewish repatriate among the literati of Hamburg in part three. In the process he ultimately renounces his link with society; in embracing the imperative to create art he submits to life in an English asylum, whether from internal or external pressures.

Human laws, meanwhile, are in the first instance Inspector Connally's business, and while they emerge as not unimportant they nonetheless appear comparatively limited and parochial. While art is portrayed as a distinctive phenomenon with its own inalienable integrity, justice is cast as something variable, susceptible to adaptation within national borders, negotiable and therefore intrinsically inferior, even if – perhaps precisely because – the price to be paid for engagement with art can preclude meaningful engagement with society.

Connally, for example, refers to a geographical variant of justice in rebutting his wife's prejudicial verdict on Greenway: 'Ich habe versucht, ihr zu erklären, dass auch die englische Justiz im Zweifel immer für den Angeklagten ausspricht.'[65] His touching, rather naive confidence is possibly an attempt to convince himself, because elsewhere its fragility has already been revealed; he loses his temper when he realises that he cannot prevent himself from telling Greenway a little white lie to disguise his wife's prejudice: 'Warum bringt mich dieser deutsche Schweinehund zum Lügen, fragte er sich, warum kann ich ihm nicht die Wahrheit sagen? Einem Engländer hätte ich gesagt, sieh mal, alter Knabe, du weisst doch, wie Frauen sind.'[66] Not that we should be any more surprised to discover that stewardship of justice is a challenge, and that faith in it needs periodic bolstering than that Greenway's journey towards artistic emancipation is hindered by personal frailties.

In a passage that ties together the themes of home, exile, justice, morality, identity and art, Connally's reflections indicate both the strength of his personal cultural roots and his awareness that artists seem to work on a different plane:

> Heimat ist, was wir für Heimat halten, dachte er, wenigstens das habe ich von John gelernt. Ich halte England für meine Heimat, und im engeren Sinne halte ich auch die englische Moral, die englischen Gesetze und die englische Mentalität für meine

Heimat. John denkt da anders, aber die englischen Gesetze und
die englische Mentalität besagen, dass ein Mensch, der einem
anderen Menschenleben ein Ende setzt, ein Mörder ist,
vorausgesetzt, dass er Gewalt anwendet. Wenn er ihn gewaltlos
umbringt, geschieht ihm nichts, denn wie bringt man jemanden
gewaltlos um? Das wissen nur die Schriftsteller [...] [67]

It therefore seems that Kreisler required a foreign setting for his novel in
order to illustrate the anthropological nature of justice in comparison with
the metaphysical mysteries of art. At the same time the choice of England
dovetails with associative images of justice that may indeed evoke nothing
more than a national tradition of writing detective fiction or, as a legacy
from Kreisler's own wartime experiences, the congenial memory of an
nation allied to the US in opposing Hitler.

In the course of exploring whether the two realms of artistic
vocation and man-made laws articulate with each other or not, Kreisler
paints an English backdrop that is two-dimensional and unconvincing but
nonetheless effective. It fulfils the requisite functions of providing an
appropriate legal environment and showing that its underlying values are
subject to a relativism that is shaped by national identity. In this way it
underlines the fact that the universal principles of art are enhanced by
cultural diversity.

The England of *Der Schattenspringer* is not a credible context in
terms of the nuts and bolts of local verisimilitude; it is a utilitarian fantasy
where justice is endowed with an idealized integrity that allows it to take on
that of art on reasonably equal terms, as well as helping it to function purely
as a detective story. In this respect the town of Bottsville and the legal
infrastructure that accompanies it fulfil a role not significantly different from
that assigned to the English justice system that wreaks retribution on the
eponymous 'Paule' in the cabaret caricature referred to previously; while it
is impossible to say whether such images of England were inspired by
Kreisler's stay in wartime Britain, they are certainly entirely consistent with
his comparatively fleeting acquaintance with the country and the particular
circumstances in which this took place.

Notes

[1] Hans-Jürgen Fink and Michael Seufert, *Georg Kreisler gibt es gar nicht* (Frankfurt am Main: Scherz/S Fischer Verlag, 2005), pp. 117-22.

[2] *Ibid.*, p. 117.

[3] *Ibid.*, p. 253.

[4] Georg Kreisler, Interview with Colin Beaven, Munich, 3 October 1996.

[5] Georg Kreisler, 'Mein Leben in Worten ohne Lieder', in *Worte ohne Lieder* (Frankfurt am Main/Berlin: Ullstein, 1988), pp. 313-26 (first published in 1986 by Paul Neff Verlag, Vienna).

[6] Georg Kreisler, 'Meine Memoiren', in *Wenn ihr lachen wollt … Ein Lesebuch* (Hürth bei Köln/Vienna: Edition Memoria, 2001), p. 131.

[7] In 2000 the recording label 'kip media', which has championed recordings of Kreisler's performances in recent years, reported on its website that 'seine Autobiographie [geht] der Vollendung entgegen – das Buch soll noch in diesem Jahr veröffentlicht werden' (http://www.kip-media.de/neues/krneu60.htm).

[8] Georg Kreisler, *Lola und das Blaue vom Himmel* (Hürth bei Köln/Vienna: Edition Memoria, 2002).

[9] Siegel's parents are variously described as Jewish immigrants from Russia (http://www.bbc.co.uk/crime/caseclosed/bugsysiegel.shtml), Hungary, and Austria ('the death certificate states Austria as the birthplace of his parents', according to an anonymous comment at http://en.wikipedia.org/wiki/Talk:Bugsy_Siegel).

[10] Hans-Jürgen Fink and Michael Seufert, *op. cit.*, pp. 84-85.

[11] Georg Kreisler, *Lola und das Blaue vom Himmel*, p. 15.

[12] Georg Kreisler, Interview with Colin Beaven, Munich, 3 October 1996.

[13] Georg Kreisler, in *Ich über mich: Georg Kreisler* (Interview with Karl Löbl, broadcast in 1992 on Österreichisches Rundfunk).

[14] Georg Kreisler, *Lola und das Blaue vom Himmel*, p. 13.

[15] Georg Kreisler, in *Boulevard Bio* (Interview with Alfred Biolek, broadcast in November 2002 on Westdeutscher Rundfunk).

[16] Georg Kreisler, Interview with Horst Wandrey, broadcast 28 February 1983 on Radio DDR II.

[17] Hans-Jürgen Fink and Michael Seufert, *op. cit.*, p. 135.

[18] Georg Kreisler, 'Offener Brief nach Wien', *Süddeutsche Zeitung*, 1 October 1996.

[19] Georg Kreisler, 'Mein Leben in Worten ohne Lieder', in *Worte ohne Lieder* (Frankfurt am Main/Berlin: Ullstein, 1988), p. 318.

[20] Christian Bauer and Rebecca Göpfert, *Die Ritchie Boys* (Hamburg: Hoffman und Campe, 2005). See also website related to associated film of the same name *At war against their home*, available at http://www.ritchieboys.com/DL/focus-en.pdf.

[21] Hans-Jürgen Fink and Michael Seufert, *op. cit.*, p. 111.

[22] Siglinde Bolbecher and Konstantin Kaiser, *Lexikon der österreichischen Exilliteratur* (Vienna: Deuticke Verlag, 2000), cited by Daniela Strigl ('Ein überfälliges Standardwerk – Das Lexikon der Exilliteratur', September 2001), available at http://www.sbg.ac.at/ger /kmueller/striglexillexikon.rtf.

[23] Georg Kreisler, Interview with Colin Beaven, Munich, 3 October 1996.

[24] *Ibid.*

[25] Kristi Fisher & Mark Fisher, 'Benjamin "Bugsy" Siegel (1904–1947), Syndicate leader and Victim' (2000), available at http://www.carpenoctem.tv/mafia/siegel.html.

[26] Georg Kreisler, *Lola und das Blaue vom Himmel*, p. 19.

[27] *Ibid.*, p. 9.

[28] Georg Kreisler, in *Ich über mich: Georg Kreisler* (Interview with Karl Löbl, broadcast in 1992 on Österreichische Rundfunk).

[29] *Ibid.*

[30] Georg Kreisler, *Lola und das Blaue vom Himmel*, p. 17.

[31] Michael Grim, 'Marcel Prawy ist tot' (2003), available at http://www.lupi.ch/ex/prawy.htm.

[32] Marcel Prawy, *Marcel Prawy erzählt aus seinem Leben* (Vienna: Kremayr & Scheriau, 1996), pp. 160ff.

[33] Marcel Prawy, interviewed in *Und immer wieder Tauben vergiften,* ed. by J. Kittner (broadcast 21 July 2002 by Österreichisches Rundfunk: ÖRF2).

[34] Tom Schlesinger, E-mail to Colin Beaven, 7 June 2001.

[35] Gerald Heath, E-mail to Colin Beaven, 24 August 2005.

[36] Tom Schlesinger, E-mail to Colin Beaven, 7 June 2001.

[37] Tom Schlesinger, E-mail to Colin Beaven, 14 July 2001.

[38] Hans-Jürgen Fink and Michael Seufert, *op. cit.*, p. 117.

[39] Georg Kreisler, Interview with Colin Beaven, Munich, 3 October 1996.

[40] Hans-Jürgen Fink and Michael Seufert, *op. cit.*, pp. 121-22.

[41] *Ibid.*, p. 167.

[42] Alfred Meyer, *My Life as a Fish* (2000), available at http://www.ritchieboys.com/DL/fish204.pdf, ch. 4, pp. 1-2.

[43] Hans-Jürgen Fink and Michael Seufert, *op. cit.*, p. 118.

[44] Georg Kreisler, in *Boulevard Bio* (Interview with Alfred Biolek, broadcast in November 2002 on Westdeutscher Rundfunk).

[45] Hans Vogel, 'On to Trier', in *World War II Experiences* (2003), available at http://www.militaryhistoryonline.com/wwii/accounts/hansvogel.aspx.

[46] Georg Kreisler, 'Zu Hause ist der Tod', in *Mit dem Rücken gegen die Wand* (Vienna: Preiser Records, 1979), text available at http://www.gkif.de/texte/liedtexte/167.doc.

[47] Georg Kreisler, in *Ich über mich: Georg Kreisler* (Interview with Karl Löbl, broadcast in 1992 on Österreichisches Rundfunk).

[48] Georg Kreisler, 'Mein Leben in Worten ohne Lieder', in *Worte ohne Lieder* (Frankfurt am Main/Berlin: Ullstein, 1988), p. 325.

[49] Georg Kreisler, 'In Deutschland', in *Gruselkabinett* (Vienna: Preiser Records, 1981), text available at http://www.gkif.de/texte/liedtexte/171.doc.

[50] Georg Kreisler, 'Der Paule', in *Everblacks Zwei* (Stuttgart: Intercord, 1974), text available at http://www.gkif.de/texte/liedtexte/040.doc.

[51] Georg Kreisler, *Der Schattenspringer* (Berlin: Edition diá, 1996).

[52] Colin Beaven, 'Multiple exile and personal integrity: the search for artistic reconciliation in the cabaret and fiction of Georg Kreisler' in *Literary Reflections of Exile*, ed. by Roger Whitehouse (Lampeter: Edwin Mellen Press, 2000) pp. 133–57.

[53] Curt Goetz, *Die Tote von Beverly Hills* (Munich: Deutscher Taschenbuch Verlag, 1963) p. 7 (first published in 1951).

[54] Georg Kreisler, *Lola und das Blaue vom Himmel*, p. 62.

[55] Curt Goetz, *op. cit.,* p. 104.

[56] Theatergruppe Triangel, *Curt Goetz* (1999), available at http://www.theatergruppe-triangel.de/haus/goetz.htm.

[57] Curt Goetz, *op. cit.,* p. 11.

[58] *Ibid.*, p. 12.

[59] Georg Kreisler, *Der Schattenspringer*, p. 14.

[60] Curt Goetz, *op. cit.*, p. 85.

[61] *Ibid.*, p. 112.

[62] Georg Kreisler, *Der Schattenspringer*, pp. 70-71.

[63] *Ibid.*, p. 71.

[64] Curt Goetz, *op. cit.*, frontispiece.

[65] Georg Kreisler, *Der Schattenspringer*, p. 75.

[66] *Ibid.*, p. 50.

[67] *Ibid.*, p. 21.

Representations of Austria

'Immortal Austria': Eva Priester as a Propagandist for Austria in British Exile

Charmian Brinson

This article considers the activities in British exile of the journalist and writer Eva Priester in promoting the view, current in the – predominantly Communist – Austrian Centre and Free Austrian Movement circles in which she lived and worked, of Austria as a nation separate from Germany, both historically and culturally, and of the desirability of the establishment of a free and independent Austria after the war. As well as examining Priester's journalistic output, the article also considers some of her historical, poetic and dramatic writings in exile, all of which, though very different in form and flavour, have Austria as their central theme.

Eva Priester, journalist, writer, historian and poet, was in exile in Britain from 1939 to 1946.[1] Born Eva Feinstein into a comfortably off, assimilated Jewish family in St Petersburg in 1910, she lived in Germany, Czechoslovakia and Austria before finally, in the mid-1930s, becoming a 'Wahlösterreicherin', an Austrian by choice. She was also a committed Communist, joining the Party in 1933, and was imprisoned for a time in Germany on account of her political activities. In Austria she met and worked with Austrian Communists of note such as the poet and dramatist Jura Soyfer, and it was at this period of her life that her close identification with Austria appears to have originated (though she could not become an Austrian citizen until after the war). In British exile, she formed one of the exceptionally active group of Austrian Communists who constituted the core of the Austrian Centre. Set up in 1939 as a meeting place for Austrians in exile in Britain, this was probably the most successful organization of Austrian exiles in any of the countries of emigration between 1939 and 1947, offering the beleaguered Austrian refugee community in London and elsewhere a wide range of cultural, political, educational and social activities, a restaurant, library, small-scale publishing house and a weekly newspaper.[2]

Although the Centre was ostensibly a non-party organization – and indeed the majority of its perhaps 3500 members had no political affiliation of any kind – it was the Communists within it who succeeded in exercising a large measure of control. Initially, and particularly in the light of the large-scale internment of 'enemy aliens' in mid-1940, the activists took care to maintain a low political profile; however, the entry of the Soviet Union into the war in June 1941 transformed the political climate in Britain, leading, *inter alia*, to the foundation of the unashamedly political Free Austrian Movement by the end of that year, in which the Austrian Centre and the Communists within the Centre played a leading role.

It is within this framework that Eva Priester carried out her work as a propagandist for Austria, both as one of the three editors of the Austrian Centre's weekly newspaper *Zeitspiegel* – the others were Jenö Kostmann and Hilde Mareiner – and in other capacities (as a dramatist, for example, or as a public speaker). It should be noted, too, that despite their period of self-imposed restraint until June 1941, the Communist exiles, like Priester, had arrived in Britain with a clear political agenda. This included the setting up of the Austrian Centre and Free Austrian Movement along Popular Front lines, i.e. as a coalition of Austrian anti-Nazi political parties – though the Social Democrats chose to absent themselves early on from this – together with leading intellectuals and artists. Their chief aim, through these organizations, was to propagate the post-war re-establishment of a free and democratic Austria (a task that was made very much easier from December 1943, after the Moscow Declaration had declared the Anschluss with Germany null and void and Austrian independence an Allied war aim). This message, which involved the affirmation of Austria's specific historical, political and cultural identity, was one in which the Austrian Communists were greatly influenced by the Communist theoretician Alfred Klahr, whose essay 'Zur nationalen Frage in Österreich' had appeared in *Weg und Ziel* in Czechoslovakia in 1937.[3] Its promotion, both to the Austrian refugee population and to their British hosts, as well as, from June 1941 at any rate, the close identification with the Allied war effort, lay at the heart of all Free Austrian endeavours, one of the chief vehicles being the newspaper *Zeitspiegel*.

Zeitspiegel, which started life in 1939 as a duplicated German-language news digest for Austrian refugees with poor English, soon grew to become the weekly newspaper of the Austrian emigration in Britain, achieving at its peak a circulation of around 3000 and offering its readership a broad coverage of news, information and culture. It was above all through *Zeitspiegel* that Eva Priester, who had learned her journalism on the staff of the celebrated liberal *Berliner Tageblatt*, was able to make her voice heard while in British exile. The range of her contributions is remarkable, indicating exceptional versatility as a writer (moreover as a writer for whom German was a second language): analyses of current events, historical essays, expositions of England and the English for her Austrian readership, poetry – she was both an accomplished poet and also a very fine translator of poetry – and numerous book, theatre and film reviews. Running through all of these, however, there is a clear common thread, namely total engagement with the Free Austrian cause.

An article entitled 'Paradies und Hölle', for instance, of 17 April 1943, i. e. from before the crucial Moscow Declaration, set out in chararacteristic fashion to present Austria as an occupied nation – a victim of Germany, therefore, rather than its ally – with Austria's true interests represented by its internal resistance movement (this last was a central tenet of the Free Austrian credo which, as it later transpired, bore only a limited relation to reality). In her article, Priester presented the position of Austrian soldiers serving in the Wehrmacht as deeply disadvantaged: they were condemned to defend hopeless positions on the Eastern front, exposed to the line of fire in Africa or sent off to fight in the frozen Arctic. How much more fortunate, she continued, were those Austrians – 'die Männer der "grünen Kader"' – who had evaded conscription and joined the Austrian Resistance up in the mountains, even if their physical conditions were equally deplorable:

> Aber sie haben die Chance, die die Männer in der Hölle nicht haben – wenn sie sterben müssen, für ihre eigene Sache zu sterben, wenn sie kämpfen, für ihre eigene Freiheit zu kämpfen, und den Tag zu erleben, an dem ihr Land [...] zu einem Land der Freien wird.

Towards the end of the war, in an article 'Götterdämmerung in Salzburg' (17 February 1945), Priester would present her views of the disastrous Austro-German connection still more starkly. Germany, so the German Foreign Office had reportedly let it be known, would consider, even if Berlin were to fall, continuing the fighting in Austria, a last terrible act by Germany against Austria to be added to the catalogue of crimes already committed:

> Die Deutschen haben unserem Land die Freiheit gestohlen, sie haben es ausgeplündert, sie haben tausende unserer Männer und Frauen zu Tode gefoltert, sie haben Millionen in ihren verbrecherischen Krieg hineingezwungen. Zahllose unserer Männer sind heute Krüppel, Tausende unserer Mädchen sind von den SS-Tieren geschändet worden, unsere zwölfjährigen und vierzehnjährigen Kinder sterben zu hunderten an den deutschen Befestigungsanlagen. Unsere Städte liegen in Trümmern und auf unseren brachliegenden Feldern der Festungszone wächst das Unkraut. Aber all dies ist noch zu wenig, all dies ist noch nicht genug! Nichts soll übrigbleiben von unserem Lande, das einmal ein Garten Europas war, als ein Haufen von Ruinen und menschlichen Gebeinen, über dem die verfluchten schwarzen Adler Deutschlands dahinflattern.

The Austrians, Priester contended, had grounds to hate the German oppressors that were just as compelling as those of the Russians, French, Czechs or Yugoslavs; therefore, it is implied, Austria had earned the right to be ranked with them among Germany's victims.

Parallel to the separatist view of Austria in the political sphere, a constant Free Austrian concern was to redefine Austrian culture, too, in autonomous terms, that is as distinct from German culture. So important was this conceived to be, in fact, that 'Kulturkonferenzen' were organized by Austrian exiles in August 1942 and again in October 1944 for this purpose. Jenö Kostmann, of the *Zeitspiegel* editorial triumvirate, had published a seminal article, programmatically entitled 'Österreichische Kulturarbeit – eine Kampfaufgabe', on 30 May 1942 in which he had exhorted his fellow Austrians in exile to defend their culture and language against German incursion, while Priester herself, a few days before the first 'Kulturkonferenz', would also publish a piece on 'Österreichische Kultur' (22 August 1942) in which she more or less dismissed the question of German cultural influence as being of secondary importance. For it had, she argued, been the Czechs, Serbs, Croats and Hungarians who had given Austrian culture its distinctive flavour. In a later piece, 'Referendar Schultz und die Weltgeschichte' (13 November 1943), Priester reflected on the process currently under way within Free Austrian circles of rediscovering 'unser Land, unsere Geschichte, das große Erbe, das uns hinterlassen wurde' in order to arrive at 'das neue Nationalbewusstsein des totgesagten und unsterblichen Österreich'. In the past, Austrians had been sadly misrepresented, not least through the Blue Danube-style cliché common in German films; now, however, 'der Name "Österreicher" [ist] zu einem Kampfbegriff geworden'.

One of Eva Priester's most regular and arguably most interesting contributions to *Zeitspiegel* was in the field of arts criticism. She wrote discerning reviews, for example, of productions at the 'Laterndl', the Austrian Centre's own theatre. In one of her most thoughtful pieces, 'Selbstkritik der Kritik' (12 October 1941), she addressed the special relationship between performance and critic in the situation of exile. A review of a 'Laterndl' production, *Laterna Magica*, appearing recently in *Zeitspiegel*, had been too harsh, she admitted;[4] considering the situation in which the Free Austrians all found themselves, it was inappropriate to adopt the stance of the 'Kritiker auf hohem Stuhl'. Rather, critic and actor should join forces as 'Kameraden, die seit einigen Jahren an einer gemeinsamen Sache arbeiten'. Yet if the critics must be held to have gone too far, then the 'Laterndl' had not gone far enough in making its message clear:

> Wir fühlten, dass es heute das Wichtigste ist, überall und ständig
> auszusprechen: 'Heute geht es um alles. Jeder von uns – du, ich
> [–] muss seine ganze Kraft einsetzen, damit wir den
> Entscheidungskampf gewinnen.' Ihr habt vom ersten Teil des
> Satzes gesprochen, aber nicht genug vom zweiten. Es genügt
> heute nicht zu sagen 'Hitler ist ein Schuft und ein Narr', man
> muss auch sagen 'das und das musst du Mann im Parkett, du
> Refugeearbeiter tun, damit wir ihn besiegen'.

In a slightly later article, 'Jasnaja Poljana und wir' (3 January 1942), Priester directed a similar exhortation, a call to actions rather than words, at her fellow German-speaking writers in exile who should publicly sever all connection with the arch-enemy, 'dem Gesindel Hitlers', in order to rescue the shared German language from its current shameful state. However: 'Es genügt nicht, es zu wissen. Man muss es hinausschreien. Es genügt nicht, es hinauszuschreien. Man muss es mit Handlungen beweisen.'

It is worth recording in this connection that, true to her own precepts, Priester did not restrict her activities to the written word alone but also played her part as a public speaker for the Austrian cause. Years later she would recall that as early as 1940 – at a time when it was still impolitic for Communists to air their views too publicly in Britain, and long before the idea of Austrian independence had been officially sanctioned – she had given a lecture in Birmingham on 'Warum muss Österreich wieder unabhängig werden?'.[5] She also participated regularly in the Austrian Centre's programme of readings and talks in London: in July 1943, for instance, she read from her own works at an event devoted to 'Österreichische Schriftstellerinnen',[6] while the following year she would address one Austrian Centre audience on the subject of 'Die Freiheitskriege (Österreichische Geschichte 1790-1815)',[7] and a second on the Austrian Monarchy between 1914 and 1918.[8]

With regard to the historical topics she often selected for her talks and her articles for *Zeitspiegel*, it is useful to recall that from around 1943 on, working in the British Museum library, Priester was engaged in preparatory research for perhaps her most significant achievement, her *Kurze Geschichte Österreichs*. This project was intended, according to the author's own preface, as a 'Neuentdeckung der Geschichte Österreichs', rendered necessary by the 'Gestrüpp der großdeutschen Darstellung' in which Austrian history had become entangled. There were certainly problems to contend with here: Priester herself, as she was the first to admit, was not a trained historian, moreover her research was further impeded by the difficult wartime conditions, including problems of access to essential literature. Her two-volume history, the first Marxist history of Austria, was nevertheless successfully completed and was published by the Party's Globus Verlag in

Vienna shortly after the war.[9] Apart from *Zeitspiegel*, Eva Priester succeeded in finding further outlets for the historical work she was producing in the later exile years. To the scholarly monthly *Kulturelle Schriftenreihe des Free Austrian Movement*, for instance, she contributed an essay on the Holy Roman Emperor Maximilian I, 'dem großen österreichischen Staaten-Erbauer', which, as the series editor Hermann Ullrich indicated in his preface, presented her subject 'in origineller, durchaus neuartiger Beleuchtung als moderner Herrscher und Reformator'.[10] As mentioned above, the Austrian Centre also ran its own publishing house, Free Austrian Books, which produced numerous publications: these were short political, cultural or literary texts which, although superficially fairly disparate in nature, all concerned themselves with aspects of Austrian aspiration and identity.[11] To *Kleines Magazin*, which combined information with entertainment for its refugee readership, Priester contributed another historical piece, this time a clear-headed view of Emperor Joseph II, culminating in a call for a new objectivity of historiography.[12] She was also able to put her Russian language skills to good use that same year, 1943, by translating Jury Herman's *Viel Glück: Aus dem Tagebuch einer Soviet [sic] W. A. A. F.*; as a portrayal of Soviet-British cooperation, this was published by Free Austrian Books to celebrate the increasing closeness of the anti-Hitler alliance.

In addition, Free Austrian Books produced a number of English-language booklets, aimed at informing a British readership of the Austrian plight as well as at propagating future Austrian independence to the British. One of these was Eva Priester's *Austria – Gateway to Germany* of September 1943, written for 'British friends of the Austrian cause' (according to the preface contributed by the Centre's President, F. C. West), which was reportedly one of the Centre's two most widely read publications.[13] This emphasized Austria's strategic significance for the further conduct of the war, following the Allied invasion of Italy; with the aim of presenting Austria as a member of the anti-Hitler alliance, it claimed that the Austrian people as a whole had already entered 'the stage of open and active resistance', marked by 'mass sabotage, mass demonstrations and strikes' (p. 13). It also stepped up the level of propaganda further by calling on behalf of the Austrian people for RAF action on Austria:

> We know that the men and women of our country will answer the bombing of their towns and their factories as the French workers answered when the RAF bombed the factories of France: 'Let your bombs fall, comrades, and hit your enemy and ours' (p. 21).

The tone here is strident, shocking in fact, born of the perceived imperatives of the propagandist's task. It is noteworthy, however, that in her poetry and dramatic sketches Priester adopted a rather different approach, even while employing these literary forms, too, to political effect.[14] In her poetry, in particular, though the certainties are undiminished, her language is considerably more differentiated and the tone frequently more tempered. As noted above, poems of hers appeared regularly in *Zeitspiegel* as well in other exile journals and anthologies. In *Die Vertriebenen: Dichtung der Emigration*, for example, a volume of poetry published jointly by the Free German League of Culture, the Austrian Centre and Young Czechoslovakia in 1941, no fewer than seven of her poems were included (more than those of any other contributor). Among these are her 'Österreichische Klage', a lament for the lost country, composed on the outbreak of war, as well as what is arguably her finest poem, the powerful anti-war allegory 'Legende'. In late 1945, these poems and others reappeared in a collection of Priester's poetry, *Aus Krieg und Nachkrieg*, published in London by Free Austrian Books to raise money for the Austrian Relief Fund; the volume was republished in Vienna the following year by the Globus Verlag. The Globus edition also featured Priester's own preface recalling the years of exile and war that had given rise to her poems as well as the faith in the future that she had attempted to capture in her work:

> Diese Zukunft war uns in den Jahren des Krieges immer gegenwärtig und ich habe, wie viele andere, die in dieser Zeit Geschichte oder Romane schrieben, versucht, an dieser oder jener Stelle den Klang ihrer fernen Schritte einzufangen.[15]

As for Priester's sketches for the 'Laterndl' – she contributed to the satirical revues *Here is the News* and *No Orchids for Mr Hitler* (both 1942) – these also bear evidence both to Priester's versatility as a writer and to the future-oriented perspective, referred to above, that was of course a part of the Free Austrian belief system. Three of the eight scenes in *No Orchids for Mr Hitler* are Priester's, two of them humorous: 'Citizen Kohn' advanced the premise that in forty years' time the word 'antisemitism' would have disappeared from use, while 'What Can I Do?', set partly in the Austrian Centre Birmingham, partly in the significantly named 'Café Freiheit, Wien', illustrated the progressive involvement of two 'typical' Austrians – Herr Frisch and Herr Fromm – in the Free Austrian cause, spurred on by perhaps over-eager Austrian Centre activists.[16] However, Priester's third scene, 'Das Urteil', represented the only serious sketch in the revue and was, in the opinion of the refugee newspaper *Die Zeitung*, particularly memorable.[17] Set in a prison cell somewhere in occupied Europe, 'Das Urteil' concluded by anticipating liberation from the Nazi yoke:

> Wir sind nicht allein. Sie werden zur Zeit kommen [...] Sie
> kommen über das Meer, auf vielen Schiffen, jeden Augenblick
> können sie kommen und in Frankreich landen und unsere Türen
> öffnen [...] Wenn du ganz genau hinhörst, kannst du ihre Schritte
> hören [...] Jetzt sind sie am Gefängnistor. Hörst du, wie das Eisen
> kracht? Jetzt haben sie die Tür eingeschlagen und sind auf der
> Treppe [...] Bald sind sie da![18]

Such visionary tones were also very much a feature of *Immortal Austria*, a 'British-Austrian Rally and Pageant' written for a mixed Anglo-Austrian audience by Eva Priester and Erich Fried. This was performed in London on 13 March 1943, to music by Hans Gál, to mark the fifth anniversary of the Anschluss. Scenes from Austrian history illustrating the surmounting of various difficulties included 'Stronger than Plague and Death', a portrayal of Vienna at the time of the plague, helped on by the legendary Viennese character der liebe Augustin; and a sketch entitled 'An Austrian Wat Tyler' depicting the Austrian peasant leader, Michael Gaissmaier, in his struggle against oppression. A further scene, 'A Concert in Bath, 1795', illustrated Haydn's success in England – as an example of past Anglo-Austrian cultural interchange – in which the question was reportedly posed: 'How is it – are all composers Austrians? Or all Austrians composers?' The final scene, 'A Garden on the Thames 1943', first focused on present-day Anglo-Austrian relations, then – according to a review by the Free Austrian writer Albert Fuchs – 'ließ sie ins Allegorische übergehend, eine Reihe von Figuren, auf die wir Österreicher stolz sind, das Wort sprechen: "Ich bin Österreich[er]"– ein stolzes Wort, alles in allem'.[19]

When, later in life, Eva Priester would reflect on what had brought together the very disparate members of the Austrian emigration in Britain, she would identify as the unifying factor 'ihr Österreichertum, genauer gesagt, ihr Bewusstsein, Österreicher zu sein und einer nationalen Gemeinschaft anzugehören, deren Land zwar von einer fremden Macht besetzt, aber nicht ausgelöscht war'. This Austrian consciousness had by no means arisen spontaneously, however; rather it had been the result 'einer jahrelangen Aufklärungsarbeit und auch einer geduldig durchgeführten organisatorischen Tätigkeit', directed by the Austrian Centre and the Free Austrian Movement and carried through by the exiled Austrian writers, among others, 'die zugleich Teilnehmer und auch Mit-Erwecker dieser Entwicklung waren'.[20] As we have seen, Priester herself played a central role here.

There were never, apparently, any doubts in Eva Priester's mind but that after the war, in line with the precepts of the Free Austrian Movement, she would return to Austria, her country by adoption. An article of hers in *Zeitspiegel*, 'Eine praktische Vision', from 7 August 1943, reviewing an exhibition of post-war rebuilding plans for London, included the unequivocal statement: 'Wenn das Volk von London nach dem Kriege seine neue Stadt zu bauen beginnt, werden wir nicht mehr dabei sein.' And an unusually reflective piece written a few weeks later, 'Englischer Herbst' (*Zeitspiegel*, 16 October 1943) which constitutes a warm appreciation of England as seen through *émigré* eyes, nevertheless concludes with the anticipation of departure:

> Es wird nicht leicht sein, die zarten Pastellfarben des englischen Herbstes zu vergessen. Der Sand rinnt rasch im Stundenglas. In das Glück des Findens mischt sich schon leise der Schmerz des Abschieds. Schon sind die weißen Felsen Dovers wieder in Sicht und der Nebel, der die Insel wie ein Tuch verhüllt. Wir wollen noch einmal durch den englischen Herbst gehen und seine reiche Milde mitnehmen in das harte Licht unserer harten Zeit.

Typically, a revue Priester wrote for Young Austria (the youth arm of the Austrian Centre), and the last their 'Spiel und Tanzgruppe' performed in March 1946, was entitled *Cheerio England!*,[21] in keeping with the FAM's policy to persuade all Young Austrians to return home.

Eva Priester herself left London for Vienna in 1946, after her seven years as a propagandist for Austria. She took Austrian citizenship two years later. Admittedly, the Austria to which she and her fellow Free Austrians returned was scarcely the country for which they had hoped and planned while in exile: they were, above all, sadly disillusioned to discover the full extent of Austrian wartime collaboration with the Germans and the relative insignificance of the internal anti-Nazi resistance. Moreover, the first post-war Austrian elections of November 1945 proved a bitter blow for the Communists who, having anticipated sizeable successes, only managed to win four parliamentary seats. Eva Priester lived the rest of her life in Austria, continuing her career as a writer and journalist and remaining a member of the Communist Party. In 1979 she was honoured by the Austrian state for her services to Austrian historiography. She died three years later, not in Austria, ironically enough, but in Russia, the land of her birth.

Notes

I am greatly indebted to the following for their kind advice and assistance: the Dokumentationsarchiv des österreichischen Widerstandes, Vienna; the Alfred Klahr Gesellschaft, Vienna; Dr Volker Kaukoreit and the Österreichisches Literaturarchiv, Österreichische Nationalbibliothek, Vienna; Dr Peter Michael Braunwarth; Professor Richard Dove; Maria Gerger; Hilde Mareiner; and Monika Warburton.

[1] For further details on Priester's biography, see autobiographical fragment from 1940 held in Eva Priester Papers, Alfred Klahr Gesellschaft, Vienna, Z155; also Heide Maria Holzknecht, 'Eva Priester: Journalistin, Schriftstellerin, Historikerin', unpubl. diss., Innsbruck, 1986, and Claudia Trost, 'Eva Priester: Ein biografischer Abriss', in *Die Alfred Klahr Gesellschaft und ihr Archiv: Beiträge zur österreichischen Geschichte des 20. Jahrhunderts* (Vienna: Alfred Klahr Gesellschaft, 2000), pp. 347-70.

[2] On this, see also Helene Maimann, *Politik im Wartesaal: Österreichische Exilpolitik in Großbritannien 1938-1948* (Vienna/Cologne/Graz: Hermann Böhlaus Nachf., 1975); *Österreicher im Exil: Großbritannien 1938-1945: Eine Dokumentation*, ed. by Wolfgang Muchitsch (Vienna: Österreichischer Bundesverlag, 1992); and Marietta Bearman, Charmian Brinson, Richard Dove, Anthony Grenville and Jennifer Taylor, *Wien – London, hin und zurück: Das Austrian Centre in London, 1939-1947* (Vienna: Czernin, 2004). The English version of the last cited, *Out of Austria: The Austrian Centre in London in World War II* (London: I. B. Tauris, 2007), is forthcoming.

[3] Republished in Alfred Klahr, *Zur österreichischen Nation* (Vienna: Globus, 1994).

[4] On this, see review of *Laterna Magica*, 'Das wieder leuchtende Laterndl', *Zeitspiegel*, 5 October 1941, p. 7; also letter from Ernst Gerhard Kempinski, 'Schauspieler contra Kritiker', *Zeitspiegel*, 12 October 1941, p. 11.

[5] See *Österreicher im Exil 1934 bis 1945: Protokoll des internationalen Symposiums zur Erforschung des österreichischen Exils von 1934 bis 1945*, ed. by Dokumentationsarchiv des österreichischen Widerstandes and Dokumentationsstelle für neuere österreichische Literatur (Vienna: Österreichischer Bundesverlag für Unterricht, Wissenschaft und Kunst, 1997), p. 108.

[6] See the Austrian Centre's eponymous monthly newsletter, July 1943.

[7] *Ibid.*, August 1944.

[8] See *Zeitspiegel*, 21 October 1944, p. 7.

[9] Vol. I of her *Kurze Geschichte Österreichs*, subtitled *Entstehung eines Staates*, appeared in 1946; vol. II, *Aufstieg und Untergang des Habsburgerreiches*, appeared in 1949.

[10] See Eva Priester, 'Maximilian I.', in *Kulturelle Schriftenreihe des Free Austrian Movement: Österreicher, die Geschichte machten*, 11, [1945], pp. 4-10. (For Ullrich comment, see p. iii.)

[11] On this, see also Charmian Brinson and Richard Dove, 'Zielgerichtete Publikationen: Die Reihe Free Austrian Books', in *Wien – London, hin und retour*, pp. 94-119.

[12] Eva Priester, 'Der Bauerngott', in *Kleines Magazin* (London: Free Austrian Books, 1943), pp. 13-14.

[13] See Georg Knepler, *Five Years of the Austrian Centre* (London: Free Austrian Books, [1944]), p. 5.

[14] For Priester's poetry, see also the present author's '"Schlaf ruhig. Die Erde ist dein": Eva Priester, a political poet in exile' in *The Austrian Lyric* (*Austrian Studies*, vol. 12) ed. by Judith Beniston and Robert Vilain, 2004, pp. 116-32.

[15] Eva Priester, Preface to *Aus Krieg und Nachkrieg: Gedichte und Übertragungen* (Vienna: Globus Verlag, 1946), [p. 6].

[16] Text reproduced under the title 'Was geht's mich an?' in *Österreichische Kulturblätter*, December 1942, pp. 13-17.

[17] 'No Orchids for Mr Hitler', *Die Zeitung*, 16 October 1942, p. 9.

[18] For text, reproduced under the title 'Irgendwo im Morgengrauen', see *Österreichische Kulturblätter*, December 1942, pp. 13-17.

[19] Though *Immortal Austria* as a whole does not appear to have survived, two drafts in the Erich Fried Archive, 'Österreichspiel' and 'Österreichspiel: Gaismaier [*sic*] überquert die Alpen', are almost certainly related to it (Österreichisches Literaturarchiv, Österreichische Nationalbibliothek, Vienna). See also Albert Fuchs, 'Immortal Austria', *Zeitspiegel*, 20 March 1943, p. 7; and Walter Pass, Gerhard Scheit and Wilhelm Svoboda, *Orpheus im Exil: Die Vertreibung der österreichischen Musik von 1938 bis 1945* (Vienna: Verlag für Gesellschaftskritik, 1995), p. 129.

[20] Eva Priester, 'Osterreichische Schriftsteller in der britischen Emigration', in *Österreicher im Exil 1934 bis 1945*, p. 437.

[21] See 'Cheerio England!', *Zeitspiegel*, 6 April 1946, p. 6.

Wien-Bilder: Paul L. Stein, Richard Tauber und das britische Kino

Christian Cargnelli

Dieser Artikel nähert sich einem bislang kaum beachteten Aspekt der Filmexilforschung: dem Werk des vertriebenen Wiener Regisseurs Paul L. Stein im Allgemeinen und seiner Zusammenarbeit mit dem gleichfalls geflüchteten Sänger Richard Tauber im britischen Kino der 1930er und 1940er Jahre im Besonderen. Im Mittelpunkt steht dabei die „exterritoriale" filmische Verarbeitung des Mythos „Wien": Wie wurden so genannte typische Topoi des Wienerischen in dieser speziellen Ausprägung des Exilfilms verarbeitet?

„We will go to a Heurige", verspricht der berühmte Tenor Van Straaten (Frank Vosper), der gerade in der Staatsoper in Bizets *Carmen* aufgetreten ist, dem jungen englischen Pärchen auf Wien-Besuch, das ihn nach London engagieren will. „A what?", repliziert Frances Wilson (Leonora Corbett), Schwester eines Londoner Impresarios. „A Heurige, typical Vienna. An old winegarden where the people of Vienna amuse themselves. A few tables under the trees, a little music, everyone's so happy, the new wine, a spring night, a beautiful woman – and that is the Heurige!"

Und schon befinden wir uns des Abends in diesem so typisch wienerischen Etablissement. Lachende Menschen, wohin man schaut, die Leute tanzen Walzer, prosten einander zu, das Quartett aus Klavier, Violine, Bassgeige und Ziehharmonika endet unter tosendem Applaus und die Gäste rufen nach ihrem lokalen Idol. Also nimmt Josef Steidler noch schnell einen zur Brust, tritt hinaus ins Freie und intoniert, den Heurigengarten durchmessend, eines der klassischen Wienerlieder schlechthin: „Wien, Wien, nur du allein, sollst stets die Stadt meiner Träume sein …"

Gestalt und vor allem Stimme verleiht diesem Josef Steidler niemand anderer als Richard Tauber, von den Nazis nach England vertrieben, der „wahrscheinlich bekannteste in den Dreißigerjahren in Großbritannien lebende Österreicher".[1]

Der Film: *Heart's Desire*, eine britische Produktion aus dem Jahre 1935, großteils entstanden in den Elstree-Studios von British International Pictures. Anders als Tauber ist der Regisseur des Films vergessen – dabei hat Paul Ludwig Stein, Exilant wie sein Star, zu diesem Zeitpunkt bereits rund 50 Filme in Österreich, Deutschland, den USA und Großbritannien inszeniert, darunter viele mit prominenter Besetzung. Und 20 weitere Filme werden bis zu seinem Tod im Jahre 1951 noch folgen.

Doch wer war dieser Paul L. Stein, wie er sich nach der Emigration nannte? Welcher Art waren seine Filme, in welchem Kontext entstanden sie? Und, nicht zuletzt, wie wird in ihnen die Erfahrung von Flucht und Vertreibung angesprochen und verarbeitet? Stein selbst gibt 1928 folgende Auskunft über sich:

> Ich bin Österreicher und in Wien geboren. Mein Vater Emil Stein war ein in Österreich und Deutschland sehr bekannter Schauspieler, und es war nur natürlich, daß ich auch für die Bühne ausgebildet wurde. Ich wurde als Junge in Wien erzogen, und meine Ausbildung verteilte sich auf die Schule und das Theater, an dem mein Vater tätig war. Im dramatischen Unterricht machte ich so große Fortschritte, daß mir mein Vater, als ich erst 17 Jahre war, schon ein Engagement bei Max Reinhardt in Berlin verschaffen konnte. Bei Max Reinhardt blieb ich 4 Jahre und spielte vor allen Dingen komische Charakterrollen in Shakespeare-Stücken; u. a. spielte ich sehr oft mit Rudolph Schildkraut zusammen. Dann kehrte ich nach Wien zurück und erzielte auch hier große Erfolge als Shakespearedarsteller.[2]

Das ist beeindruckend und ziemlich gut ausgedacht. Immerhin stimmt, dass Stein 1892 in Wien geboren wird und aufwächst – und zwar als Sohn des jüdischen Kaufmanns Emanuel Stein und dessen Gattin Marie, wohnhaft Obere Donaustraße 87 im zweiten Wiener Gemeindebezirk Leopoldstadt, wo ein großer Teil der jüdischen Wiener Bevölkerung lebte.[3]

Mit Reinhardt haben ja bekanntlich fast alle gearbeitet – tatsächlich ist Stein in seinen späten Teenagerjahren allerdings kein Bühnenstar, sondern zunächst einmal Eleve an der Schauspielschule des Reinhardt'schen Deutschen Theaters in Berlin: 1910 gibt er, in Reinhardts Regie, den Flaut in einer Sommeraufführung des *Sommernachtstraums* im Föhrenwald in Nikolassee; als Zettel tritt der spätere Charakterdarsteller und Entertainer Paul Graetz auf, mit dem Stein bis in die gemeinsamen Jahre des Exils freundschaftlich verbunden bleibt.

Nach Anfängen in der deutschen Provinz ist Stein 1915/1916 in der ersten Saison an der neueröffneten, von Reinhardt geleiteten Berliner „Volksbühne" (Theater am Bülowplatz) engagiert. Klein- und Kleinstrollen bilden hier ebenso sein Repertoire wie danach in Königsberg (in der Direktionszeit Leopold Jessners) und von 1916 bis 1919 als Ensemblemitglied des Deutschen Volkstheaters in Wien.[4]

Als Stein 1928 die zitierten autobiografischen Auskünfte erteilt, hat er in Hollywood bereits fünf Filme inszeniert, für Warner Bros. und für den Filmpionier und führenden Produzenten Cecil B. DeMille. Wie etliche andere mitteleuropäische Filmschaffende wird er in den zwanziger Jahren von der amerikanischen Filmindustrie engagiert, um die Filmbranche der

Alten Welt durch Abwerbung zu schwächen und gleichzeitig das technische Know-how und die Expertise des in deutschen Studios geschulten Personals, ihr Spezialwissen und ihren kulturellen Background gezielt für eigene Zwecke einzusetzen – vorzugsweise in Produktionen mit (historischem) europäischem Hintergrund. Zu den bekanntesten Acquisitionen zählen die Regisseure Ernst Lubitsch, Michael Kertesz (= Curtiz), Friedrich Wilhelm Murnau, Paul Leni und E. A. Dupont, der Produzent Erich Pommer und die Darsteller Emil Jannings und Conrad Veidt.[5]

Steins grandiose „Neuerfindung" seiner selbst kann als durchaus typisch angesehen werden. Es scheint, als würde der in Hollywood erfolgreiche Regisseur – er macht 1927/28 noch einen „Zwischenstopp" in Berlin für das Melodram *Seine Mutter/Ehre Deine* Mutter – sich der gleichen Selbstvermarktungsstrategie bedienen, die viele europäische Filmschaffende in der Neuen Welt anwandten: sich retrospektiv eine Karriere schaffen, eine neue, glamourösere Identität. Es muss ja nicht gleich ein erfundener Adelstitel inklusive famoser militärischer Karriere sein wie bei Erich von Stroheim. Den Erwartungen, die Hollywood an die Immigranten knüpfte, dem Bild, das Amerika von der Alten Welt hatte, kamen solcherlei Nachstellungen romantischer Fantasien von Europa (Versiertheit in Sachen europäischer Geschichte und Kultur, Intellektualität, Bildung) bereitwillig entgegen.

Dazu passt gut die Erklärung, die Paul L. Stein 1934 in London dem gleichfalls exilierten Journalisten Peter Witt für seinen Wechsel vom Theater zum Film gibt. Der Regisseur erzählte ihm, so Witt, „how, many years ago he, the most successful actor in Vienna, suddenly and without any real reason, gave up his work and turned his enthusiasm to films".[6] „Ohne jeden Grund" ist ziemlich charmant formuliert – tatsächlich ging mit der schauspielerischen Karriere offenbar überhaupt nichts (mehr) weiter.

Die Hand voll Filme, die Stein 1919 in Wien inszeniert, deuten schon voraus auf die Genres, die seine Karriere bestimmen werden: Lustspiele und Melodramen. In der Komödie *Das kommt davon*, ebenfalls von 1919, tritt er als junger Mann namens Sebastian Flockerl auf, dem im Wiener Strandbad Gänsehäufel seine Jacke gestohlen wird. „Badeszenen ausgezeichnet", befinden *Paimann's Filmlisten*.[7] Der Regisseur des Films, Rudolf Stiassny, wird Stein 15 Jahre später bei den Dreharbeiten zu *Blossom Time* (1934) als „Quartiermacher" in Wien nützlich sein.[8]

1919 übersiedelt Stein nach Berlin und inszeniert bis 1926 nicht weniger als 25 deutsche Filme, zu Beginn einige für die eigene Firma Stein-Film, dann für die Ufa und andere Gesellschaften. 1920 etwa entstehen drei Streifen mit Pola Negri: *Martyrium, Arme Violetta* und *Die geschlossene Kette*. Was die Filmgeschichtsschreibung bislang zu Stein beizutragen hatte, nämlich wenig, wird noch übertroffen vom geradezu grotesken biografischen Eintrag zu seiner Person im als Standardwerk geltenden Band *Österreicher in Hollywood* des Filmarchiv Austria: Laut diesem hätte er mit *Martyrium* „den ersten Pola-Negri-Film" inszeniert – die Actrice war zu diesem Zeitpunkt allerdings schon in mindestens 25 Filmen aufgetreten, darunter in einigen Lubitsch-Klassikern wie *Die Augen der Mumie Mâ* (1918) und *Madame Dubarry* (1919).[9]

Die Genres von Steins deutschen Arbeiten: Melodram, Gesellschaftsdrama, Kostümfilm. Populäres Entertainment, keine Kunstfilme oder Experimente. Ein einziger dieser Streifen, *Liebesfeuer* (1925), bedient sich eines Wiener Sujets: das lustige Husarenleben am Vorabend des Ersten Weltkriegs. „Solche Geschichten aus dem lieben alten Österreich", so mit unverhohlener Ironie das Berliner *Reichsfilmblatt* „(im kalten Berlin brav und nicht immer mit echten Farben nachgespielt) haben es vielleicht in sich".[10]

Und dann: Hollywood. Gleich Steins erster Film dort, *My Official Wife* (1926), hat, unter anderem, Wien zum Schauplatz. Irene Rich spielt die Tochter eines russischen Adeligen, die der Deportation nach Sibirien dadurch entgeht, dass sie nach Wien flüchtet. Und hier, in der Stadt der Musik, gelingt ihr „a great success as a cabaret singer". Die Rezension im britischen *Bioscope* vermeldet auch „brilliant scenes at a Viennese café"[11] – genau für derlei melodramatische Konfektion europäischer Konvenienz hat man Stein geholt. Den charismatischen Charakterschurken gibt ein anderer Wiener, Gustav von Seyffertitz.

Bis 1932 dreht Stein in Hollywood Film auf Film, insgesamt 16 an der Zahl: Romantic Comedies, Murder Mysterys, Spionagefilme, Ehedramen. Was auffällt: Meistens spielen Frauen die Hauptrollen, stehen weibliche Stars im Zentrum der Handlung – zunächst Irene Rich, später Ann Harding, Jeanette MacDonald und vor allem Constance Bennett. Und: Steins amerikanische Filme sind überwiegend in Europa oder an exotischen Schauplätzen angesiedelt: Wien, Paris, London, Spanien, Norwegen, Arabien. In *A Woman Commands* (1932) etwa liebt und leidet sich Pola Negri in ihrem ersten amerikanischen Tonfilm durch ein ungenanntes osteuropäisches Königreich – welterfahren eben, diese Regisseure aus Europa.

„Let Them *All* Come!" titelt 1931 ein langer Artikel im britischen *Picturegoer*, der auf die (zunehmende) Internationalisierung des britischen Films Bezug nimmt und das Hereinströmen ausländischer Filmschaffender ausdrücklich begrüßt.[12] Ab 1933 gesellen sich zu den paar Dutzend freiwillig in England Arbeitenden jene, die nach der Vertreibung aus Nazideutschland, manchmal vorübergehend, Exil in England nehmen. Paul Stein gehört zu letzteren und seine Geschichte bislang zu den wenig bekannten Kapiteln in diesem Kontext.

„I wanted to go back to Berlin", erzählt er 1934 rückblickend dem *Picturegoer*:

> Just as a murderer is always magnetically drawn back to the scene of his crime, so I too was drawn back to Berlin and to the places of my unforgettable years of apprenticeship. But there I was up against the trend of political events. German filmcraft, which has been completely shattered by political experiments, is hardly the basis on which I can work out my ideas.[13]

Was Stein damit gemeint hat, erscheint aus heutiger Sicht klar; ob die britische Leserschaft die Botschaft ebenfalls verstanden hat, darüber lässt sich nur spekulieren.

Nach einem ersten Abstecher in Londoner Ateliers anno 1932 (mit dem arg verrissenen Woman's Film *Lily Christine* für die britische Tochter des US-Majors Paramount) lässt sich Stein 1933 permanent in Großbritannien nieder – die renommierte britische Produktionsfirma B. I. P. (British International Pictures) nimmt ihn unter Vertrag.

„It is very slight and obvious Viennese romance", urteilt Lionel Collier unbarmherzig über Steins ersten B. I. P.-Film *The Song You Gave Me* (1933).[14] Die musikalische Komödie, mit der Amerikanerin Bebe Daniels und dem Ungarn Victor Varconi in den Hauptrollen international besetzt, ein Remake des deutschen Films *Das Lied ist aus* (1930), zu dem der später nach London und Hollywood vertriebene Walter Reisch das Drehbuch schrieb, hinterlässt in der britischen Filmgeschichte keine nennenswerten Spuren, weist aber schon voraus auf bessere, erfolgreichere Arbeiten Steins im gleichen Genre, Ambiente, Stil: „Wien"-Filme made in Great Britain.

> Die Welt will „Wien". Das ist momentan ganz unpolitisch gemeint. Die Welt, von der hier die Rede sein soll, ist die Welt des Theaters, des Films, der Unterhaltung und Zerstreuung in jeder nur erdenklichen Form. Eine Scheinwelt also. In dieser Welt ist Wien eine Großmacht allerersten Ranges.[15]

Schöner als Harry W. Gell, Generaldirektor der Wiener Filiale des Hollywood-Majors Fox, es hier 1934 im populären Magazin *Mein Film*, gewissermaßen dem Wiener Pendant des vielgelesenen Londoner *Picturegoer*, ausdrückt, kann es wohl nicht auf den Punkt gebracht werden: Nicht Realismus ist angesagt, wenn es um Erfolg an der Kasse geht, sondern die Verwendung, Verwertung, Ausbeutung jener „zeitlosen" Topoi, jener Mythen, für die „Wien" seit jeher so bekannt und beliebt ist. Wenig überraschend erwähnt der Artikel österreichische Operetten, Theaterstücke

und Romane, Lehár, Strauß und Stolz ebenso wie Fritz Kortner, Paul
Hörbiger und Elisabeth Bergner:

> Diese Stadt exportiert seit Generationen ihren Überschuß an
> Talent nach allen Himmelsrichtungen, ein Talent, das einer
> glücklichen und gesegneten Lebensauffassung entspricht.[16]

Keine Rede davon, dass eine Reihe dieser Erfolgreichen und
Hochtalentierten zu diesem Zeitpunkt längst nicht mehr in Deutschland
arbeiten kann und sich nach ihrer alles andere als freiwilligen „Remigration"
nun in Wien im Exil wiederfindet, unter ihnen die Darsteller Peter Lorre und
Oskar Homolka und der Drehbuchautor und Regisseur Rudolf Katscher, der
später nach England gehen und dort als Rudolph Cartier das moderne BBC-
Fernsehspiel begründen wird.

Schon Steins übernächster britischer Film geht ganz in „Wien" auf,
erzählt eine Episode aus dem Leben Franz Schuberts, dem prototypischen
„Ikon der Entsagung"[17] des Wiener Biedermeier. *Blossom Time* (1934) wird
nicht zuletzt dank Richard Tauber in der Rolle des Komponisten zu einem
phänomenalen Erfolg – es ist sein Eintritt in den englischen Film. Stein
gegenüber *Mein Film*:

> Wenn ich nun darangehe, in England einen wienerischen Film zu
> inszenieren, der selbstverständlich auch für Amerika bestimmt ist,
> so kommt mir der Gedanke, warum es nicht möglich sein sollte,
> solche Wiener Filme echt in Österreich zu drehen. Und von der
> Erwägung ausgehend, daß man in einem Film dem Ausland kein
> Österreich, wie es nicht ist, vortäuschen, sondern Österreich und
> Wien zeigen soll, wie es ist, habe ich mich entschlossen, die
> Außenaufnahmen für den Schubert-Film [...] nach Wien zu
> verlegen.[18]

Ein bisschen „geschwindelt" darf dabei ruhig werden – so wird der
Prater, den das Liebespaar Jane Baxter & Willy Eichberger im Fiaker
durchquert und dort vom wehmütigen Schubert erspäht wird, vom
Laxenburger Schlosspark dargestellt – weil im „echten" Prater, wie der
britische Regieassistent Frank Cadman erklärt, „Anachronismen in Form von
den überall befindlichen elektrischen Lampen und Telephonleitungen nicht
zu vermeiden gewesen wären ... "[19] Der weit überwiegende Teil des Films
freilich, darunter die imposanten Innenräume des Ballsaals und der
Karlskirche, entsteht im Studio in Elstree.

Das Filmteam reist im Frühjahr 1934 getrennt von London nach
Wien: Stein, Tauber und Kameramann Otto Kanturek nehmen den Umweg
über Frankreich und Italien, um nicht unter Umständen den

Nationalsozialisten in die Hände zu fallen – alle drei sind zu diesem Zeitpunkt bereits Exilanten in Großbritannien.

Blossom Time, im Verein mit drei britischen Kollegen geschrieben von Franz Schulz, einem höchst produktiven Drehbuchautor des deutschen Kinos, der 1934 in die USA emigriert, erzählt die Geschichte der unglücklichen Liebe Schuberts zu Therese Grob (im Film: Vicki Wimpassinger, gespielt von Jane Baxter) – und gibt Richard Tauber ausreichend Gelegenheit zu singen. Buchstäblich mitten im Film intoniert Schubert, weil der vorgesehene Sänger plötzlich seine Stimme verloren hat, seine Lieder im Redoutensaal selbst, gleich vier hintereinander, darunter „Frühlingsglaube" und „Ungeduld" („Thine is my heart") auf Englisch und das „Ständchen" auf Deutsch. Letzteres beginnt mit der Zeile „Leise flehen meine Lieder" – so nannte Willi Forst seine ein Jahr zuvor in Wien entstandene filmische Schubert-Biografie mit Hans Jaray. „Wo Forst ein Ikon auffüllt", so Franz Marksteiner, „wird in Steins Film eine Figur Richard Tauber angepaßt".[20] Jaray nähert sich seinem Schubert rührend-naiv-ehrerbietig; sein Schubert leidet viel tragischer als derjenige Taubers – entsagen müssen sie allerdings beide. Immerhin hilft der „britische" Schubert schlussendlich noch tatkräftig mit, die Unerreichbare in den Hafen der Ehe zu führen.

Blossom Time steht ab 24. August 1934 sieben Wochen lang auf dem Spielplan des Regal Cinema (Marble Arch) – eine überdurchschnittliche Laufzeit. Etliche weitere wichtige und wesentlich von ExilantInnen geprägte Produktionen erreichen in diesem Herbst ebenfalls die Londoner Kinos – ein Indiz für die überragende Bedeutung des Exilfilms in Großbritannien: *Catherine the Great* mit Elisabeth Bergner (Regie: Paul Czinner), *Chu Chin Chow* mit Fritz Kortner (Kamera: Mutz Greenbaum, Bauten: Ernö Metzner), *Little Friend* mit Kortner (Regie: Berthold Viertel, Kamera: Günther Krampf, Bauten: Alfred Junge), *Evensong* mit Kortner und Carl Esmond alias Willy Eichberger (Kamera: Greenbaum, Bauten: Junge), *Jew Süss* mit Conrad Veidt und Paul Graetz (Regie: Lothar Mendes, Bauten: Junge) und *The Private Life of Don Juan* (Regie & Produktion: Alexander Korda, Drehbuch: Lajos Biró, Musik: Ernst Toch).[21]

Die Londoner Kritik erfreut sich vor allem an den musikalischen Elementen des Films. Im Jahresrückblick des *Picturegoer* etwa heißt es:

The most important of the year's musical crop, and the most important film to come out of the British International Studios at Elstree for long enough, was *Blossom Time*, in which the great German tenor Richard Tauber gave both a full-length vocal concert and an excellent imitation of Franz Schubert.[22]

Die Bedeutung, die die filminteressierte Öffentlichkeit dem britischen Filmdebüt Taubers beimisst, spiegelt sich nicht zuletzt in der breiten Berichterstattung über die Dreharbeiten und die Hintergründe des Produktionsprozesses wider. Die am Tag der Premiere erscheinende Ausgabe von *Film Weekly* etwa widmet *Blossom Time* neben einer ausführlichen, äußerst positiven Rezension eine vierseitige Fotostrecke und einen zweiseitigen Artikel, in dem Paul Stein seine Zusammenarbeit mit Tauber darlegt.[23]

Der Leistung des Sängers wird in der Presse ausnahmslos höchstes Lob zu Teil – Plot und Ausstattung freilich stoßen auf weniger Gegenliebe. Der Film leide an einer

> story that is hackneyed and a development that is pedestrian [...] A story of artless simplicity is jumbled with a „Gay Vienna" atmosphere of sophistication and elaborate, if rather too obviously studio-made, spectacle and settings.[24]

Ähnlich der Tenor der Kritik im *Jewish Chronicle*, dem Organ der jüdischen Gemeinde Großbritanniens:

> Schubert's music and Tauber's fine voice and superb technique – attractions enough surely; so that it may be churlish to speak of the utterly artificial and sugary little novelette story that forms the plot.[25]

Und selbst die *Times*, die *Blossom Time* zu dessen Nachteil mit *Congress Dances* (1931), der englischen Version des großen Ufa-Erfolges *Der Kongress tanzt*, vergleicht – „a film which in some particulars it quite obviously imitates" – und vor allem die Sentimentalität und den schleppenden Fortgang der Handlung kritisiert, kommt um ein Lob der musikalischen Gestaltung und Taubers Darstellung nicht herum:

> This is really a concert, a very good concert, of Schubert's songs. The music is treated with respect and sung with feeling by Mr. Richard Tauber disguised as the composer...[26]

Für die Nazipropaganda gegen jüdische Entertainer im Exil stellt Tauber eines der bevorzugten Angriffsziele dar. *Der Stürmer* etwa hetzt Mitte der 1930er Jahre nur sporadisch gegen KünstlerInnen – aber jedenfalls wiederholt gegen den „Operetten-Rundfunkjuden" Tauber.[27] Auch im berüchtigten antisemitischen Propagandafilm *Der ewige Jude* (1940, Regie: Fritz Hippler), einem, wie es im Titelvorspann heißt, „Filmbeitrag zum Problem des Weltjudentums", wird der Tenor, wie etwa auch Kortner, Lorre oder Lubitsch, böse desavouiert und verunglimpft.

In Paul Steins nächstem Film *Mimi* (1935), einer Adaption von Henri Murgers Roman *Scènes de la vie de bohème*, auf dem die bekannte Oper basiert, ist Tauber nicht dabei – hier wird nicht gesungen. Puccini ohne Musik, das sei, wie Lionel Collier im *Picturegoer* anmerkt, „like playing Hamlet without the ghost".[28] Und sein Kollege E. G. Cousins, der von Mai 1931 bis Mai 1939 die Dreharbeiten britischer Filme besucht und darüber eine wöchentliche Kolumne verfasst, belauscht den Regisseur am Set: „I love to listen to Stein directing. ‚Be kvite kviet, everybody, *please* – which is the good old Anglo-Saxon vord *shut tup*!'"[29]

Zwischen Bewunderung und Herablassung: Eine Inhaltsanalyse der Ausgaben des *Picturegoer*, des populärsten britischen Filmmagazins der 1930er Jahre, ab 1933 fördert zu Tage, dass hier, zuweilen in ein und derselben Nummer, jene ambivalente Haltung gegenüber den europäischen Filmschaffenden zum Ausdruck kommt, die auch in der Branche herrschte: Zum einen waren, wie erwähnt, das technische Know-how und der Input an Qualität, den die Zuwanderer einbrachten, willkommen und für die Weiterentwicklung der britischen Filmindustrie von instrumentaler Bedeutung; zum anderen begegnete man diesen Einflüssen ob ihrer (vermeintlichen) „non-Britishness", die sich unter anderen in kontinentalen Stoffen, Genres, Kamera- und Schauspielstilen manifestierte, mit ironischer Skepsis bis offener Ablehnung.[30]

Wesentlich in diesem Zusammenhang erscheint die Rolle der Association of Cinematographic Technicians (ACT). Im Juni 1933 als ordentliche Gewerkschaft formiert und mit dem Ziel angetreten, die schlechten Arbeitsbedingungen der Kameraleute, Cutter und übrigen Studiotechniker zu verbessern, sah sie sich, obzwar am linken Rand des politischen Spektrums angesiedelt und keineswegs antisemitisch orientiert, durch den Zustrom von Flüchtlingen ab 1933 mit zusätzlichem Druck auf dem Arbeitsmarkt konfrontiert und setzte 1935 „ein Komitee ein, das die Anzahl der in England arbeitenden Ausländer überprüfen sollte. […] Aus dieser Spannung zwischen politischem Idealismus und politischer Praxis entwickelten sich die Interventionen der ACT oft zu einem ideologischen Eiertanz".[31]

Nun aber zurück zum Anfang, zum zweiten Film des Duos Stein/Tauber und Höhepunkt und Herzstück ihrer Zusammenarbeit. *Heart's Desire* verhandelt zentrale Topoi des Exils: Entwurzelung, Fremdsein, Sprachverlust. Natürlich wird Josef Steidler, anders als sein Darsteller, nicht nach England vertrieben, sondern kommt aus freien Stücken – und doch evoziert seine Geschichte, wenn auch nicht explizit politisch, so doch deutlich genug, das Schicksal des Exilanten. Nicht nur, weil das Drehbuch des Films von einem anderen Flüchtling stammt: Bruno Frank (und drei britischen Autoren).

Ein Heurigensänger namens Josef Steidler wird von einer jungen Engländerin und ihrem Bräutigam, einem aufstrebenden Komponisten, bei der Ausübung seines Jobs entdeckt - und zwar für „höhere" Aufgaben, nämlich: Operette in London zu singen. Vorher muss er aber noch Englisch lernen, sein Freund und Manager Florian (Paul Graetz) hilft ihm dabei:

> Florian: „Have you a chill or influenza, as the case may be?"
> Josef: „Hör schon auf! Ich bleibe, wo ich bin!"
> Florian: „I only understand English!"
> Josef: „I stay where am I."
> Florian: „I am."
> Josef: „You are."

Dieser ziemlich komische und von den beiden Protagonisten glänzend gespielte Dialog dürfte nicht all zu weit von der Wirklichkeit entfernt sein: Taubers Schwierigkeiten mit der englischen Sprache sind wohldokumentiert.[32]

Der Sprachkundige in diesem Dialog, Paul Graetz, großartiger Charakterkomiker und Kabarettist in Berlin, ehe er nach England flüchten muss und dort unter anderem in *Jew Süss* (1934) und den drei vorangegangenen Stein-Filmen (*Red Wagon*, *Blossom Time* und *Mimi*) brilliert, geht 1937 nach Hollywood. Kaum ist er dort angekommen, versagt ihm das Herz.[33]

Josef Steidler liebt Wien, wo alle seine Freunde leben und alle Welt ihn gern hat. Aber das englische Fräulein hat's ihm angetan. Am Westbahnhof bereitet ihm der ganze Heurige einen grandiosen Abschied – und seine eigentliche, die Wiener Herzdame, nämlich, bleibt unendlich traurig zurück.

Heart's Desire findet einfache, aber einprägsame Bilder und Szenen für den Übergang vom Vertrauten zum Fremden. Vor dem Hintergrund der schneebedeckten österreichischen Berge singt Josef im Zugabteil das Volkslied „Morgen muss ich fort von hier". Applaus und heimische Hausmannskost – doch da schneit die Engländerin herein: „Josef! Lunch, please!" Wehmütig schaut er aus dem Fenster des Zuges, aus dem Off ertönt kurz und instrumental „Wien, Wien, nur du allein", Überblendung auf London, Busse in den Straßen und schwungvolle, großstädtische Schlagermusik. „Florian, it is all so strange here."

Tauber bei einem Wien-Besuch im Sommer 1935:

> Ich spiele darin einen Menschen, dessen ganzes Wesen und Handeln von der Liebe zu seiner Heimatstadt Wien, von dem

> Heimweh nach dieser Stadt beeinflußt wird. Und dieses Gefühl
> habe ich jedenfalls echt empfunden ... [34]

Abgesehen davon, dass Tauber, wenn man den biografischen Quellen
Glauben schenkt, politisch naiv war, sich mit Politik nie wirklich
auseinandergesetzt hat und Vertreibung, Emigration oder Exil kaum deutlich
angesprochen hätte – in der Wiener Zeitschrift *Mein Film* wäre das anno
1935 auch nicht opportun gewesen. Gerade noch Phrasen wie „aufgrund der
geänderten Verhältnisse" lassen sich nach 1933 dort finden – und auch diese
nur sporadisch. Was in Berlin, Wien, London oder Hollywood im Film
passiert, steht – mit deutlichem Übergewicht des Österreichischen – einfach
nebeneinander. In den Wiener Kinos laufen Nazifilme und britische
Produktionen einträchtig Seite an Seite, Deutschland ist schließlich der
wichtigste Absatzmarkt österreichischer Produktionen. Dem langjährigen
Chefredakteur Friedrich Porges nützt diese Blattlinie nichts: Mit dem
„Anschluss" wird er zum Flüchtling und geht 1938 ins britische Exil (und
1943 in die USA).

Ob die Wiener Leserschaft Taubers Heimwehgefühle als
Äußerungen eines Österreichers im Exil verstanden und interpretiert hat?
Man möchte es, seiner exponierten Stellung als Angriffsziel der Nazis
wegen, fast annehmen.

In *Heart's Desire* entsteht nun „ganz Wien" in London:

> In den Elstree-Studios sind Alt-Wiener Gäßchen und eine
> Heurigenschenke von künstlerischer Hand erstaunlich echt
> errichtet worden und eine richtige Urwiener Atmosphäre schwebt
> über diesem Fleckchen am Ufer der Themse. [35]

Etwas weniger urwienerisch ist in den britischen Drehberichten und
Rezensionen vom Heurigen als „Austrian beer-garden", „Viennese
Biergarten" oder einfach „*biergarten*" die Rede. [36]

Richard Tauber singt drei eigene Kompositionen in *Heart's Desire*,
zwei Lieder von Schumann – und hat als Venezianer am Olympic Theatre in
der Operette *Venetian Moon* natürlich einen rauschenden Erfolg. Die von
ihm Angebetete bekommt er nicht. „Florian, how soon can we be back in
Vienna?" Und Josef schaut auf und in das große Alpenpanorama-Foto in
seiner Garderobe – und dieses überblendet ins Alpenpanorama hinter dem
fahrenden Zug, während es wieder Richtung Wien geht. „I never realised
that Austria was so beautiful!"

Im Finale des Films scheinen sich London und Wien, das Englische
und das Wienerische, dann auf wundersame Weise zu vermählen. Josef
Steidler tritt hinaus in den Heurigengarten und singt noch einmal „Wien,
Wien, nur du allein" – und zwar die englische Fassung „Vienna, City of My

Dreams". Er hat, vielleicht, also doch ein bisserl was mitgenommen aus der
Fremde und gibt es jetzt dem britischen Kinopublikum zurück.

> Die authentisch wienerischen Filme entstanden exterritorial,
> anderswo – nachdem zuvor der Begriff des Authentischen vom
> Kino verändert worden war. Ob sie aus echten Wiener
> Erfahrungen stammen oder aus begehrlichen Vorstellungen von
> Fremden spielt keine Rolle. So und so nähert das Wienerische
> sich immer dem Klischee. Da ist das Filmbild dann gleich
> nebenan.[37]

Paul Stein, der 1938 britischer Staatsbürger wird,[38] dreht bis zu
seinem Tod noch 16 weitere Filme in England: musikalische Romanzen,
Agentenfilme, Komödien und Krimis. Am 21. Mai 1937 schreibt er an
seinen Freund, den Exilanten und legendären Agenten Paul Kohner in
Hollywood:

> There is no film industry here in England. Still, it remains a fact
> that some people are making pictures. So don't regret the fact that
> you are still stuck over there and even if life seems to be very
> monotonous sometimes, it doesn't matter – you are far away from
> Europe where, one day, not in the near future, political troubles
> will start which will end in a war. [...] You know how much I
> love Europe, you know how much I enjoy travelling around in
> France, in Switzerland, in Austria and in Czechoslovakia, but,
> frankly, in the depths of my heart I am longing to go back to the
> States, to Hollywood, maybe to settle down there and try to get a
> little peace after all these years of excitement.[39]

Wie aus der Korrespondenz mit Kohner hervorgeht, möchte Stein nach
Hollywood – hat aber gleichzeitig Angst, wieder von vorne beginnen zu
müssen.

Und einmal lässt er gay old Vienna noch im Film auferstehen, 1945,
zu einer Zeit, als im britischen Kino andere Genres regieren als die
kontinental angehauchte Operette. „Once upon a time, in old Vienna, the
Waltz was considered a naughty and immoral dance ... " Mit diesem Schrift-
Prolog beginnt *Waltz Time* – und sogleich stimmen ein *gypsy troubadour*
und seine Partnerin in den Straßen Wiens, also des Ateliers in Elstree, den
mitreißenden Titelsong des Films an, „Waltz Time in Vienna", geschrieben
vom gebürtigen Wiener und nach England vertriebenen Hans May.

Die Geschichte dreht sich um die junge Kaiserin Maria (Carol Raye)
und ihre große Liebe, den Grafen Franz von Hofer (Peter Graves), und damit
verknüpft, die Love-Story der Tochter des Premierministers (Patricia
Medina) und eines feschen Offiziers (Thorley Walters). Verwicklungen,
Maskerade, eine Menge Songs – und am Ende erklärt die Kaiserin den zuvor

verpönten Walzer zum „official court dance" und heiratet in einer prächtigen Hochzeitszeremonie ihren Count. Und Richard Tauber im priesterlich-weißen Ornat steht inmitten seines Bubenchors auf der Kanzel und singt mit ihm „Break of Day" – eine Parallele zu jener Szene in *Blossom Time*, wo er in der Karlskirche zur Hochzeit des Grafen von Hohenberg mit Vicki mit seiner Schulklasse ein Lied zum Besten gibt.

Tauber tritt in *Waltz Time* lediglich als Gast auf. Vor dem Finale singt er dasselbe Lied schon in seiner Schäferhütte, als die Kaiserin im Fiaker vorbeifährt; in die Handlung selbst ist er nicht integriert. Doch sein Name, in den Credits extra herausgestellt, mag mit dazu beigetragen haben, dass dieses Recycling wienerischer Motive ein großer Erfolg wird. Paul Stein an Kohner: „In my opinion the film stinks – but the public is always right."[40]

Aus der Korrespondenz mit Kohner entsteht ein lebendiges Bild der schwierigen wirtschaftlichen Situation im England der unmittelbaren Nachkriegszeit. „Every food parcel from California is more than welcomed!!"[41] schreibt Stein im Herbst 1945; Kohner schickt ihm regelmäßig Lebensmittel. „Your last parcel arrived safely", heißt es dann im Frühjahr 1947, „[...] the salami is very good – but no more during the summer I am afraid."[42]

Paul L. Stein stirbt im Mai 1951 in London. Ausführliche Nachrufe oder Würdigungen bleiben aus – es scheint, als hätte die britische Öffentlichkeit auf diesen verlässlichen, durchaus erfolgreichen Regisseur, fast zwei Jahrzehnte lang eine fixe Größe ihres Unterhaltungskinos, vergessen.

In einem Leserbrief an das Branchenblatt *The Cinema* erinnert sich Arthur Dent, Managing Director des in den 1930er Jahren führenden britischen Filmverleihers Wardour Films, der unter anderem auch *Blossom Time* und *Heart's Desire* in die Kinos brachte, an seinen Weggefährten:

> So Paul Stein is dead. The man who did more in blending successfully art and industry in entertainment films than anyone I know is no more. His *Blossom Time* was a landmark in the industry and Paul will always be associated with it. It was a stroke of genius to bring Richard Tauber over for the leading role and Paul was able to bring the film in to schedule. [...] His charm of manner and good temper were proverbial – in fact it was said of him that his manner could almost charm a bird off a tree.[43]

Ein echter Wiener eben. Gewissermaßen.

Anmerkungen

[1] Charmian Brinson, Richard Dove, „Zielgerichtete Publikationen. Die Reihe Free Austrian Books", in Marietta Bearman, Charmian Brinson, Richard Dove, Anthony Grenville, Jennifer Taylor, *Wien – London, hin und retour: Das Austrian Centre in London 1939-1947* (Wien: Czernin, 2004), S. 99.

[2] *Filmkünstler. Wir über uns selbst*, Hrsg. Hermann Treuner (Berlin: Sibyllen-Verlag, 1928), o. S.

[3] Geburtsmatrikel Paul Ludwig Stein, Reg. Nr. 275/1892, Israelitische Kultusgemeinde Wien.

[4] Die Informationen zu Steins Theaterarbeit entstammen dem *Neuen Theater-Almanach* (1913f.), dem *Deutschen Bühnen-Jahrbuch* (1915ff.) und den Programmzetteln des Deutschen Volkstheaters Wien.

[5] Siehe dazu: Thomas Elsaesser, „Heavy Traffic. Perspektive Hollywood: Emigranten oder Vagabunden?", in *London Calling. Deutsche im britischen Film der dreißiger Jahre*, Red. Jörg Schöning (München: edition text + kritik, 1993); Thomas Elsaesser, *Weimar Cinema and After. Germany's Historical Imaginary* (London: Routledge, 2000), S. 361ff.; Graham Petrie, *Hollywood Destinies. European Directors in America, 1922-1931*. Revised edition (Detroit: Wayne State University Press, 2002); Jan-Christopher Horak, „Sauerkraut & Sausages with a Little Goulash: Germans in Hollywood, 1927", *Film History*, vol. 17, no. 2/3 (2005).

[6] Paul Stein, „Heading for British Supremacy", *Picturegoer Weekly*, 3. März 1934, S. 10.

[7] *Paimann's Filmlisten*, Nr. 15 (31. Jänner bis 6. Februar 1919).

[8] Hans Taussig, „Sommertagstraum in Laxenburg", *Mein Film*, Nr. 440 (Juni 1934), S. 11.

[9] Rudolf Ulrich, *Österreicher in Hollywood* (Wien: Filmarchiv Austria, 2004), S. 489.

[10] Go., „Liebesfeuer", *Reichsfilmblatt*, Nr. 38 (1925), S. 41.

[11] *Bioscope*, 21. Oktober 1926, S. 55.

[12] John K. Newnham, „Let Them *All* Come!", *Picturegoer Weekly*, 7. November 1931, S. 7.

[13] Paul Stein, „Heading for British Supremacy", *Picturegoer Weekly*, 3. März 1934, S. 10.

[14] Lionel Collier, *Picturegoer Weekly*, 13. Januar 1934, S. 27.

[15] Harry W. Gell, „Die Welt will ‚Wien'", *Mein Film*, Nr. 442 (Juni 1934), S. 24.

[16] Ebenda.

[17] Franz Marksteiner, „Schubert heiß ich. Bin ich Schubert?", in *Aufbruch ins Ungewisse. Österreichische Filmschaffende in der Emigration vor 1945*, Hrsg. Christian Cargnelli, Michael Omasta (Wien: Wespennest, 1993), S. 85.

[18] Paul Ludwig Stein, „Amerika-Film für Europa", *Mein Film*, Nr. 428 (März 1934), S. 4

[19] Hans Taussig, „Sommertagstraum in Laxenburg", *Mein Film*, Nr. 440 (Juni 1934), S. 11.

[20] Marksteiner, a. a. O., S. 82.

[21] Großbritannien ist sicherlich jenes Land, das von der Diaspora mittel- und osteuropäischer Filmschaffender am meisten profitiert hat. Die ImmigrantInnen vom Kontinent waren in mannigfaltiger Weise instrumentell für den Aufschwung und die Weiterentwicklung des britischen Kinos in den 1930er Jahren. Siehe dazu: „Deutsche Künstler im englischen Film.

Eine vorläufige Bilanz", *Pariser Tageblatt*, 12. Dezember 1934, S. 4; Kevin Gough-Yates, „The British Feature Film as a European Concern. Britain and the Émigré Film-Maker, 1933-1945", in *Theatre and Film in Exile. German Artists in Britain, 1933-1945*, Hrsg. Günter Berghaus (Oxford/New York/München: Berg, 1989), S. 135-66; Kevin Gough-Yates, „Exiles and British Cinema", in *The British Cinema Book*, Hrsg. Robert Murphy (London: British Film Institute, 1997), S. 104-13. Verwiesen sei auch auf den 2007 erscheinenden Sammelband zur Konferenz „German-speaking Emigrés in British Cinema, 1925-1950", die im Juli 2005 an der University of Southampton (UK) abgehalten wurde.

[22] E. G. Cousins, „The Year on the British Sets", *Picturegoer Xmas Annual*, Dezember 1934, S. 16.

[23] Paul L. Stein, „How We Made Richard Tauber's First British Film", *Film Weekly*, 24. August 1934, S. 8f.

[24] M. D. P. [d. i. Malcolm D. Phillips], „Richard Tauber's British Debut", *Picturegoer Weekly*, 28. Juli 1934, S. 16.

[25] *The Jewish Chronicle*, 24. August 1934, S. 34.

[26] *The Times*, 27. August 1934, S. 8.

[27] „Der emigrierte Richard Tauber", *Der Stürmer*, 14. Jg., Nr. 15 (April 1936).

[28] Lionel Collier, *Picturegoer Weekly*, 10. August 1935, S. 25.

[29] E. G. Cousins, *Picturegoer Weekly*, 16. Februar 1935, S. 26.

[30] Siehe etwa Graham Greenes berühmt-berüchtigte, xenophob-antisemitische Rezension des Exilfilms *The Marriage of Corbal* (1936), produziert von Max Schach, inszeniert von Karl Grune, photographiert von Otto Kanturek (*Spectator*, 5. Juni 1936), nachgedruckt in Graham Greene, *The Pleasure Dome*, Hrsg. John Russell Taylor (London: Secker & Warburg, 1972).

[31] Tim Bergfelder, „Rooms with a View. Deutsche Techniker und der Aufstieg des Filmdesigners", in *London Calling. Deutsche im britischen Film der dreißiger Jahre*, Red. Jörg Schöning (München: edition text + kritik, 1993), S. 66.

[32] Siehe etwa Michael Jürgs, *Gern hab' ich die Frau'n geküßt. Die Richard-Tauber-Biographie* (München: List, 2000), *passim*; Paul L. Stein, „How We Made Richard Tauber's First British Film", *Film Weekly*, 24. August 1934, S. 8f.

[33] In seinem Nachruf in der *Pariser Tageszeitung* vom 19. Februar 1937 schreibt Pem (d.i. Paul Marcus), Exiljournalist in London: „Paul Graetz, der einst bei Reinhardt gespielt hat und zu den Begründern des zweiten "Schall und Rauch" gehörte, war die Inkarnation echtesten Berlinertums. Für ihn hat Kurt Tucholski [sic] die meisten jener Chansons geschrieben, die immer das große Herz und die herrliche Schnauze verkörperten, die um Verständnis für jenes Berlinertum warben."

[34] „Richard Tauber auf der Durchreise…", *Mein Film*, Nr. 498 (Juli 1935), S. 5.

[35] C. T. J., „Heurigenfilm mit Richard Tauber", *Mein Film*, Nr. 488 (Mai 1935), S. 8.

[36] *Picturegoer Weekly*, 1. Juni 1935, S. 30; *Monthly Film Bulletin*, vol. 2, no. 2 (August 1935), S. 133; *The Jewish Chronicle*, 18. Oktober 1935, S. 48.

[37] Frieda Grafe, „Wiener Beiträge zu einer wahren Geschichte des Kinos", in *Aufbruch ins Ungewisse. Österreichische Filmschaffende in der Emigration vor 1945*, Hrsg. Christian Cargnelli, Michael Omasta (Wien: Wespennest, 1993), S. 227.

[38] *Pem's Privat-Berichte*, 14. September 1938, S. 55.

[39] Brief von Paul L. Stein an Paul Kohner vom 21. Mai 1937, Sammlung Paul Kohner, Filmmuseum Berlin – Deutsche Kinemathek.

[40] Brief Stein an Kohner, 15. September 1945, Sammlung Paul Kohner, Filmmuseum Berlin – Deutsche Kinemathek.

[41] Ebenda.

[42] Brief Stein an Kohner, 30. April 1947, Sammlung Paul Kohner, Filmmuseum Berlin – Deutsche Kinemathek.

[43] Arthur Dent, „To Paul Stein", *The Cinema. News and Property Gazette*, 9. Mai 1951, S. 27.

Fritz Rosenfeld, Filmkritiker

Brigitte Mayr & Michael Omasta

Der bedeutendste österreichische Filmkritiker der Ersten Republik, Dr. Fritz Rosenfeld, war in Großbritannien, wohin er 1934 von Wien aus über Prag emigrieren musste, besser als Kinderbuchautor Friedrich Feld bekannt. Rosenfelds in der sozialdemokratischen *Arbeiter-Zeitung* erschienene Artikel wurden bislang in keinem filmhistorischen Kontext kommentiert; genau dies ist aber – aufgrund seiner Leistungen, der Vielseitigkeit und Sachkenntnis bei der Arbeit als Kritiker, Redakteur und Autor – von großer Wichtigkeit. Unser besonderes Interesse dabei gilt Texten über gleichfalls aus Österreich vertriebene Filmschaffende sowie den kritischen Schriften, die er während des Kriegs für die deutschsprachige *Zeitung* (London) verfasst hat.

Filmkritik der zwanziger- und dreißiger Jahre. Welche Namen fallen einem dazu ein? Bücher zu Balázs, Kracauer und Arnheim gibt es, ihre Schriften sind wiederaufgelegt. Wer aber kennt Fritz Rosenfeld? Er war der bedeutendste Filmkritiker der Ersten Republik. In seiner regelmäßig in der *Arbeiter-Zeitung*, dem Zentralorgan der Sozialdemokratischen Partei, erscheinenden Rubrik „Die Welt des Films" analysierte er das Medium in seiner kapitalistischen Verfasstheit und bewertete dessen ideologische Funktion. Mit seiner journalistischen Arbeit lieferte er einen maßgeblichen Beitrag zum Aufbauwerk des „Roten Wien", das sämtliche Lebensbereiche umfasste: sozialer Wohnbau, Volkswohlfahrt, Schulreform, Freizeitkultur. Rosenfeld war einer der ersten in Österreich, der auf die nicht genutzten Möglichkeiten von Film und Kino für die sozialistische Agitation und Kulturpolitik verwies und sich vehement für die Eroberung des Kinos durch das Publikum einsetzte.

Der 1902 in Wien als Friedrich Rosenfeld Geborene schreibt bereits während seines Studiums der Germanistik, Anglistik und Kunstgeschichte für sozialdemokratische Zeitschriften und stößt 1923 zur Kulturredaktion der *Arbeiter-Zeitung*, wo er sich nach kurzer Zeit als *der* Filmkritiker des Landes etabliert. In dieser Eigenschaft versteht er sich selbst als einen „Warnenden", seine Kritik als „Wegweiser durch das dornenvolle Gestrüpp unseres Kinos".[1] Filmkritik ist dabei in einem doppelten Sinn zu verstehen: einmal als Filmbesprechung, zum anderen als grundsätzlich vorgetragene Gesellschaftskritik. Neben dem bekannten Argument, der Film begünstige die Flucht aus dem Alltag, indem er eine Scheinwirklichkeit vorspiegelt, versucht Rosenfeld das Problem mit den Kategorien der politischen Ökonomie anzugehen. In der Filmproduktion sieht er den nüchtern

kalkulierenden Vorgang einer Warenproduktion, die den Gesetzen
kapitalistischer Rationalität folgt. Diesem Profitinteresse des Kinokapitals
stehen aber die Interessen der Kinobesucher entgegen, für die der Film „ein
Stück Erlebnis" ist, ein Gebilde, von dem „geistige und seelische
Wirkungen" ausgehen. In seinem Beitrag „Film und Proletariat. Versuch
einer Soziologie des Kinos" argumentiert er, dass durch die weitgehende
Unmöglichkeit, sich im kapitalistischen Produktionsprozess zu
verwirklichen, die Massen:

> [mit einem] ungeheuerlichen Erlebniswunsch, mit einer Fülle
> ungestillter Lebenssehnsucht ins Kino strömen: ihre Seele ist ein
> unbestellter Acker, in den man den Samen eines Traums von der
> Umgestaltung unserer ungerechten Welt, aber zugleich auch das
> Bewußtsein senken kann, daß alles so sein muß, wie es ist, daß
> die kapitalistische Gesellschaftsform die einzig mögliche, die
> Justiz gerecht, die Bankdirektoren edle Götter und die Kaiser und
> Könige Sendboten des Himmels sind.[2]

Fast wortgleich wettert er gegen den Militarismus – etwa anlässlich der
Premiere von *Morgenrot*: „Am Sterben verdient der Kanonenfabrikant
Hugenberg, und deshalb läßt er seine Filmfabrik, die Ufa, Propagandafilme
für den Tod drehen; ein Geschäft fördert das andere."[3] Und er polemisiert
gegen den Schund und reaktionären Kitsch, nicht zuletzt der österreichischen
Produktion. Damit zieht er sich den Unmut der heimischen Filmbranche zu
und gerät in einen jahrelangen Konflikt mit der von den Sozialdemokraten
gegründeten Kinobetriebsgesellschaft (Kiba), deren kommerziell orientierte
Programmpolitik er strikt ablehnt. Im Gegenzug zu dieser „absichtlich
antifortschrittlichen Programmierung" fordert er in seinem wohl
berühmtesten Artikel „Sozialdemokratische Kinopolitik"[4] den
Zusammenschluss aller Arbeiterkinos, die politische Kontrolle der
Kinoführung in einer Bildungszentrale, die Schaffung einer Filmleihstelle,
eines Uraufführungstheaters und einer „Besuchergemeinschaft", um den
Kinos einen Grundstock an festem Publikum zu sichern. All seine gut-
gemeinten Vorschläge nützen nichts: 1930 wird ihm auf Weisung des
Parteivorstandes die Rezension von Filmen der Kiba für die *Arbeiter-Zeitung*
untersagt.[5]

    Rosenfelds sehr entschiedene Position veranschaulicht einen
Paradigmenwechsel in der sozialdemokratischen Kulturpolitik. Galt das
Kino, nebst Alkohol und Klerikalismus, noch Anfang der zwanziger Jahre
wegen seiner demobilisierenden Wirkung im Klassenkampf als Hauptfeind
der Arbeiter/innen/schaft (in der Anklage der Bildungsfunktionäre reduziert
auf die Formel, dass – anstelle in die politischen Veranstaltungen die Massen
ins Kino strömten), werden nun (zumindest theoretisch) auch die Potentiale

der neuen Kunstform anerkannt, die „bis in die entlegensten Täler und zu den ungebildetsten Menschen vordringen, sie mitreißen, aber auch beeinflussen kann".[6]

In seinem Artikel „Warum wir Filmreferate bringen" von 1925, der in der sozialdemokratischen Frauenzeitschrift *Die Unzufriedene* erscheint, wendet sich Rosenfeld – im Gegensatz zu vielen Autoren, die keine Rücksicht auf das Medium nehmen, in dem sie abgedruckt sind – ganz speziell auch an die Leserinnen[7] und geht auf den Zusammenhang von Kino- und Frauenpolitik ein. So wie es seine persönliche Aufgabe sei, die Arbeiter vor misslichen Produkten der Filmindustrie zu warnen, sei es die Aufgabe, ja Pflicht „einer Zeitschrift, die das Sprachrohr arbeitender, freier, aufrechter Menschen" ist, „ihre Leserinnen vor dieser Art von Kitsch und anderen Formen des Schundfilms zu warnen".[8] Mit seinen Filmkritiken will er vor dem Kinobesuch beraten, will davor bewahren, sich alberne Geschmacklosigkeiten ansehen zu müssen und enttäuscht zu werden. Ganz der Aufklärungsarbeit verpflichtet, will er in vertrauenswürdigen Zeitungen – und „das sind einmal nur die sozialistischen Blätter" resümiert er lapidar – dafür sorgen, dass man und frau mit der Kinokarte „nicht die Katze im Sack kauft".[9] Aufschlussreiche Informationen auch in der kürzesten Rezension, lautet das Motto.

Seines Erachtens nach „gute Filme" erhalten meist längere Besprechungen, ob nun Eisensteins *Panzerkreuzer Potemkin* oder Chaplins *Lichter der Großstadt*, dessen Arbeiten immer ganz enthusiastisch aufgenommen werden, obwohl Chaplin ja eigentlich eine der Symbolfiguren des kapitalistischen Films ist. Ab 1924 bietet Rosenfeld in der *Unzufriedenen* zwar in der von ihm redigierten Rubrik „Welche Filme sollen wir uns ansehen" eine Form der Filmetikettierung an, aber eben ganz und gar nicht in der Weise, wie die Branchenblätter das handhaben, die mit ihren plakativen und stereotypen Reklametexten meist nur als Sprachrohr der jeweiligen Produktionsfirmen fungieren. Retrospektiv, in einem Artikel für *Die Zeitung*, erläutert er genauer, wogegen er anschreibt:

> Es gibt wirklich Kritiker, die von ihrem Handwerk herzlich wenig verstehen. Das ist teilweise Schuld der Zeitungen, die mit der Filmkritik nur zu oft einen beliebigen Reporter betrauen, der gerade nichts zu tun hat oder zu seiner Unterhaltung gerne ins Kino gehen möchte. Woher soll er die zur sachlichen Beurteilung eines Films notwendigen Kenntnisse nehmen? Einige Kritiker suchen ihren Mangel an Sachkenntnis und Urteilskraft hinter Sternen und Ziffern zu verbergen. Sie dünken sich damit wohl sehr modern, kurz, knapp und „amerikanisch". In Wirklichkeit handeln sie nach einem ganz alten Prinzip, dem des Schulmeisters, der Noten gibt. Er sagt dem bedauernswerten Schüler nicht, was er gut und was er schlecht gemacht hat, er malt

mit roter Tinte, „gut" oder „genügend" unter die letzte Zeile. „Nicht genügend" gibt es für diese Art von Filmkritikern ja ohnehin nicht; die Inseratenabteilung würde es nicht dulden.[10]

Leidenschaftlich tritt Rosenfeld für den Russenfilm ein, begeistert sich für Chaplin, Clair, Murnau, Siodmak, verfasst seitenlange Aufsätze über Granowsky und Pabst, bewundert Greta Garbo, widmet sich nicht nur den Regisseuren, sondern auch dem beruflichen Umfeld von Autoren, Kameraleuten, Technikern, Ausstattern und Kinomusikern, reißt in seinen Artikeln „Der visuelle Mensch", „Die Flucht aus der Wirklichkeit", „Der Wiener Film von gestern und morgen", „Wir und das Kino", „Der Kampf um den Tonfilm", „Der Arbeiter und der Film" stets brennende Themen der Zeit an.[11] Dabei macht der Film nur einen Teil seines Interesses, das Schreiben nur einen Teil seiner Aktivitäten aus:

> Ich arbeitete in der Feuilletonredaktion, ich war Theaterkritiker, ich schrieb allein die Filmseite für die Sonntagsausgabe, ich mußte zu Tanzabenden gehen, ich wurde von den Sektionen der Partei, auch in der Provinz, zu Vorträgen eingeladen, ich hatte bei den Filmvorstellungen, die die Kunststelle veranstaltete, die einleitenden Worte zu sprechen – und ich kann heute nicht mehr verstehen, wie ich das alles geschafft habe. Ich war eben noch jung und sehr enthusiastisch.[12]

1930 tritt Rosenfeld zudem mit einem Roman aus der Filmindustrie als Schriftsteller in Erscheinung: *Die goldene Galeere* ist seine literarisierte Analyse der Filmindustrie, seine darin skizzierte Theorie war eine für die politische Praxis. Und diese wiederum ist nur aus seinem politischen Engagement heraus zu verstehen, versucht er doch mehrfach im Roman zu unterstreichen, dass das Publikum begeisterungsfähig für den realistischen Film, für den Film der sozialen Anklage sowie für den revolutionären Film sei. Diese spezielle Betonung Rosenfelds hat stark mit der bereits zuvor angesprochenen Entwicklung der österreichischen Kinopolitik in den späten zwanziger Jahren zu tun. Rosenfeld beteiligte sich innerhalb der Sozialdemokratie nicht nur intensiv an der – gegen die pragmatische Realisierung dieser Politik gerichteten – Diskussion, er prägte diese Auseinandersetzung maßgeblich.[13]

Lange vor dem Kino aber kommt für Rosenfeld das Schreiben selbst, der Autor, das Buch. So schenkt er in seinen Rezensionen auf der Feuilletonseite neben dem Film der Literatur die größte Aufmerksamkeit:[14] Unter den fremdsprachigen Autoren schätzt er besonders Emile Zola, „den Klassiker der sozialen Dichtung", Romain Rolland, Henri Barbusse, Anatole France, Maxim Gorki, „den Kämpfer, der vom hellsten Optimismus beseelt ist", Upton Sinclair, „„den unerbittlichen Feind und Ankläger der kapitalistischen Ordnung", Jack London, den Deutsch-Amerikaner B. Traven und Martin Andersen-Nexö, „den sozialen Dichter par excellence". Für Rosenfeld haben weder Kant, Fichte, noch Schiller, weder Richard Wagner noch Nietzsche „den bürgerlichen Geist revolutioniert", sondern die russischen Romanciers, Zola, Darwin und Marx. In seinen Augen zählt allein die zeitgenössische internationale Literatur. Beiwörtern wie „proletarisch", „revolutionär" oder „sozialistisch" ist er eher abgeneigt, er spricht lieber von „sozialer Dichtung". Dies sind die Werke von Schriftstellern, die von pazifistischer Gesinnung, Humanismus und Nächstenliebe beseelt sind (und also die Idee einer gewaltsamen Revolution ablehnen), von Vertretern eines „ethischen Sozialismus", denen der überzeugte Reformist Rosenfeld seine umfangreichen, meist im progressiven Blatt *Der Kampf* erschienenen, Studien widmet und deren Werke er dem Arbeiterpublikum nahezubringen versucht. Diese Schriftsteller sind in Österreich und Deutschland Alfons Petzold, den er tief verehrt, Heinrich Mann, „der deutsche Zola", Leonhard Frank, „der größte Erzähler, den das deutsche Proletariat heute besitzt" und Ernst Toller, dem er 1923 einen seiner ersten Artikel in der *Arbeiter-Zeitung* gewidmet hatte und der „uns so nahe [steht], weil seine Probleme Probleme der Massen, Zeitthemen, Gegenwartsfragen sind".

Auch Rosenfelds erstes Kinderbuch, *Tirilin reist um die Welt*, das er 1931 veröffentlicht und in dem sich ein Junge auf die Suche nach einem Märchenland macht und lernt, dass er es erst erreichen kann, wenn es soziale Gerechtigkeit gibt, behandelt ähnliche Fragestellungen.

Die Zerschlagung der Demokratie im Februar 1934 zwingt die Redaktion der *Arbeiter-Zeitung* fast geschlossen zur Flucht in die Tschechoslowakei; Rosenfeld findet in Prag eine Stelle als Lektor und Dramaturg bei einer Niederlassung der Paramount:

> Daß ich in Prag für eine amerikanische Filmgesellschaft arbeitete, verursachte mir keinerlei Gewissensbisse – ich hatte die kapitalistische Filmindustrie immer angeprangert, das wußte man in Hollywood, aber man bot mir doch einen Posten an, weil ich ja keinerlei Entscheidungsmacht erhielt – ich war nur als Berater tätig. Ich las die neuen Romane und ging zu den Premieren der neuen Stücke und berichtete, was sich für Hollywood eignen würde und was nicht. Das meiste kam ja von Anfang an nicht in Frage. Ich half bei Straßenaufnahmen in Prag für den Lubitsch-Film *Blaubarts achte Frau* und hielt Interviews mit Sängerinnen, die nach Hollywood engagiert werden wollten. Dabei vergab ich mir nichts.[15]

Daneben arbeitet er als freier Journalist und ständiger Theater-Korrespondent einer jugoslawischen Zeitung.

Bei der Besetzung Prags durch deutsche Truppen muss Rosenfeld erneut fliehen und kommt 1939 nach England, wo er als „feindlicher Ausländer" ein halbes Jahr lang auf der Isle of Man interniert wird. In London gelingt es ihm vorerst nicht, in seinem angestammten Beruf als Journalist zu arbeiten. Er nimmt einen Job als Metalldreher in einer Fabrik an, dann ist er für die BBC im „Monitoring" tätig, das heißt er hört deutsche bzw. tschechische Sendungen ab und übersetzt sie ins Englische. Von einem sehr emotionalen Gespräch mit Friedrich Feld (wie er sich nun nennt), das im Oktober 1942 von London nach Österreich gesendet wird, ist erfreulicherweise der O-Ton erhalten:

> We think of our fatherland, and when the noise of the machines seems to deafen us, then someone here and there starts to sing. We sing our old songs, the song of the Viennese workers. We think of Vienna, of Austria as it was before the Nazis trampled it down. We remember our friends at home and wonder what they will be thinking when they stand at the machine to produce weapons and munitions just as we do. For we are all Austrians. We are almost handling the same things here as you over there. Only it serves another purpose: the weapons which you put out help Hitler. The weapons produced by us help to beat Hitler. But we can let you know what we think, what we feel when we turn through our machines 1.000, 14.000 pieces daily, when we sharpen and bore a weapon that will fight for a great cause: the homecoming for us, freedom for you, and a free Austria for us all.[16]

Nur mehr sporadisch publiziert er Filmkritiken in der deutschsprachigen Emigrantenpresse, meist sind es aber nur historische Rückschauen, was er im Kino alles gesehen hat oder ein Aufsatz hie und da, etwa über Orson Welles (gegen den er gewisse Vorbehalte hat und in dem er „nur die Ziellosigkeit eines experimentierenden Talents" erkennt). In der *Zeitung* erscheint von 1942 bis 1944 in 20 Folgen und unregelmäßigen Abständen seine Kolumne „Filmsilhouetten", in der er Leute porträtiert, die er schon vor dem Exil geschätzt hat, wie Greta Garbo, Greer Garson oder Katharine Hepburn, aber auch Emigranten und Emigrantinnen wie Marlene Dietrich, Stroheim oder Lubitsch:

> Nicht viele Filmregisseure dürfen sich dessen rühmen, daß das große Publikum ihre Namen kennt. Man spricht von einem Garbo-, einem Dietrich-, einem Gary Cooper-Film und kümmert sich wenig um den Mann, der ihn gedreht hat. Ernst Lubitsch ist eine der ganz wenigen Ausnahmen. Wer immer in seinen Filmen auftritt, sie sind in erster Linie „Lubitsch-Filme". Es gibt sogar einen „Lubitsch-Stil" [...] – der war immer kritisch, auf seine eigene Weise. Er versuchte sich in politischer Ironie in

Ninotschka, er holte in *Sein oder Nichtsein* zu dem
vernichtendsten satirischen Schlag aus, den die Naziwelt im Film
bisher einstecken musste. Wie alle, die in Hollywood arbeiten, hat
auch Lubitsch zuweilen Kompromisse machen müssen: aber selbst
seine schwächeren Filme tragen den Stempel einer Persönlichkeit,
die europäischen Geschmack mit amerikanischer brillanter
Technik, satirische Angriffslust mit Beherrschung aller Tricks,
Geist mit Können vereint.[17]

Liest man seinen exzellenten Stroheim-Beitrag aufmerksam, entdeckt man
einen Hinweis, dass er nun auch wieder im Exil ins Kino geht und sich neu
angelaufene Filme ansieht:

Der Schauspieler und Regisseur Erich von Stroheim, seiner
Herkunft nach Österreicher, seiner Wahl nach Weltbürger, der
teils in Hollywood, teils in Paris wirkte und wirkt, ist eine
Erscheinung, die in der Geschichte des Theaters und des Films
wohl einzigartig da steht. Stroheim hat sich als Regisseur nicht
durchsetzten können, er ist zu eigenwillig, um ein fügsames
Rädchen in der Hollywood-Produktionsmaschine zu sein. Er ging
nach Frankreich, er spielte den kastenstolzen aristokratischen
Offizier in der *Großen Illusion,* er gab in *Gibraltar* und anderen
Filmen eine lange Reihe meisterhafter Porträts kaltherziger
Diplomaten, politischer Intriganten, Spitzel und Spitzelvernichter.
Das „Dritte Reich" brachte ihm einen neuen Typ: die Bestie in
Gestapo-Uniform, die Dreckgeburt aus Sadismus und brutalem
Machtwahn. Er hat ihr in dem Remarque-Film *So endet unsere
Nacht* ein Denkmal gesetzt. Er ist niemals ein beliebter „Star"
gewesen, dazu fehlt ihm und den Typen, die er mit den bren-
nenden Farben eines aus tiefstem Herzen kommenden Hasses
hinmalt, die Gefälligkeit: er ist „negativ", er spielt Menschen, um
sie zu verdammen. Erich von Stroheim, der Kämpfer gegen das
berufsmäßige Schlächtertum, gegen eine verwesende dummstolze
Adelskaste, hat wahrhaftig ein reines Gewissen: er hat der Welt
oft genug intensivst vorgespielt, worunter sie heute so unsäglich
leidet.[18]

Mitten im Krieg gelangt in der Schweiz auch seine Komödie *Das glückliche
Ende* zur Uraufführung. Paradoxerweise widerspricht der Titel aber ganz
Rosenfelds traurigem Resümee zur schweren Zeit seines Exils: „Natürlich
war ich in der Emigration deprimiert, wer war es nicht?"[19]

   Ab 1946 ist Rosenfeld Redakteur, anfangs eigentlich „Monitor", der
Nachrichtenagentur Reuter. In dem Beitrag „Die Ohren der Welt",[20] den er
in dieser Zeit für die *Arbeiter-Zeitung* schreibt, schildert er seine Arbeitswelt
als – wie er sich selbst bezeichnet – „Übersetzungsmaschine". Eine ähnliche
Beschwerde geht aus einem 1948 geschriebenen Brief hervor:

> Meine Hörspiele haben Erfolg in der Schweiz (deutsch und
> italienisch), in Holland, Belgien, Norwegen, Dänemark, der
> Tschechoslowakei, Finnland und werden auch in Österreich und
> Deutschland gespielt, und in Wien sind mehrere Kinderbücher
> und ein Band Legenden in Vorbereitung. Aber all das klingt wohl
> sehr schön auf dem Papier, enthebt mich aber nicht der
> Notwendigkeit, mir mein tägliches Brot hier sehr schwer mit
> nervenaufreibender   Übersetzungsarbeit   und   unter   sehr
> ungünstigen äußeren Umständen zu verdienen. Unsere Abhörstelle
> liegt weit draußen, ich muss drei Nächte in der Woche dort in
> einem kellerartigen Raum schlafen und von dem leben, das ich
> mir mitbringe und selber koche.[21]

Seit Ende des Krieges beschickt er auch die neu gegründete *Arbeiter-Zeitung*
gelegentlich wieder mit Beiträgen. Ein verspätetes Angebot, in Wien die
Feuilletonredaktion zu übernehmen, schlägt er aus. Einer der Gründe mag
sein, dass ihn die internationale politische Lage – der Kalte Krieg und die
damalige Entwicklung des Kommunismus – anödete:

> Dazu kommt das bedrückende Schauspiel, daß in Deutschland und
> Österreich die früheren Nazis und Faschisten, besonders
> Schriftsteller, Schauspieler etc., blühen und gedeihen und von
> einer wirklichen Reinigung kaum die Rede sein kann.[22]

1948 wird er britischer Staatsbürger, womit:

> [...] fast genau 14 Jahre des Wanderns zu einem Ende kommen.
> Ich lebe hier auch sehr kosmopolitisch, im Büro gibt es alle
> Nationalitäten, da man ja Vertreter aller Sprachen braucht. Und
> sonst gibt es Inder, Chinesen und Neger rundum. Ich kann es mir
> gar nicht mehr vorstellen, wie man in Wien oder Prag gelebt hat –
> wo man nur von Leuten umgeben war, die alle dieselbe Sprache
> redeten und aus demselben Kulturkreis stammten.[23]

Nach Österreich also kehrt er nicht mehr zurück. Mitte der fünfziger Jahre,
nach einer Intrige jüngerer *AZ*-Redakteure, beendet er seine Mitarbeit ganz
und storniert sein Abonnement.

Weit erfolgreicher verläuft seine schriftstellerische Karriere, der er
sich nach seinem Abschied von Reuter 1962 wieder verstärkt widmet. Unter
dem Pseudonym Friedrich Feld veröffentlicht er Dutzende Kinder- und
Jugendbücher, die in viele Sprachen übersetzt, als Hörspiele im Rundfunk
gesendet und auf Schallplatte vertrieben werden.

Fritz Rosenfeld stirbt 1987 in Bexhill, Sussex. Richtig in Pension ist
er nie gegangen. Bis kurz vor seinem Tod bleibt er überaus aktiv, wenn auch
in ungewohnter Rolle: als politischer Kommentator für eine Schweizer
Zeitschrift, in der er gegen den Thatcherismus wettert.

Obwohl der österreichische Film ihm immer zu klein, zu unbedeutend, zu verlogen war, ist es doch vielleicht typisch für den Emigranten Rosenfeld, dass er im Exil in England wiederholt auf das Thema der Repräsentation von Österreich im Film zurückgekommen ist. Folgende Gedanken zum Wiederaufbau einer österreichischen Filmindustrie erschienen in der *Zeitung*:

Niemand weiß heute, ob Wiens Ateliers nach dem Krieg noch stehen werden, ob es Baumaterial und Kostüme geben wird, ob Autoren, Regisseure, Schauspieler, technisches Personal neu erstehen und aus allen Winkeln der Welt nach Wien zurückströmen werden; aber wenn es in absehbarer Zeit wieder eine österreichische Produktion geben sollte, muß sie sich von der der Epoche zwischen den beiden Kriegen wesentlich unterscheiden. Es gibt keine Produktion mit eigenem Gesicht, die gleichzeitig finanziell von anderen Ländern und ganz besonders von einem anderen Land abhängig ist; wer sagen will, was er zu sagen hat, muß eben auf die finanzielle Rückendeckung verzichten – er muß den Mut zur Unabhängigkeit haben. Das mag wieder kleinere und billigere Filme bedeuten, aber auch bessere und – wirklich österreichische. Aber nun – was ist „Österreichisch"? Gewiß nicht die klebrige Vergangenheitssentimentalität, die k. und k. Uniformen, die Spießer in Stößer und Bratenrock, die feschen Grafen und die anderen Operettengespenster. Der weinselige Patriotismus, der in Verzückungskrämpfe verfällt, wenn festgestellt wird, daß im Prater wieder die Bäume blühen, muß endgültig verschwinden. Der Teil des Publikums, der darauf noch hereinfällt, wird von Hollywood mit Vienna-Syrup feinster technischer Qualität reichlichst versorgt.[24]

Zum Teil verdankt Österreich die Aufmerksamkeit seiner Musik; die unsterblichen Melodien der Walzerdynastie Strauß sind dem Ohr der Kinobesucher in aller Welt vertraut und werden eben deshalb im Tonfilm immer wieder gern gehört. Zum anderen Teil verdankt es seine Beliebtheit aber einer Legende: der stark verzerrten, doch weitverbreiteten Vorstellung, daß es ein leichtlebiges Ländchen sorgloser Menschen sei, die vom frühen Morgen bis spät in die Nacht hinein in Grinzing und Sievering beim Heurigen sitzen, trinken, singen und tanzen. Wenn ein Filmsujet recht unglaubhaft war, und die Gestalten sich so benahmen, daß es zweifelhaft erschien, ob sie ihre fünf Sinne beisammen hatten, kurz, wenn der Operettenunsinn ins Extrem zu gehen begann, verlegte man den Film einfach nach Österreich: dort ist alles möglich, dort nimmt man nichts ernst, dort hat man nur Sinn für Wein, Weib und Gesang. Die Filmproduzenten in London und Paris, besonders aber die Hollywoods, bewunderten das Wien der Legende, und wenn sie einmal Österreich besuchten, waren sie zumeist unangenehm überrascht, ein Land vorzufinden, das sich gar nicht so sehr von anderen unterschied und dessen Volk von Arbeit lebte, nicht von Gesang.[25]

Der Krieg hat die Bilanz von Geben und Empfangen wesentlich verschoben. Hollywood wird erst wieder in reicherem Maß zu schenken beginnen, wenn der Krieg vorüber ist: die vom Faschismus auch geistig und künstlerisch ausgehungerten Nationen Europas werden jahrelang aus Hollywoods Film-magazinen ihre Kinoprogramme bestreiten, wie sie aus Amerikas Kornkammern ihr Brot empfangen werden.[26]

Anmerkungen

„Fritz Rosenfeld, Filmkritiker" (Arbeitstitel) ist ein Forschungsprojekt von Brigitte Mayr und Michael Omasta im Rahmen von SYNEMA – Gesellschaft für Film & Medien in Kooperation mit dem Filmarchiv Austria. In dessen Verlag soll im Herbst 2007 die zweibändige Publikation *Proletarisches Kino in Österreich* erscheinen, wobei Band 1 – *Arbeiterfilm während der Ersten Republik* – von Christian Dewald, Band 2 – *Fritz Rosenfeld, Filmkritiker* – von Michael Omasta und Brigitte Mayr herausgegeben wird.

[1] Fritz Rosenfeld, „Warum wir Filmreferate bringen", in *Die Unzufriedene: Eine unabhängige Wochenschrift für alle Frauen*, 52 (1925), S. 3.

[2] Fritz Rosenfeld, „Film und Proletariat. Versuch einer Soziologie des Kinos", *Arbeiterjahrbuch 1934*, Karlsbad 1934, S. 17-32 (S. 21).

[3] Fritz Rosenfeld, „Die Welt des Films – *Morgenrot; Ein neuer Kriegshetzfilm der Ufa*", *Arbeiter-Zeitung*, 5.3.1933, S. 19.

[4] Fritz Rosenfeld, „Sozialdemokratische Kinopolitik", *Der Kampf*, 4 (1929), S.192-97 (S. 196).

[5] Vgl. Verein für Geschichte der Arbeiterbewegung, Protokolle der Sitzungen des Parteivor-stands vom 1.9.1926 und 29.4.1929, zit. nach *Arbeiterkultur in Österreich 1918-1934*, Endbericht, Teil I (Wien: Österreichische Gesellschaft für Kulturpolitik, 1983), S. 224.

[6] Fritz Rosenfeld, „Der Arbeiter und der Film' – Vortrag gehalten am 30.1.1930 in der Arbeiterkammerstunde des Wiener Radios", *Bildungsarbeit*, 2 (1929), S.17-21 (S. 17).

[7] Vgl. zur Adressierung speziell der Leserinnen: Monika Bernold, „Kino. Über einen historischen Ort weiblichen Vergnügens und dessen Bewertung durch die sozialdemokratische Partei Wien 1918–34" (Diplomarbeit, Universität Wien, 1987).

[8] Fritz Rosenfeld, „Warum wir Filmreferate bringen", a. o. O, S. 3f.

[9] Ebenda.

[10] Fritz Rosenfeld, „Kritiker des Films", *Die Zeitung*, 6.4.1945, S. 7.

[11] Fritz Rosenfeld, „Der visuelle Mensch", *Arbeiter-Zeitung*, 16.5.1926, S. 21; Fritz Rosenfeld, „Die Flucht aus der Wirklichkeit", *Arbeiter-Zeitung*, 29.8.1926, S. 17; Fritz Rosenfeld, „Der Wiener Film von gestern und morgen", *Arbeiter-Zeitung*, 11.2.1932, S. 7-8; Fritz Rosenfeld, „Wir und das Kino", *Der jugendliche Arbeiter*, 2 (1928), S. 3-5; Fritz

Rosenfeld „Der Kampf um den Tonfilm", *Arbeiter-Zeitung*, 2.6.1929, S. 11; Fritz Rosenfeld, „Der Arbeiter und der Film", a. o. O., S. 17-21.

[12] Für biografische Hinweise danken wir Fritz Hausjell, nach dessen Artikel „‚Gedankt hat man es mir nicht.' Anmerkungen zum Leben des exilierten österreichischen Sozialisten Fritz Rosenfeld und seinen Beiträgen zu Theorie und Kritik des Kinofilms" in Friedrich Stadler (Hrsg.), *Vertriebene Vernunft II. Emigration und Exil österreichischer Wissenschaft* (Wien/München: Verlag Jugend und Volk, 1988), S.848-62 wir hier (S. 852ff) Rosenfeld im Originalton zitieren können.

[13] Vgl. genauere Ausführungen zu *Die Goldene Galeere* als eine literarisierte Theorie des Films für die politische Praxis bei Fritz Hausjell, a. o. O., S. 849.

[14] Wir folgen neben den angeführten Originalzitaten aus Rosenfelds Literaturkritiken für die *Arbeiter-Zeitung*, den *Kampf*, den *Sozialdemokrat* und die *Bildungsarbeit* auch im sonstigen Wortlaut den Ausführungen von Jürgen Doll in Ders., *Theater im Roten Wien. Vom sozialdemokratischen Agitprop zum dialektischen Theater Jura Soyfers* (Wien/Köln/Weimar: Böhlau-Verlag, 1997), S. 37-41.

[15] Zitiert nach einem Brief Fritz Rosenfelds vom 14. Oktober 1987 an Fritz Hausjell, a. o. O., S. 861, Fußnote 73: „es war dies Rosenfelds Antwort auf die Frage ‚Wie beurteilen Sie den Einfluß der Emigration auf Ihre geistigen Arbeiten? Sie arbeiteten in Prag für Hollywood, obwohl Sie zuvor die kapitalistische Filmproduktion stark kritisiert hatten? War dies schlicht der Preis fürs Überleben-können?'"

[16] Dokumentationsarchiv des österreichischen Widerstandes – DÖW Akte 8483: Radiogespräch Friedrich Feld, 31.10.1942, Radiosendung des BBC London nach Österreich.

[17] Fritz Rosenfeld, „Ernst Lubitsch – Filmsilhouetten III", *Die Zeitung*, 25.9.1942, S. 6.

[18] Fritz Rosenfeld, „Erich von Stroheim – Filmsilhouetten I", *Die Zeitung*, 11.9.1942, S. 3.

[19] Vgl. Anmerkung 15, zitiert nach einem Brief Fritz Rosenfelds vom 14. Oktober 1987.

[20] Fritz Rosenfeld, „Die Ohren der Welt", *Arbeiter-Zeitung*, 25.5.1947, S. 3.

[21] Brief von Fritz Rosenfeld an Josef Luitpold Stern (Wien) vom 9.2.1948. Kopie im Verein für Geschichte der Arbeiterbewegung, Wien, Mappe „Fritz Rosenfeld".

[22] Ebenda.

[23] Ebenda.

[24] Fritz Rosenfeld, „Neuaufbau des Films", *Die Zeitung*, 23.3.1945, S. 9.

[25] Fritz Rosenfeld, „Österreich im Film", *Die Zeitung*, 8.1.1943, S. 7.

[26] Fritz Rosenfeld, „Hollywood und Europa", *Die Zeitung*, 2.4.1943, S. 6.

'Kennen wir uns nicht aus Wien?': Emigré Film-Makers from Austria in London 1928-1945

Tobias Hochscherf

From the mid-1920s onwards, Austrians formed a vital émigré group within the British film industry. Whether they came voluntarily or as refugees, their contributions and expertise helped to establish a viable national cinema and to consolidate the studio system. In addition to the storylines of individual films, their influence is particularly visible in the organization of production and the improvement of standards. In this respect, film-making in Britain was shaped considerably by the work of technicians and art directors who introduced pioneering camera techniques, rationalized production processes, and increased the importance of *mise en scène*. Actors and producers from Vienna also soon became central figures within the London exile community and the British cinema.

For the British cinema, the 1930s stand out as a time of consolidation and expansion. The introduction of protectionist laws had spread optimism and boosted investment. In fact, the thriving film business was among the most dynamic industries in pre-war Britain.[1] Between 1935 and 1937 alone, 640 new film companies were founded. The increase of firms and production facilities was accompanied by new developments in the market. Following the overwhelming international success of Alexander Korda's historical epic *The Private Life of Henry VIII* (1933), highly capitalized film companies such as the Gaumont British Picture Corporation increasingly sought to conquer overseas markets.

What seems to be a genuinely British success story, however, was in fact the outcome of international cooperation. As the cast and credits of the era clearly illustrate, foreign personnel – most of them from German-speaking countries – played a pivotal role in the making of British films. The producer Alexander Korda, for instance, began his career working in Vienna and Berlin. For his box-office hit *The Private Life of Henry VIII*, a film he both produced and directed, he employed numerous other émigrés: the sets were designed by his brother Vincent Korda, Viennese-born Lajos Biró was co-author of the script, and the German composer Kurt Schröder was responsible for the music.

This article examines the various contributions of German-speaking émigrés from Austria to the British film industry. It advances the assertion that, as far as the film business is concerned, the crucial years of 1933 for Germany and 1938 for Austria were not the beginning of migration processes. The reciprocal interactions, transactions and career paths of individuals such as Alexander Korda, Emeric Pressburger, or Oskar F. Werndorff, for instance, underline the cosmopolitan character of cinema in the 1920s and 1930s. This implies that our understanding of émigré contributions to the British cinema depends on taking into account the various migration processes of the era in the context of pan-European co-operation that existed well before the Nazis came to power. Thus it will be argued that from the mid-1920s onwards, various migration processes, multi-faceted ways of inter-European co-operation, and the unprecedented mass purge of continental film practitioners as a result of Nazi policies, fundamentally affected film-making in the UK. Besides directors (such as Berthold Viertel, Paul L. Stein, and Wilhelm Thiele), script-writers (including Walter Reisch, Robert Neumann, and Lajos Biró) or actors (such as Adolf Wohlbrück, Richard Tauber, and Hans Wengraf), it was especially the work of German-speaking technicians and art directors who revolutionized the modes of studio production. The cinematographers Otto Kanturek and Günther Krampf and the set designer Oskar F. Werndorff, all born in Vienna, introduced pioneering camera techniques, for instance, rationalized production processes, and increased the importance of *mise en scène*. Furthermore, the producers Max Schach and Alexander Korda were central figures within the London exile community and can be regarded as the most important independent producers at that time in England.

Given the numerous links between the Austrian and German film industries, a basic thesis of this article is that it is not possible to differentiate clearly between Austrian and German film-makers. Attracted by the vibrant culture and the film scene in Berlin, many Austrians learned their craft in Germany, in particular in the UFA studios – one of the biggest and most modern production facilities outside Hollywood. Calling them Austrian film-makers seems problematic given that many of them never worked in their home country. The great number of German-speaking Hungarians, Czechs, and other film-makers who worked for the German/Austrian film industry make simplistic national distinctions even more difficult. Once again Alexander Korda's career path serves as a good example. Born in Hungary, he started to work in the film business in Budapest before he became a producer in Vienna from 1919 to 1923. From 1927 to 1930 he worked in Berlin before he eventually came to Britain in 1932 after some time in Paris and Hollywood. The itineraries of Korda's fellow countryman Josef Somlo also illustrate the mobile and global character of the film business. Born in Papá, Hungary, Somlo studied law in Budapest. After his graduation he began to work as the managing director of Viennese-based film companies in 1908. From 1919 to 1922 he then acted as head of UFA's foreign department in Berlin before founding his own production company with

Hermann Fellner (Fellner & Somlo Film GmbH, later Felson Film GmbH). In 1933 he came to Britain as a refugee, where he was involved in numerous film productions until 1958.

The careers of Alexander Korda and Josef Somlo – one could equally take other film personnel such as Sam Spiegel or Peter Lorre – raise the question as to whether they should be regarded as Hungarian, Austrian, or German. Perhaps a bit of each? In the following, the expression 'German-speaking' is used to acknowledge the complex international character of the film industry in general and in Germany and Austria in particular prior to 1933 and 1938.

This article is structured chronologically. The first part outlines the migration processes of film-makers from Austria in the period from 1928 to 1933, while the second part deals with the group of mainly Jewish refugees who came to Britain between 1933 and 1945. Following this general overview, the final two sections illuminate the problems faced by film-makers in Britain and describe émigré film genres.

By outlining the diverse migration processes undertaken by émigrés and by inserting émigré films into their historical context, the findings of this analysis are of wider interest. They illuminate crucial developments in the British cinema, inter-European co-operation, and the position of Whitehall regarding the many refugees from Germany and Austria. Moreover, this examination also raises general questions of cultural imagery, national cinema, and intercultural exchange.

Film Europe: Early Austrian Emigrés in Britain before 1933

Britain was comparatively late in developing a recognized national cinema. When American market dominance was all too obvious with British films accounting for only five per cent of those shown in 1925, a growing number of voices demanded governmental protection.[2] With the Cinematograph Films Act in 1927, quota legislation was implemented which was designed to strengthen British production; it ruled that distributors and exhibitors must acquire and show a minimum number of domestic films. The implementation of the new protectionist legislation profoundly changed the industry as it prompted investment, spread optimism, and accelerated the formation of new enterprises.

An increase in the production of British films went hand in hand with an internationalization of the industry. In order to increase the production value of films the affluent British film industry increasingly looked abroad for foreign talent. Among their new employees was a significant number of German-speaking personnel who found temporary or permanent employment in Britain, in particular for major productions aimed at an international market such as *Moulin Rouge, Piccadilly* (both Ewald André Dupont, 1927/28 and 1928) or *The Woman He Scorned* (Paul Czinner, 1929). The latter film demonstrates that German-speaking film-makers of various nationalities usually worked together on these films. While Czinner, who not only directed the film but also wrote the original story, started his career in Vienna, his assistant Herbert Selpin was born in Berlin. Moreover, the protagonists of *The Woman He Scorned*, the Weimar film star Pola Negri and one of Czinner's favoured actors Hans Rehmann, were born in Poland and Switzerland respectively. The numerous examples of German-speaking film-makers in Britain underline that 'seen from a purely industrial perspective, 1933 was in no way the beginning of a widespread emigration, but rather the politically motivated intensification of a process that had started in the early 1920s'.[3]

Growing concerns about Hollywood's unchallenged hegemony led to a double strategy in Europe. On the one hand, countries like Germany or England tried to protect their market by the introduction of quota legislation. On the other, they tried to compete with Hollywood by increasing pan-European co-operation.[4] Although no equivalent of the US Office of the Motion Picture Producers and Distributors Association existed in Europe, producers were able to establish manifold networks and personal contacts on the basis of inter-European partnerships and joint ventures from the mid-1920s onwards. A main consequence of the cultural and technical interchange that took place under the heading of 'Film Europe' was that a number of German-speaking film-makers enjoyed good relations with decision makers in the British film industry. Later, when the Nazis set into motion the unparalleled exodus of film workers first from Germany and then from Austria, such contacts proved invaluable in finding new jobs. This explains why it was émigrés such as Alexander Korda, Josef Somlo and Oskar F. Werndorff with already established links to British companies and individuals who were successfully able to pursue careers in the diaspora.

After the introduction of sound at the end of the 1920s, film-makers from Austria and Germany were especially important for the production of remakes of popular continental films and multi-language productions; that is films made with the same plot that were shot with a different cast in a different language for varying national markets.[5] This trans-European cooperation, which also included a common exchange of film personnel, led to the phenomenon that 'film industries of the 1920s and 1930s witnessed an increasingly mobile workforce and the emergence of a new type of film professional, the mobile freelancer'.[6]

The many long-term contracts given to German-speaking technicians and art directors against the common practice of signing up film-makers for individual productions only suggest that they were seen as vital for the future development of the studios and for the training of prospective staff. Michael Balcon later noted that at Shepherd's Bush: '[we] also started training schemes at a local technical school, and many of the first-class British technicians received their early instruction under the supervision of the men we had brought in from the Continent.'[7]

Like many of his German-speaking colleagues, Oskar F. Werndorff came to Britain in the context of German-British co-productions in the late 1920s (*Die letzte Nacht/The Queen Was in the Parlour, Der fesche Husar/The Gallant Husar, Der Geisterzug/The Ghost Train, The Wrecker/Der Würger*). Besides his work as set designer, he also directed the multi-language production *The Bells* (1931). After he had gained recognition and established contacts through these early works, he was given a permanent post as head of the art department at the Gainsborough studios in Islington (where he created sets for Hitchcock's *The Thirty-Nine Steps* and *Sabotage*). Acknowledging the émigrés' pivotal role, Tom Ryall rightly points out that the artistic aspirations of major British studios are represented by 'the European sophistication'[8] of British films made by foreigners. In fact, it was especially the production companies' endeavour to produce films for the international market that allowed the relatively few German-speaking émigrés to fill key positions in major British studios. Besides Werndorff, other film practitioners from Austria were also able to establish themselves in the British film business before 1933 – among them the author Lajos Biró, the cinematographer Günther Krampf, and the directors Paul Czinner and Geza von Bolvary. While they usually started their English careers in one of the many trans-European co-productions (Geza von Bolvary, for instance, directed *Der Geisterzug/Ghost Train*), they increasingly became involved in British productions. Together with other continentals who came to Britain in the late 1920s (above all film-makers from the Weimar Republic), they helped to consolidate the British film industry. Thus the contribution of set designers such as Oskar F. Werndorff or cinematographers such as Günther Krampf was vital for the astounding boom of the British film industry from 1932 to 1937. When they were given permanent senior posts in the major studios in or surrounding London, they not only helped to raise the production values of individual films but also managed to streamline production processes, to modernise the studios and to train future staff. In fact, their expertise helped the aspiring British industry to equal the artistic accomplishments of Hollywood and Weimar Germany, and to produce the technical innovations required to make films for the international market. Last but not least, these early immigrants also paved the way for refugees from Germany and Austria who came to Britain after 1933.

Goebbel's *Filmpolitik*: Emigrés in British Cinema after 1933

After only a few weeks in power, the National Socialist Party (NSDAP) established the Reich Ministry of Enlightenment and Propaganda under the leadership of Joseph Goebbels in order to regulate all aspects of cultural affairs through *Gleichschaltung* ('co-ordination'). For the film industry this meant fundamental changes, as it implied both the eradication of all political opponents and groups seen as racially inferior – above all German Jewry.[9] The developments in the German film business after the takeover by the Nazis and the resultant industrial reconstruction which took place alongside its political policies eventually caused the migration of some 2,000 film-workers. This meant that about twenty to thirty per cent of the whole industry fled to other countries.[10] All in all, about 400 German-speaking emigrés from Germany or Austria were involved in British film production at some stage between the late 1920s and 1945.[11] Despite this unparalleled purge, it must be noted that not every German-speaking film-maker in Britain was a refugee. The international character of the film industry also meant that some expatriates from the Third Reich or Austria came for economic reasons. Some of these eventually returned to their home country and resumed successful careers under the Nazis. An example here is the Austrian cinematographer Hans Schneeberger who returned to Germany after he had worked for Alexander Korda. Schneeberger's decision illustrates that the migration of film workers in the 1920s and 1930s was neither a one-way movement nor was the Third Reich film industry isolated. For example the German-speaking art director Andrej Andrejew, who made his first films in the Weimar Republic in the 1920s and worked frequently in both England and France throughout the 1930s continued to design sets for French productions during the Nazi occupation before returning to Britain in 1946 for Alexander Korda's production of *Anna Karenina* (Julien Duvivier, UK 1947).

The fact that many Austrians came to London some time before the Anschluss in 1938 has to do with the history and structure of the film business. With its internationally acclaimed, innovative productions – exemplified above all by German expressionism – Weimar cinema had become Hollywood's only rival. Above all the UFA studio complex attracted both Germans and foreigners, among them a large number of film-makers from Austria. Because most of them were Jewish or, according to the classification of the Nuremberg laws, 'half- or quarter-Jews', they were forced to leave Germany when it became more and more evident that the film business was one of the first industries the Nazis wanted to be *judenfrei*. Among the Austrians who fled from Berlin to London were prominent names such as the author and director Rudolph Bernauer, the producers

Isidore Goldschmidt (Isadore Goldsmith), Alex Strasser, Paul Merzbach, Joe May and Karl Grune, the actors Adolf Wohlbrück (Anton Walbrook), Magda Sonja and Peter Lorre, and the composer Ernst Toch. In view of the many Austrians who participated in British productions the feature columnist and chronicler of exile, Paul Marcus,[12] noted in his émigré newsletter on the occasion of several film premieres in winter 1936 that that one can speak about 'Viennese Weeks' in London.[13]

This first wave of Austrian refugees came to London at a fortunate time. The film industry was prospering and in need of well-trained and experienced staff. Consequently, finding a new job in the thriving British industry was still relatively easy for this first group of exiles. The positive economic outlook, however, only partially explains why Austrian refugees from Berlin preferred London to Vienna. The relatively small size of Austrian production might be one reason, yet their decision also seems to have been politically motivated.

Although Austria, sharing as it did a language and a history of many joint film projects with Germany, could theoretically have employed German exiles, its film industry was highly dependent on the German film market under Nazi control. Constant pressure from NSDAP officials, economic difficulties as a result of films being banned in Germany, along with domestic Austrian anti-Semitism, meant that Austria was a safe refuge for Jewish and other refugee film-makers for a limited period of time only.[14] In March 1934, the association of the film industry in Berlin offered to give advice to Austrian companies to help prevent Austrian productions being banned. The efforts of the Nazi *Filmpolitik* proved entirely successful. From 1935, all major Austrian production companies followed the Nazi directives by banning the employment of Jewish film-makers – although exceptions were still granted to those who 'only' had Jewish ancestors or a Jewish spouse. This led the exile publication *Pariser Tageblatt* to express doubts about the independence of the Austrian cinema in August 1935 by means of the rhetorical headline 'Österreich-Film unabhängig?'[15]

Unable to find work, many Jewish Austrian and other German-speaking film-makers thus had to leave Austria as early as 1934, many of them through the '*grüne Grenze*' via Czechoslovakia where the cities Prague and Brno developed into lively Austro-German cultural centres until the Munich agreement in 1938. The only way to stay and work in Austria was to establish independent production companies which employed a high number of refugee film practitioners from the Third Reich.[16] However, while some of the films produced by independent companies like *Mit Salto in die Seligkeit* (Fritz Schulz, 1934) or *Der Pfarrer von Kirchfeld* (Jacob and Luise Fleck, 1937) were successful at the box office, they also provoked fierce opposition from Nazi supporters. Although Austria was still a safe country of exile the situation was deteriorating quickly. Protests against films made with Jewish personnel underline the anti-Semitic resentment that ran deep in Austrian society. In addition to independent films made by mainly Jewish film-makers in Austria, Nazi sympathizers and conservative voices also ran campaigns against the release of critical foreign films. The British émigré movie *Jew Süss* (Lothar Mendes, GB 1933/34), for instance, which criticized the pogroms and contained some exceptionally clear attacks on Nazi policies[17] was reviled in the Austrian press as a 'Jewish *tendenzfilm* [*sic*] which grossly insults the feelings of Catholic people'.[18] Disillusioned with Austria as a safe place to live and work, many film-makers thus left the country for England before its formal annexation by the Third Reich. Examples include the composer Nicholas Brodsky, the author and director Rudolf Kacser (Rudolph Cartier), and the actors Gitta Alpar and Oskar Homolka. The latter's itinerary exemplifies a journey typical of Austrian film exiles. Like many of his countrymen he had worked in Berlin since the mid-1920s and had gone to Vienna shortly after 1933. About a year later he moved to London, where he was cast by fellow émigré Berthold Viertel for his Empire film *Rhodes of Africa*, before eventually being granted a visa for the US in 1937. As this case illustrates, Britain was often seen as a country of transit. Notwithstanding the many refugees who found a new home in and about London, Hollywood was the preferred final destination for most film exiles.[19]

The remaining mainly Jewish film practitioners fled after the Anschluss in 1938 – again many of them to England. Among them were many who had previously worked with British film companies and who had friends or good contacts among the refugees who had already found work in Britain. Richard Tauber, for instance, had already featured as a leading actor in four English musical films before he finally left his beloved Austria in 1938. Other examples of film personnel who fled to Britain after 1938 are the actors Sybille Binder, Ludwig Stössel, Hans Wengraf, the authors Anton Kuh and Friedrich Porges, the publisher of the Viennese film journal *Der Film*. Among the large group of German-speaking film-makers in Britain it was especially the strong presence of German-speaking producers from Austria like Vienna-born Max Schach or the Hungarian Alexander Korda who had worked for years as directors and producers in Austria that helped many fellow-refugees to find employment. Lajos Biró, for example, constantly followed Alexander Korda, who became a close friend over the years, to the various places where he worked including Vienna, Berlin, Hollywood, Paris, and London.[20] Korda's preference for foreign film-makers, among them many he knew from his time in Berlin and Vienna, even led to the popular joke that the five Union Jacks that marked the entrance of the Denham studios represented the five British employees.[21]

For many refugees who had to leave Austria after the Anschluss, the situation on the British job market was increasingly difficult as a consequence of a financial crisis of the film business in 1936/37. After the first devastating accounts of the scale of the crisis appeared in the *Financial Times* on 13 July 1937, those in Britain who mistrusted the activities of German-speaking and particularly Austrian Jewish film-makers interpreted the financial problems as evidence for their concerns. Subsequently, the unions, some journalists, and members of the public were quick to blame producers such as Alexander Korda and Max Schach for the crash.[22] By primarily blaming German-speaking Jewish émigrés for the crisis, the unions and other figures often fostered already existing resentment and anti-Semitic conspiracy theories. In August 1938, for instance, the diplomat and author Sir Bruce Lockhart wrote in his diary:

> Last night Bayliss-Smith, who is a leading chartered accountant and represents the creditors in some of the biggest cinema financial messes in this country, says the cinema industry here has cost the banks and insurance companies about £4,000,000. Most of this is lost by Jews – like Korda and Max Schach. [...] In Bayliss-Smith's opinion and he would not say so lightly, Korda is a much worse man than Schach. Schach is just a slick Jew who sees financial moves ahead of the other fellow. Korda is a crook and, according to Bayliss-Smith, an evil man.[23]

British Immigration Policies, the Internment of Emigrés and Anti-German Resentments in Britain

Anti-Semitic resentments in European countries meant that émigré film practitioners were constantly in danger of being deported to the Third Reich because of passport, labour or residence misdemeanours.[24] Britain was no exception: 'Curt Siodmak [...] spent several weeks riding the English Channel ferry from Dover to Calais and back, because neither the French nor the British would let him disembark without a residency permit.'[25] If refugees were granted leave to land at Dover this was done under the condition that they did not remain in the United Kingdom longer than one month. Rudolf Kacser's passport meticulously documents his monthly day trips to France in order to apply for a renewal of his residence permit.[26]

The main reason for the great difficulties in giving an exact figure for exile films is that many of the émigrés who were not in possession of a valid visa or work permit (including both paid and unpaid employment) are not mentioned in the cast and credits of films. Accordingly it is very difficult to reconstruct the uncredited film personnel. The film *Pagliacci* (Karl Grune, UK 1936), which was produced with the help of numerous German-speaking émigrés, serves as a good example. Whereas director Karl Grune, producer Max Schach, composer Hanns Eisler, cinematographer Otto Kanturek, set designer Oskar F. Werndorff, singer Richard Tauber and production manager Fritz Brunn are mentioned, neither Bertolt Brecht nor Fritz Kortner, who collaborated on the script, are named in the credits because they were not in possession of a valid work permit for Great Britain.[27] Further examples are the Austrian authors Hans Kahan and the director Carl Mayer. Like so many of their fellow exiles, Kahan's contribution to the script of Basil Dean's *I See Ice* (1938) remains uncredited as does Carl Mayer's involvement in the George Bernard Shaw adaptations *Pygmalion* and *Major Barbara*.

After the outbreak of war the climate for German-speaking exiles deteriorated significantly. Xenophobic hysteria and ethnic discrimination, fuelled by fears of espionage, sabotage and a possible German invasion led to the internment of thousands of German exiles in England, on the Isle of Man or overseas. Although the British authorities sought to intern enemy aliens only, paradoxically many of the internees were Jews and/or anti-Nazi activists who had fled Germany to escape persecution.[28] Among the internees were also numerous film-workers: set designers Alfred Junge and Hein Heckroth, cinematographers Rudolf Kacser and Karl Kayser, director and actor Erich Freund or script writer Emeric Pressburger.

After internment many German-speaking émigrés remained under MI5 and police surveillance. In particular they were closely observed after applying for British citizenship – often rumours and gossip were used as sources of information. The police file on Rudolf Kacser, for example, states that 'he is not well regarded in film circles' and that he 'lacks ability to prepare satisfactory scenarios and is considered not intelligent enough for the work'. Beside a meticulous assessment of the financial and professional situation of refugees, the reports also investigated their private lives, as Kacser's file illustrates:

> Another aspect of his character is his association with women. [...] For the past three years applicant has been intimately associated with a British woman who a few months ago married a well-known personality in the British film industry. Enquiries show that this young woman, whose parents are quite rich, maintained applicant for the greater part of the period that they were associated. But in view of her recent marriage to an Englishman who may not know of her association with applicant, I have not interviewed the lady.[29]

Furthermore, the trade union Association of Cinematograph Technicians and other public organizations or figures viewed the ever-increasing number of German-speaking émigrés in Britain with growing concern. They repeatedly criticized the employment of foreign film-workers because of fears, caused by various factors ranging from economic concerns to xenophobia or anti-Semitism, that the British film industry was dominated by foreign film-makers to the detriment of British employees. Interestingly, prominent film critics like Graham Greene often drew upon the same rhetoric of decadence and otherness that German anti-Semites drew upon in order to describe Jewish film-makers pejoratively.[30] In his now notorious review of Karl Grune's *The Marriage of Corbal* (UK 1936) Greene wrote:

> England, of course, has always been the home of the exiled; but one may at least express a wish that *émigrés* would set up trades in which their ignorance of our language and culture was less of a handicap: it would not grieve me to see Mr Alexander Korda seated before a cottage loom in an Eastern country, following an older and better tradition. The Quota Act has played into foreign hands, and as far as I know, there is nothing to prevent an English film unit being completely staffed by technicians of foreign blood. We have saved the English film industry from American competition only to surrender it to a far more alien control.[31]

Emigré Film Genres

Since the British job market for film personnel was saturated in the late 1930s, émigrés generally had to choose 'film genres that were under-represented in the film industries of host countries, and in which they could demonstrate their special talents'.[32] For Austrian film-makers this often meant that they had to participate in the production of films such as *Heart's Desire* and *Waltz Time* (1935 and 1945, both Paul L. Stein) that alluded to the idealized, nostalgic views of Austria as a country of grandeur, music and Viennese *Gemütlichkeit*.[33]

This mythical perception of Austria was both a blessing and a curse for the émigrés. While the light-hearted musicals set in 'old Vienna' provided jobs at difficult times, it also meant that Austrian actors were increasingly typecast to play clichés and so were limited in their artistic self-expression. What is perhaps even more significant about these films, however, was that they play down Austria's active role in the pogroms against Jews and other minority groups. The latter point in particular was criticized repeatedly by Austrian refugees. For example, in a feature column, the London exile publication *Die Zeitung*, underlines the absurdity of the idealized filmic Austria:

Das Jahr 1938, der Untergang Österreichs im braunen Meer, hat [an den idealisierten Kinobildern] nichts geändert. Er hat nur die Verwirrung in den Hirnen der Filmschreiber vergrößert. Sie feierte ihren Triumph erst kürzlich in dem Hollywood-Produkt 'They Dare not Love'. Da läuft im Jahre 1938, in den Tagen der Besetzung ein 'Prinz Kurt von Ratenberg' in altösterreichischer Erzherzogsuniform herum, der sehr fesch und angeblich die letzte Hoffnung des Vaterlandes ist, vor den Nazis nach Amerika flieht und sich dort dessen besinnt, was er seiner Heimat schuldig ist. Das Wien der Märztage 1938 sieht aus wie das von etwa 1890: der erste Weltkrieg scheint noch nicht begonnen zu haben und gewiß hat es kein 1918 gegeben. So werden wir Zeugen, wie der Film ein Stück Geschichte, das wir vor wenigen Jahren selbst miterlebt haben, bereits verdreht, um es der Schablone anzupassen, die ja so bequem und kommerziell so einträglich ist. Armes Österreich; es ist bitter, von den Feinden gefoltert, aber es ist durchaus nicht süß, von den Freunden mißverstanden zu werden.[34]

Adopting a similar critical perspective, some Austrian film-makers even sought to deconstruct both the myth of Austria as the first victim of Nazi aggression as well as the idealized romantic images of Austria in general and of Vienna in particular. The 1936 British production *Land Without Music* (Walter Forde), for instance, counteracts the myth of a peaceful and liberal Austria that was the first victim of the Nazi war of conquest. Interestingly, many of the participating film-makers were from Austria: the script was written by the Viennese author Rudolph Bernauer, Max Schach produced the film, Oscar Straus composed the music and the actor Richard Tauber played the main protagonist. It tells the story of a star singer who returns to his beloved Ruritanian birthplace, the land of music of the title, only to find that any form of musical activity is prohibited because Austria threatens its music-loving neighbour with war if the debts resulting from the idleness of its people are not immediately repaid. What at first seems to be a fantasy is in fact a sophisticated filmic experiment that ironically mocks popular notions of the Danubian monarchy. In fact, the Austria of *Land Without Music* threatens to invade its own myth, the country of music and a harmonious, peaceful society.

While *Land Without Music* rather playfully deals with the mythical Austrian idyll, other exile film projects were more serious in their criticism. A surprisingly direct critical statement is the Gaumont-British film proposal 'City Without Jews'. Banned by the censors in Britain, the script, which had already been made into a silent movie in Austria in 1923/24 by Hans Karl Breslauer, was an adaptation of an anti-Nazi novel by Austrian writer Hugo Bettauer. The film project was unique as it not only deals with the issue of anti-Semitism but also addresses the role of Jewish exiles. The script describes how Christian Socialist and German Nationalist parties in Austria pass a law that expels all Jews from the country, including baptized Jews and children of mixed marriages. After a brief period of enthusiasm and prosperity, the country experiences a severe crisis which leaves half its people on the verge of starvation because all the leading brains in science, finance, art and commerce were Jewish.

It is no coincidence that the script of 'City Without Jews', which is set in contemporary Vienna, was submitted to the British Board of Film Censors in June 1933. After having eliminated the Austrian parliament in March 1933, Chancellor Engelbert Dollfuß sought to install an authoritarian Catholic corporatist state with the backing of fascist Italy. His Christian Social party was not only deeply conservative but also anti-liberal and anti-Semitic. The script can thus be read as a representation of these events. It also includes a warning about the real strength of anti-Semitism in Austria prior to the Anschluss. The cheering crowds celebrating the expulsion of Jews in the proposed film anticipate the thunderous applause that welcomed German troops marching into Austria on 12 March 1938.[35]

Whether they were directors, authors, actors, cinematographers, or art directors, the work of film-makers from Austria enriched the British cinema. By way of their expertise and imagination they helped to consolidate the studio system. It was not coincidence that it was an émigré film, *The Private Life of Henry VIII*, that put British cinema on the international map. When the Second World War ended, few refugee film-makers returned to Germany or Austria. While the Holocaust was a main reason not to return to their home countries, many film-makers also found a new *Heimat* in Britain. Most of those who stayed continued to make films in England. Furthermore, the emergence of television also offered new job opportunities. For example, Rudolph Kacser, who had many difficulties with the British authorities until he was finally naturalized years after the war, became one of the leading TV producers and directors responsible for landmark productions such as the 1958 science fiction series *Quatermass and the Pit*.

Notes

[1] Margaret Dickinson and Sarah Street, *Cinema and State: the Film Industry and the British Government, 1927-1984* (London: BFI, 1985), p. 76.

[2] Sarah Street, 'British Film and the National Interest, 1927-39', in *The British Cinema Book*, ed. by Robert Murphy, second edition (London: BFI, 2003), pp. 28-34 (p. 28).

[3] Tim Bergfelder, 'The Production Designer and the *Gesamtkunstwerk*: German Film Technicians in the British Film Industry of the 1930s', in *Dissolving Views: Key Writings on British Cinema*, ed. by Andrew Higson (London: Cassell, 1996), pp. 20-37 (p. 21); see also Thomas Elsaesser, 'Heavy Traffic: Perspektive Hollywood: Emigranten oder Vagabunden?', in *London Calling: Deutsche im britischen Film der dreißiger Jahre*, ed. by Hans-Michael Bock, Wolfgang Jacobsen and Jörg Schöning (München: text + kritik, 1993), pp. 21-41.

[4] See *'Film Europe' and 'Film America': Cinema, Commerce and Cultural Exchange 1920-1939*, ed. by Andrew Higson and Richard Maltby, Exeter Studies in Film History (Exeter: University of Exeter Press, 1999).

[5] See Joseph Garncarz, 'Made in Germany: Multiple-Language Versions and the Early German Sound Cinema', in *'Film Europe' and 'Film America'*, pp. 249-73.

[6] Bergfelder, *op. cit.*, p. 21.

[7] Michael Balcon, *Michael Balcon Presents: A Lifetime of Films* (London: Hutchinson, 1969), p. 58.

[8] Tom Ryall, 'A British Studio System: The Associated British Picture Corporation and the Gaumont-British Picture Corporation in the 1930s', in *The British Cinema Book*, ed. by Robert Murphy, 2nd edn (London: BFI, 2001), pp. 35-41 (p. 37).

[9] See Julian Putley, 'Film Policy in the Third Reich', in *The German Cinema Book*, ed. by Tim Bergfelder, Erica Carter and Deniz Göktürk (London: BFI, 2002), pp. 173-81 (p. 173).

[10] Author's estimate made on the basis of casts and credits of British feature films made 1928-1945.

[11] Figure according to the author's research for a PhD thesis at the University of Liverpool.

[12] Paul Marcus's newsletter *Pem's-Privat-Berichte* was published from May 1936 to September 1939 and September 1945 to May 1972.

[13] Pem (= Paul Marcus), *Pem's-Privat-Berichte*, 31 (3 December 1936), p. 62.

[14] See Jan-Christopher Horak, 'German Exile Cinema, 1933-1945', *Film History*, 4 (1996), 373-89 (p. 376, especially endnote 10).

[15] Anon., 'Österreich-Film unabhängig?', *Pariser Tageblatt*, 16 August 1935, p. 4.

[16] See Anon., 'Film-Österreich am Scheidewege', *Pariser Tageblatt*, 3 May 1935, p. 4; on independent émigré productions, see *Unerwünschtes Kino: Der deutschsprachige Emigrantenfilm 1934-1937*, ed. by Armin Loacker and Martin Prucha (Wien: Filmarchiv Austria, 2000).

[17] See Susan Tegel, 'The Politics of Censorship: Britain's "Jew Süss" (1934) in London, New York and Vienna', *Historical Journal of Film, Radio, and Television*, 2 (1995), pp. 219-45.

[18] Cited after Tegel, *op. cit.*, p. 232.

[19] On Austrians in Hollywood see Rudolf Ulrich, *Österreicher in Hollywood*, second edition (Vienna: Filmarchiv Austria, 2004).

[20] See C.A. Lejeune, 'The Private Lives of London Films', *Nash's Magazine*, September 1936, p. 8.

[21] Paul Tabori, *Alexander Korda* (London: Oldbourne, 1959), p. 9.

[22] On the cases of Alexander Korda and Max Schach see: 'Finance for British Films', *The Times*, 2 May 1939, p. 5; Kevin-Gough Yates, 'The European Film Maker in Exile in Britain, 1933-1945', (unpublished doctoral thesis, Open University, UK, 1991), pp. 160-67; Sarah

Street, 'Alexander Korda, Prudential Assurance and British Film Finance in the 1930s', *Historical Journal of Film, Radio and Television*, 2 (1986), pp. 161-79; Rachael Low, *The History of the British Film 1929-1939: Film Making in 1930s Britain* (London: Allen & Unwin), pp. 198-208 and pp. 218-29; Bergfelder, 'The Production Designer...', pp. 31-32.

[23] Bruce Lockhart, *The Diaries of Sir Bruce Lockhart* (London: Macmillan, 1973), p. 392; in the original Schach's name is mis-spelt 'Schacht' throughout.

[24] Horak, *op.cit.*, p. 377.

[25] *Ibid.*

[26] Passport of Rudolf Kacser (aka Rudolf Katscher, later known as Rudolph Cartier), National Archives, HO 405/26875; file opened by Home Office upon author's request.

[27] Horak, *op.cit.*, p. 383.

[28] Cf. Louise London, *Whitehall and the Jews, 1933-1948: British Immigration Policy, Jewish Refugees and the Holocaust* (Cambridge: Cambridge University Press, 2001).

[29] Police Report dated 1 January 1947, pp. 6-7, National Archives, HO 405/26875.

[30] Cf. 'Der Mann mit der Zigarre', pictures of Jewish film personnel from a Nazi propaganda publication, reprinted in Asper, *op.cit.*, p. 14.

[31] Graham Greene 'The Marriage of Corbal', *The Spectator*, 5 June 1936, reprinted in *The Pleasure Dome: Graham Greene – The Collected Film Criticism 1935-40*, ed. by John Russell Taylor (London: Secker & Warburg, 1972), pp. 78-79.

[32] Horak, *op.cit.*, p. 379.

[33] For the influence of the Viennese operatic tradition see Stephen Guy, 'Calling All Stars: Musical Films in a Musical Decade', in *The Unknown 1930s. An Alternative History of the British Cinema, 1929-1939* (London/ New York: I. B. Tauris, 2000), pp.99-118 (esp. p. 104).

[34] F. R. 'Österreich im Film', *Die Zeitung*, 8 January 1943, p. 7.

[35] See Wolfgang Benz, *Geschichte des Dritten Reiches* (Munich: C.H. Beck, 2000), p. 159.

Imaging the Future through the Past: Austrian Women Exile Writers and the Historical Novel

Andrea Hammel

Using the genre of the historical novel Hermynia Zur Mühlen and Hilde Spiel, two women writers who went into exile in Britain, show alternative moments in Austrian social, cultural and political history in an attempt to connect a future imagined Austria with the past. Both writers create narratives that show the failures as well as the possibilities in Austria's historical development, paying special attention to multiculturalism, Jewish emancipation and gender relations.

The historical novel was a popular genre for exile writers: Helmut Koopmann in '"Geschichte ist die Sinngebung des Sinnlosen": Zur Ästhetik des historischen Romans im Exil'[1] points to the booming production of historical novels in the early years of exile, a view supported by Alexander Stephan.[2] Stephan also outlines the discussions surrounding the genre of the historical novel and its suitability as antifascist literature. He points out that many historical novels were not conceived with a post-1933 agenda in mind and that a number of exile writers finished historical projects in exile, which they had started before 1933. Hermynia Zur Mühlen's project for a series of historical novels based on an Austrian aristocratic family was started in Vienna, the first stage of her flight. As it was first published in Berne and Prague in serialized form and eventually - in an English translation by Zur Mühlen herself - as *We Poor Shadows*[3] in book form by Frederick Muller in London in 1943, it should not be seen as a spontaneous reaction to a certain situation, but a long-term project, albeit started after she had to flee National Socialist Germany. The case of *Die Früchte des Wohlstands*[4] is different again as it was definitely started after Spiel's arrival in London.

Debates surrounding the genre focused mainly on the relevance of historical themes in literature and the debating parties were to be found in all political groups: 'Gestritten wurde von Marxisten und Bürgerlichen vor allem über die Frage nach Gegenwartsflucht und Zeitbezogenheit des historischen Romans.'[5] Kurt Hiller's polemic against historical themes in literature is often quoted. He accuses the writers of escapism when centring their works on historical figures such as 'Katharina von Rußland, Christine von Schweden, Josephine von Frankreich, über Ferdinand den Ersten, Philipp den Zweiten, Napoleon den Dritten'.[6] But Hiller is not condemning a whole genre, acknowledging that books about Moses Mendelssohn might well have a useful contribution to make at a time when the project of Jewish emancipation had finally failed. Thus Hilde Spiel's choices of historical subjects, such as the Jewish family in *Die Früchte des Wohlstands*, seem less inevitably directed towards escapism. The subgenre of the family saga also provides a fundamentally different platform from the obviously popular biographical genre with its focus on one famous life. The possibilities of the generational structure of the family saga has so far not been analysed in the criticism on historical novels written in exile. Furthermore, in a family saga like *Ewiges Schattenspiel*, it is the interconnections between private and public life and again, as in other novels by women exile writers, the focus on the everyday, which sets it apart from other historical novels. Hiller's lament that no one writes about 'was wertvolle reale Menschen in wertvollen realen Nächten entfremdet und zusammentreibt'[7] is not borne out by the narrative development in *Ewiges Schattenspiel* or *Die Früchte des Wohlstands*.

Georg Lukács also recognised the centrality of the historical novel for exile literature: 'This democratic protest movement has created a new type of historical novel which, chiefly in the literature of the German-antifascist emigration, has become a central problem of letters in our day.'[8] In his study on the historical novel, conceived in 1936/7, Lukács praises the exiled writers for overcoming what he sees as the previous problem of historical narratives, namely the lack of connection between history and the present. He sees the historical novel as a tool against the misuse of history by the National Socialists and proclaims the works to be 'a humanist declaration of war against fascist barbarism'.[9] But it is not only this positive assessment of the genre of the historical novel that makes Lukács an important contributor to this debate. His outline of the development of historical narratives is also significant for the analysis of Zur Mühlen's and Spiel's novels. Lukács sees the French Revolution, the revolutionary wars and the rise and fall of Napoleon as the beginning of history as mass experience. Whereas earlier wars had been waged by professional armies, the French had to create a mass army against the coalition of absolute monarchies. Thus the purpose of the war had to be made clear to the masses by means of propaganda, which had the effect of increasing individuals' awareness of the influence of history:

> Now if experiences such as these are linked with the knowledge that similar upheavals are taking place all over the world, this must enormously strengthen the feeling first that there is such a thing as history, second that it is an uninterrupted process of changes and finally that it has a direct effect upon the life of every individual.[10]

It is interesting that Zur Mühlen set *Ewiges Schattenspiel* during the period succeeding the Napoleonic wars and that especially in the characters Victoire and Joseph this effect of history on the individual is illustrated.

In my analysis I shall make the link to the historical developments of the 1930s and 1940s, while trying to show how it is the concepts of everyday life, gender and multiculturalism that hold open the narratives and prevent *Ewiges Schattenspiel* and *Die Früchte des Wohlstands* from slipping either into an escapist or a pessimistic mode.

Hermynia Zur Mühlen's historical novel *Ewiges Schattenspiel* is firmly anchored in Austrian history: it focuses on one Austrian aristocratic family, the Herdegens, living in Vienna and Bohemia. *Ewiges Schattenspiel* is the first part of a three-part family saga. The third part, *Als der Fremde kam*, is set in the 1930s and centres on Clarisse Herdegen, a direct descendent of the early Herdegen family. This third part was also published in Britain, whereas the second part has never been published and is deemed lost.

The narrative of *Ewiges Schattenspiel* follows the family history through five generations from 1814 to 1848/9. The oldest member of the family is Grandmaman Inez, originally a Spanish Catholic. She is the matriarch of the family and shown as a traditional but influential woman. Her son Carl Herdegen is married to Ludmilla, and they have five children: Stanislas, Joseph, Antoinette, Marie Christine and Franz. The members of this middle generation all marry and have children with the exception of Franz, and at the end of the novel the late Inez's great-great-grandson Joseph is born during the gunfire of 1848.

The narrative is rooted in the tension between continuity and change. The family's geographical location marks the position of continuity: this is represented by the country estate, Wohan, in Bohemia, rather than in their Palais in Vienna. When Carl and Ludmilla's oldest son Stanislas has to withdraw from his diplomatic career because he has got the country girl Bozena pregnant, he is sent to Wohan. When Victoire plans to leave her husband Joseph and move back to her country of origin, France, because Austria is at war again with France and Joseph is in the Austrian army, Joseph's little brother Franz elopes with her to Wohan instead to diffuse the situation. When Joseph is finally dismissed from the civil service because of his reformist ideas, he moves to Wohan. The manager of the estate is used to members of the family retreating to the estate and contrasts values in politics with those rooted in the land:

> Doch hatte er schon viele Männer kommen und gehen gesehen, die sich an Ziel und Hoffnung geklammert hatten. Elegante Perücken tragende Hofleute, die bereit gewesen waren, für eine

> Gunstbezeugung des Königs oder der jungen Königin, alles zu
> opfern [...] Monsieur de Venelles kannte noch eine andere
> Ewigkeit: die der sich immer wieder vollziehenden Erneuerung
> des Lebens. Saat und Blüte und Frucht, den Schlaf des Winters
> und wieder Saat, Blüte und Frucht. (ES 186/187)

The generational structure of the novel is supported by an omniscient narrator who moves from character to character, and therefore moves along with the generations and gives the narrative continuity. This typical family saga cycle of birth, youth, frustrated dreams, settling into middle age, old age and death can be read as representing a resigned mood. The character Victoire is shown as a striking example of the effects which the disappointments of life can have on a person. The vivacious young woman with strong political convictions, who is involved in high politics, becomes melancholic and depressed in old age. However, Zur Mühlen makes clear that her frustrations are based on evident political disappointments and also on her position as a woman in a patriarchal society.

Zur Mühlen manages to weave several critical undercurrents into the historical narrative: firstly, the failure and success of understanding between the different European nations; secondly, the break-up of class divisions; and thirdly, the position of women.

The theme of European multiculturalism is related less to the different nations of the Habsburg Empire, which is the focal point of Spiel's *Die Früchte des Wohlstands*, as we will see in the next section, but rather to European politics following the Congress of Vienna 1814/1815. The Congress is viewed with historical hindsight as a potential source of a new European political landscape, which did not materialize. Frequent criticisms such as the wasteful extravagance of the countries' leaders while the population was going hungry are expressed through the eyes of the common people. "'Die fremden Fürsten fressen uns arm", sagt ein ältlicher mürrischer Mann. "Sitzen da in Wien, tun nichts als Feste feiern, tanzen, spielen, essen und trinken. Wer zahlt's?"'[11] These scenes of discussions in the streets intermittently appear in the development of the novel, almost like a commentary, or like the chorus in a classical Greek drama. This has the effect of questioning the centrality of the aristocracy at the heart of the novel and the political developments, while at the same time keeping to a description of the status quo. The complaining old man of the commentary above gets arrested by the secret police, another often commented upon feature of Austrian society at the time. Victoire also appears in police reports,[12] but of course, being Gräfin Herdegen, she is not arrested.

The country estate Wohan, far away from the platform of high politics in Vienna, allows for more transgressive developments across class and national boundaries. Here the non-aristocratic characters actually interrelate with the Herdegens. First and foremost, there is Bozena, a farmer's daughter who is seduced by Stanislas, the eldest son of Carl and Ludmilla Herdegen. Grandmaman Inez forces the couple to get married, against the wishes of the eighteen-year old Stanislas and his mother Ludmilla. What on the one hand is a dogmatic and cruel move, is shown in a more differentiated way in the narrative. Bozena is not depicted as a simple peasant girl who is grateful that the young count will marry her. She has her own sexual desire and is shown to fancy the second gardener. By forcing Stanislas to marry a woman situated below him in the class structure, rather than just paying her off as suggested by the arrogant Ludmilla, Inez acknowledges the equality of all human beings, a view which is based on her Christian faith. Bozena's parents provide another case for the depiction of the interrelationships across class boundaries. Whereas her mother is completely overawed by the idea that her daughter is to marry a Herdegen, her father displays family pride in the fact that even his grandfather had not been a serf, but a free farmer with his own land. Zur Mühlen creates a rupture in the class-constrained narrative by deploying her usual irony against the notion of an objective hierarchy between the classes: when Stanislas comes to asks Bozena's parents for the permission to marry her, Bozena's mother falls into a lament about the situation and tells him what great chances Bozena would have had with the second gardener Wenzel. Stanislas replies: "'Ich ... ich," stotterte Stanislas in seiner hilflosen Verlegenheit, "bin doch auch eine gute Partie.'"[13] Thus Zur Mühlen's narrative provides space for small transgressions in an otherwise restrictive society. But by not engaging in the romantic notion that everyone lives happily ever after in such a marriage across class boundaries, Zur Mühlen avoids the pitfalls of romantic escapism, which would re-enforce rather than weaken the nineteenth century class structure. Bozena and Stanislas are both shown as unhappy.

Claudio Magris has identified this recreation of a sense of security in the works of post World War I writers in his book *Der Habsburgische Mythos in der österreichischen Literatur*.[14] He sees the writers creating models of the monarchy and the state as a guarantor for continuity. Quoting Stefan Zweig and Joseph Roth, Magris points out that these authors did acknowledge the mediocrity and ineffectualness of the monarchy and imperial administration, but that the Habsburg Empire nevertheless became their ideal fatherland in their memories and their literature.[15]

Continuity on the public political level is discussed in a different way in *Ewiges Schattenspiel* than in equivalent books by male authors. There are no descriptions of old male politicians who walked slowly, spoke slowly and stroked their well-kept grey beards as Stefan Zweig describes in *Die Welt von Gestern*.[16] There is Grandmaman Inez, who was in her youth a friend of the Empress Marie Therese, which certainly serves as a mark of continuity and guarantees her influence with Emperor Francis I. This influence, however, is only used to intervene on behalf of her family and their political aspiration. Order and continuity lie not, as in Joseph Roth's *Radetzky Marsch*, with uniforms and military parades, in which Roth, 'die Liebe zur Ordnung und Symmetrie als Abwehr des Chaos erblickt'.[17]

Zur Mühlen's narration of history stays very much behind the scenes, inside the bosom of the family. In the beginning of the novel, during the Congress of Vienna, a ball is held in the Palais Herdegen, but the reader is only introduced to the events in the boudoir where Marie Christine gets ready for the evening or to the conversations in one of the side rooms, where the eldest son Joseph meets his future bride Victoire.

Significantly the narrative development of the family saga with its births and deaths is interspersed with short chapters based on historical figures and events. These stylistically different chapters, like the following focussing on Napoleon, create a rupture in the main narrative:

> Auf einer windumtobten Insel im Mittelmeer wachte ein Mann. Er wollte nicht schlafen. Im Schlaf kamen Träume. Eisige Winternächte in einem ungeheuren Land, Schnee, ein grauer gefrorener Fluß ... Glühende Hitze, hochragende Pyramiden ... Paris, jubelnd, selig ... Eine schlanke, weinende Frau ... Sieg um Sieg ... Kaiser von Frankreich ... Die Habsburgerin im Ehebett ... Ein Knabe, sein Sohn ... Der König von Rom ... Ein grauer Oktobertag ... Leipzig ... Oktober, das ist sein Schicksalsmonat ...Auch in Rußland ... Paris, stumm, grollend ... eine fremde Stadt ... Elba... (ES 23)

These interruptions can be read as Zur Mühlen's questioning the traditional manner of historical narration. These stream-of-consciousness passages do not mark the pomposity of an official historical meta-narrative, but the fragmented nature of human historical consciousness. Thus showing historical events as impinging intermittently on the consciousness of the characters opens up the novel to a far more modern reading than a traditional description of historical events would have done. Writing as a refugee in 1930s Austria gave Zur Mühlen a heightened insight into the differentiated historical consciousness and led her to question official versions. Although figures such as Metternich and Napoleon, who are awarded room for interruptions in the narrative of the novel, are important, their real importance and the real tension between continuity and change lie with the Herdegen family and its generations. Although most of the characters' attempts at political reform fail, it shows the possibilities of 'what could have been.' Obviously, for Zur Mühlen a reconnection of the development of Austria with these revolutionary and reformist moments was the desired outcome of a postwar cultural and political re-establishment of the country, and she sought to aid this process with her contribution to this alternative culture.

Ewiges Schattenspiel explores strong anti-German sentiments, chiefly centred on Antoinette's Prussian husband Graf Bredar. He is described as pompous and boring and does not talk to her, or allow her to go out and demands that she bear him many sons. Pointing out the difference between the two countries is clearly one of the aims of this passage, which fits in with the programme of the Free Austrian Movement. Zur Mühlen, however, not only outlines the negative feature of Germanness, but also points to the positive features of the multicultural Austrian Empire. The following explanatory discourse is embedded in a dialogue between Joseph and Victoire at the beginning of their relationship. He explains the difference between language and nationality:

> 'Wir wollen ans andere Ende des Parks gehen, wo die Zelte stehen. Dort können Sie die Nationaltänze der Böhmen und Ungarn sehen.'
>
> 'Der Böhmen und Ungarn?' staunte Victoire. 'Wie kommen die her? Das sind doch fremde Völker, die eine andere Sprache reden?'
>
> 'Es sind Österreicher, Mademoiselle. Was bedeutet die Sprache? Wäre die ausschlaggebend, müßte ich ein Deutscher sein.'
>
> Victoire lachte. Der Gedanke erschien ihr äußerst drollig. (ES 42/42)

Thus Zur Mühlen ridicules the idea that Germany and Austria should be joined, purely because both countries' official language is German.

By crossing class and national boundaries in her narrative and exploring the interconnections of private and public sphere, Zur Mühlen successfully subverts the Habsburg myth of her male colleagues. Konstanze Fliedl has summed up this achievement as follows:

> Wie manche andere ihrer exilierten Schriftstellerkolleginnen, Hilde Spiel etwa oder Elisabeth Freundlich, griff sie zum Genre des historischen Generationsromans, um zu zeigen, wie die Geschichte kein privates Schicksal ungeschoren läßt. Und die Retrospektive auf die Monarchie war bei allen diesen Autorinnen kein nostalgischer 'habsburgischer Mythos', sondern ein halb

utopischer Versuch, sich ein tolerantes Zusammenleben von
Sprach- und Volksgruppen vorzustellen.[18]

It has been argued that *Ewiges Schattenspiel* marks a retreat from Zur
Mühlen's former radicalism. This is not the case: Zur Mühlen manages to
create an emancipatory discourse of multiculturalism and the position of
women without using history as a mere backdrop or a nostalgic memory.
Ewiges Schattenspiel, written in the 1930s, is successful in providing an
alternative narrative space to the obliteration of radical elements in Austrian
history.

      Illuminating these radical moments is also an important part of Hilde
Spiel's work. Edward Timms praises Hilde Spiel for being able to portray
'one of the most illuminating accounts of the debate about Jewish
emancipation'[19] in her biography *Fanny von Arnstein oder die
Emanzipation: Ein Frauenleben an der Zeitenwende 1758-1818*[20] and thus
being able to show in fiction what historians have failed to investigate,
namely the failure to establish a policy for pan-European Jewish
emancipation at the Congress of Vienna. Spiel tries to outline similar
moments of possible radical change in her novel *Die Früchte des
Wohlstands*, another attempt by a woman exile writer to represent both the
radical and the reactionary strands in Austrian history and politics in order to
provide cultural models for the future.

      She started to work on this historical novel about Vienna in English
and a first draft of the manuscript was finished by 1943. Even earlier
extracts, which were translated into German, were published in *Die Zeitung*,
a London exile journal, in November 1941 entitled 'Österreichische
Fragmente'[21] appearing alongside a short story by Zur Mühlen entitled 'Das
fliehende Feld'. Spiel also published parts of the manuscript in the *Kulturelle
Schriftenreihe des Free Austrian Movement*, which was published as a
supplement of *Zeitspiegel*, on 'Österreichische Schriftsteller im Exil' in
April 1946. In this issue Zur Mühlen was represented with a piece entitled
'Das Wort. Eine Legende'. The table of contents indicates that 'Die Früchte
des Wohlstands' is one of the 'Beiträge und Vorabdrücke aus
unveröffentlichen Werken.'[22] Spiel and Zur Mühlen obviously worked
within similar circles in the exile organisations. During the war Spiel seems
to have been a staunch supporter of the stance taken by the Free Austrian
Movement promoting the distinctiveness of Austria from Germany in a
cultural and political sense. Her name appears on a list of delegates
representing Austria at the Seventh International PEN Congress in
September 1941. Since January 1939 the Austrian PEN in London was
recognised as the official representative of Austria in the international PEN
community.[23]

Die Früchte des Wohlstands was only published for the first time in book form in 1981, translated into German by Hilde Spiel herself. Like Zur Mühlen, Spiel saw the distinctiveness of Austrian culture and history in its ability to provide the possibility for a multicultural society. In the interview with Anne Linsel she describes why Austria is special: 'Es setzt sich zusammen aus der Vielgestaltigkeit der Einflüsse, die sich in eineinhalb Jahrhunderten – mit Ausnahme der sieben Jahre des Anschlusses – in Österreich manifestierten.'[24]

Spiel places much emphasis on the Jewish contribution to Austrian culture, a theme which is not strongly developed in Hermynia Zur Mühlen's historical novel. Spiel's non-fictional writing includes a book on the Viennese Jew Fanny von Arnstein, often described as her masterpiece, and a large part of her essays are about issues concerning cultural difference and understanding. Even one of her last works *Vienna's Golden Autumn* (1987) gives a good impression of her vision of a multicultural Austria with a strong Jewish component and proclaims that the liberal Jewish bourgeoisie was the last proponent of multicultural Austria: 'Dieses liberale, stark jüdisch durchsetzte Bürgertum war eben die letzte Selbstverwirklichung universalen Österreichtums, ehe es an Traditionalismus, nationaler und sozialer Unrast dort scheiterte.'[25] In comparison to the height of Austria's multicultural society coinciding with the reign of Franz Joseph I, postwar Austria has lost its 'Urbanität und Weltoffenheit' which has been substituted by 'gleichmacherische Provinzialität'.[26]

One of Spiel's prime concerns is to show that the Austrians of Jewish descent have been an integral part of Austrian society for many centuries. She even argues that at times it was only the assimilated Jews who saw themselves first and foremost as Austrian nationals and who felt a real duty to the Austrian state because most of the other Austrian citizens would claim to have their roots in one of the distinct ethnic parts of the Austrian monarchy.

Spiel realizes that the irrational reverence for German culture above any other created problems for the Jewish intelligentsia and that the *laissez-faire* policy linked to nineteenth century liberalism led to economic chaos like the stock market crash on 9 May 1873. This interrupted the liberal phase for a decade. After the recovery in 1883, a polarization occurred in Austrian society. On the one hand, there was, according to Spiel, the liberal, anticlerical, rational bourgeoisie and on the end of the spectrum there stood the lower classes, who had been turned to racial hatred by the nationalistic parties and the clergy.

Die Früchte des Wohlstands portrays this division as well as the possibility of a multicultural society. Spiel explained the choice of her subject for the novel as a desire to escape the depressing present as well as the search for her roots in a Jewish family in multicultural Austria.[27]

The novel has three main strands: firstly, the history of an assimilated Viennese Jewish family, secondly, the crisis of the liberal bourgeoisie and the consequences of Austria's rapid industrialization and thirdly, the interrelationship between class, ethnicity and gender. The narrative is framed by two historical events, the world exhibition in Vienna in 1873 and the burning of the Ringtheater in 1881. Stephanie Benedict and Milan Todor embody the generation in which the fruits of prosperity seem ripe and ready to be picked. Stephanie's family comes from an assimilated Jewish background, her father Carl Benedict had come to Vienna from Moravia in 1843 with high hopes of becoming a teacher or a doctor. As no university would accept him because of his Jewish background, he became a textile merchant. Although his career turned out to be successful and prosperous Carl Benedict always regretted that he was not allowed to enter a profession and that 'Dieser klare Geist, dieser tiefe Ernst, diese Entschlossenheit [...] nichts anderem dienen [sollten] als dem Schacher mit Waren.'[28] As a consequence he has high hopes for his children. Milan, on the other hand, comes from a Croatian farming family. His family is not poor, either, but his circumstances and education are necessarily very different from Stephanie's. As a younger son from a rural background he comes to Vienna to seek his fortune. Contrary to the newly arrived Carl Benedict in the 1840s, Milan in the 1870s has no feigned or genuine aspirations to look for anything but wealth. Parallels are shown between the position of the Jewish population and the position of other non-German ethnic groups.

Rapid industrialization has brought wealth to Vienna and the world exhibition is only one outward sign of this development, albeit the most obvious one. The negative aspect of increasing industrialization is the rapid, often destructive pace of modern life and the corrupt business men who make their profit from other people's misfortune. Spiel shows how the little investors are ruined and how the profiteers are often to be found in public offices. As an image for growing industrialization Spiel uses the railways which cut through the landscape and interrupt the social order in all provinces of the Habsburg Empire but at the same time bring the different parts of Austria closer together:

> In jenem Jahr rollten viele Züge.
>
> Sie rollten durch das träge, mährische Flachland, das stille, satte, pflaumenfarbige Slawonien, durch die ungarische Ebene, die blau im Himmel verrann, und durch die grünen und goldenen steirischen Wälder.

> Die Züge bäumten sich auf. Viehherden längs der Schienen, noch
> ungewohnt des Lärms, der durch ihre Weiden riß, stoben verstört
> davon. Bauern, die Furchen tretend hinter ihren schweren Gäulen,
> beschatteten die Augen mit der Hand und starrten. Die Züge,
> dampfend und zischend von feurigem Rauch, stampften durch den
> hellen Tag, durch die stille, sternenlichte Nacht, dahin zur Stadt,
> zur Stadt, zur fernen Stadt des Kaisers. (FW 5)

A train carries Milan to his hopeful future in Vienna but the railway brings
about his near downfall as well. He is conned out of all his money by a
dubious investment in the Galician railway. Although his loss is due to a
criminal profiteer, even respectable investors like Carl Benedict lose money
due to the fall in value of railway shares after the stockmarket crash in 1873.
Ultimately though, the financial chaos manages to bring together people of
different ethnic and social backgrounds such as Milan and Carl Benedict.
Milan starts working for Carl and as he is a child of the new era, a natural
salesman with his eyes firmly on success, he rises fast in Benedict's firm and
eventually even marries his daughter Stephanie. It is really the boom and
bust atmosphere which weakens old hierarchical structures and works in
favour of a certain kind of multiculturalism.

It has been argued that Spiel is advocating a natural homogeneity of
the Habsburg monarchy without any conflicts.[29] This is not the case. Spiel
rightly points out that the economic success of the Habsburg Empire did
contribute to keeping it together in the later decades of the nineteenth
century. This worked not only in the geographical sense but also to pacify
middle-class subjects such as the Benedicts for whom economic success
acted as a substitute for liberal freedom and real political participation.
Actual conflicts are incorporated in the novel. Milan's brother-in-law has to
give up his position in the civil service because of national and ethnic
problems and Milan has to lend him money. The most broadly illustrated
conflict is the fate of the Orthodox Jew Simon Wolf who was at one point
Milan's teacher. It is shown how the less fortunate in the new society are
looking more and more for scapegoats. Antisemitic and nationalistic
thinking spreads among these groups. Simon Wolf is beaten up by a group of
young thugs and the police turn out to be more sympathetic to the
perpetrators than to the victim.

The political structure is shown to encourage the search for
scapegoats rather than reform. In turn it is first and foremost the Jewish
industrialists who are blamed for the social injustices. Hilde Spiel shows the
intertwining of social and economic factors well, although she sometimes
seems to idealize rural life – the escape to Milan's hometown in Croatia is
shown as their only chance to escape the hedonistic ways of city life – or to
schematize people from the provinces like Milan. The possibilities of

nineteenth century Austrian multiculturalism such as social and ethnic mobility are exemplified by the main characters in the novel. At the same time she shows its limits: the widening economic division in society prevents ultimately the functioning of a multicultural Austria. Spiel explains the inconsistency of the political system and its ruler which opens up and closes down opportunities at the same time:

> Das österreichische Pendel schwang in diesem Jahr 1876 so munter wie eh und je. Wie immer schlug es ein wenig heftig nach der ungarischen Seite aus ... Es war eine konfuse, eine unzulängliche Staatskonzeption. Bald sollte sie ein neues Jahrhundert durch Methoden ersetzen, die dem Staate weit wirksamer dienten als die Politik des Irgendwie. Gemessen an dem Leid, das diese neue Ordnung über die Menschheit bringen sollte, waren die Leiden der alten Schlamperei freilich nur Nadelstiche. (FW 164)

In this way Spiel connects nineteenth century Austrian history with the contemporary events in Europe. Hilde Spiel's life project promoting multiculturalism and Jewish emancipation indicates her way of dealing with history and narration. Spiel wants to show that European history has always been multicultural while being antisemitic, racist, class-bound and misogynist at the same time. Additionally Spiel's historical narration does not only focus on political developments on a large scale but also on individual stories.

Contrasting the historical setting of *Ewiges Schattenspiel* and *Die Früchte des Wohlstands* the difference in the position of the family in society and in the narratives is striking. Whereas the development of Zur Mühlen's novel takes place almost entirely within the family, economic ties are considered more important in Spiel's historical novel. Spiel presents this development in her historically reflexive narrative. The first half of the 19th century is exemplified by the houses in the Vienna Seidengasse: 'Dort rollte in seinem ewigen Kreislauf von Geburt, Heirat, Krankheit, Tod das menschliche Drama ab, begleitet und übertönt von der täglichen Tragikomödie des Broterwerbs.'[30] The 1870s and 1880s champion a different model of the separation of public and private sphere:

> In diesem Zeitalter der Industrialisierung hatte sich das Leben auf nie zuvor gekannte Weise von seinem Ursprung entfernt. Mittel wurde zum Selbstzweck, der Schreibtisch weitete sich zur Welt, vor der Börsenkulisse wurden die Frau und die Kinder zu unbeachtetem Mobilar oder bloßen Ornamenten. Allmählich erschien das Geflecht der Handelsbeziehungen wichtiger als die Familienbande. (FW 90)

These extracts show how different the representations of historical events are in *Die Früchte des Wohlstands* from those in Zur Mühlen's *Ewiges Schattenspiel*, which is dependent on dialogues. Claudio Magris identifies the 'feuilleton' as the literary form, which became especially prominent after the break-up of the monarchy, and was aimed at expressing 'eine endlose Abwandlung des ewigen Themas der *Austriazität*'.[31] Spiel became champion of this literary genre during and after the Second World War. The passages outlining the historical development in *Die Früchte des Wohlstands* could all be taken as separate feuilletons. Magris sees this form as a vehicle for the perpetuation of the Habsburg myth as 'ein Werk der Selbsttröstung'.[32] Spiel's elegant portrayals of Austrian history can be read in this way, but at the same time they contain moments of subversion. She writes about the decline of the salon of Fanny von Arnstein and the withdrawal into private life, and thus links newly ordered family relationships with the position of the Jews:

> Diese Tolerierten erfreuten sich, wie ihr Name besagte, der Duldung, wenn auch nicht der Achtung von Wien. Dennoch hatten sie noch vor wenigen Jahrzehnten in besserem Ansehen gestanden. [...] als der Kongreß in Wien tanzte, obgleich er nicht von der Stelle ging, waren die Leidesdorfs mit ein paar anderen Häusern ihres Glaubens unter den großen Gastgebern der Kaiserstadt gewesen. [...] Es waren andere Zeiten gewesen, und sie waren dahin. [...] Im größten Kaiserreich knabberte man an den bittersüßen Früchten der Reaktion. Man war reich, doch man gab keine Feste mehr. Die Häuser hatten Raum für eine Schar von Kindern, doch es war in ihnen kein Salon. (FW 37/38)

As in *Ewiges Schattenspiel* the representation of gender relations are interwoven with the ideal of multiculturalism and the breaking up of the class structure in *Die Früchte des Wohlstands* and are bound up with the family structure narrative. The Viennese upper-middle class Jewish woman Stephanie marries Milan from a Croatian farming background but their relationship is difficult. Stephanie does not love Milan but gives in to the will of her father, who hopes that the marriage will help Stephanie 'den Fluch meiner Rasse abzustreifen'.[33] In the same way for Milan it is probably not love but obtaining what has seemed unobtainable – to be accepted by the rich urban family to such an extent that he can marry one of its members – that makes him marry Stephanie. For most of the plot their relationship is not very successful due to their disparate backgrounds and expectations. Both the male and the female character are shown to have expectations and sexual desires: Stephanie fantasizes about the young composer with whom she had been romantically involved. Milan finds comfort in the arms of big blonde

women. Only when they finally manage to communicate with each other
does their relationship have a chance to develop.

The novel's ending is explicitly negative. Both Stephanie and Milan
die in the Burgtheater fire of 1881. This historical event has often been seen
as the final death knell for the liberalism of the earlier decade, which had
already been undermined from many directions. Nine hundred people died
on the evening of 7 December during a performance of Offenbach's
Hoffmanns Erzählungen. The number of Jews among the dead was
significant, which led to antisemitic comments about the catastrophe, most
famously by Richard Wagner. His comments were recorded by his wife
Cosima in her diary. On 17 December she wrote: 'Daß 416 Israeliten bei
dem Brand umkamen, steigert R's Teilnahme für das Unglück nicht.'[34] The
entry of the next day is even more shocking: 'Er sagte im heftigen Scherz, es
sollte alle Juden in einer Aufführung des "Nathan" verbrennen.'[35]

The ending can be read both as the ultimate failure of certain liberal
tendencies and the cumulative effect of other reactionary, antisemitic and
sexist tendencies in nineteenth century Austrian history. The unchecked
industrialization is criticized in the final passage of the novel when the dying
Milan remembers not his economic success in Vienna, but the rivers in
Croatia.

But there is a gender difference, even in death: while the male
character surrenders completely to nostalgia in the final passage of the book,
the female character Stephanie questions the decisions she has made in her
life:

> Das ist die Strafe, dachte sie, meine Strafe, nun werde ich
> bestraft. Aber wofür? Was war meine Schuld? Irgendeinmal habe
> ich falsch gewählt. An irgendeiner Wegkreuzung hab ich die
> falsche Straße eingeschlagen. Aber wann war das? Ich weiß es
> nicht mehr. Meine Zeit ist um. Vergib mir, Gott. Ach meine
> armen Kinder - (FW 305/206)

This can be read as a sign of agency and it is significant that the
character of a Jewish woman asks these questions. Both at the end of the
liberal part of the nineteenth century and during the Second World War,
Austrians had to ask themselves about the decisions and policies that had led
to the problems of their country and, in the wider sense, the problems of the
whole of Europe. Therefore it becomes clear that both Jewish and women's
emancipation are depicted as necessary elements of future political progress.
Die Früchte des Wohlstands is less successful at outlining utopian hope than
Ewiges Schattenspiel, but it gives extremely poignant accounts of the
moments when political change might have happened. Thus even in the
1930s and 1940s both Spiel and Zur Mühlen are among a very small group

of exiled women writers who are able to show historical connections which can be used to imagine a brighter future for a post-Second World War Austria.

Notes

[1] Helmut Koopmann, "'Geschichte ist die Sinngebung des Sinnlosen": Zur Ästhetik des historischen Romans im Exil' in *Schreiben im Exil*, ed.. by Alexander Stephan und Hans Wagner (Bonn: Bouvier, 1985), p. 18.

[2] Alexander Stephan, *Die deutsche Exilliteratur, 1933-1945* (Munich: C. H. Beck, 1979), p. 194.

[3] Hermynia Zur Mühlen, *Ewiges Schattenspiel* (London: Frederick Muller, 1943).

[4] Hilde Spiel, *Die Früchte des Wohlstands* (Frankfurt: Ullstein, 1991).

[5] Stephan, *Die deutsche Exilliteratur*, p. 197.

[6] Kurt Hiller, 'Profile', 1937, quoted in Walter A. Behrendsohn, *Die humanistische Front. Einführung in die deutsche Emigranten-Literatur*, vol. 1, (Zurich: Europa, 1946), p. 118.

[7] *Ibid.*

[8] Georg Lukács, *The Historical Novel*, transl. Hannah and Stanley Mitchell (Harmondsworth: Penguin, 1969), p. 307.

[9] Lukács, *The Historical Novel*, p. 325.

[10] Lukács , *The Historical Novel*, p. 20.

[11] Zur Mühlen, *Schattenspiel*, p. 45.

[12] Zur Mühlen, *Schattenspiel*, pp. 73-74.

[13] Zur Mühlen, *Schattenspiel*, p. 33.

[14] Claudio Magris, *Der habsburgische Mythos in der österreichischen Literatur* (Salzburg: Otto Müller, 1988).

[15] Magris, *Der habsburgische Mythos*, p. 8.

[16] Stefan Zweig, *Die Welt von Gestern* (Stockholm: Bermann-Fischer, 1944), p. 40.

[17] Magris, *Der habsburgische Mythos*, p. 262.

[18] Konstanze Fliedl, 'Noblesse und Gesinnung. Zwei Romane von Hermynia Zur Mühlen' *in Literatur und Kritik*, April 1997, pp. 85-86.

[19] Edward Timms, 'The Pernicious Rift: Metternich and the Debate about Jewish Emancipation at the Congress of Vienna' in *Leo Baeck Institute Yearbook XLVI*, 2001, p. 7.

[20] Hilde Spiel, *Fanny von Arnstein oder die Emanzipation: Ein Frauenleben an der Zeitenwende 1758-1818* (Frankfurt: Fischer Taschenbuch, 1992).

[21] Hilde Spiel, 'Österreichiche Fragmente' in *Die Zeitung*, nos. 218-221, 21.11.-15.11.1941, accessed via http://deposit.ddb.de, 17.9.2003.

[22] Facsimile reproduced in Bolbecher/Kaiser, 'Exilbedingungen und Exilkultur', p. 14.

[23] Klaus Amann, *P. E. N. Politik, Emigration, Nationalsozialismus, Ein österreichischer Schriftstellerklub* (Vienna, Cologne, Graz: Böhlau, 1984), p. 66.

[24] Anne Linsel, *Hilde Spiel. Die Grande Dame. Gespräch mit Hilde Spiel in der Reihe Zeugen des Jahrhunderts* (Göttingen: Lamuv, 1992), p. 81.

[25] Hilde Spiel, *Vienna's Golden Autumn* (London: Weidenfeld and Nicholson, 1987), p. 41.

[26] Hilde Spiel, *Glanz und Untergang. Wien 1866-1938*, transl. Hanna Neves (Munich: List, 1988), p. 25.

[27] Spiel quoted in Waltraud Strickhausen, 'Hilde Spiels historischer Roman *Die Früchte des Wohlstands*' in *Exil 10*, 1990, p. 31.

[28] Spiel, *Früchte*, p. 40.

[29] Konstanze Fliedl, 'Hilde Spiel's Linguistic Rights of Residence' in *Austrian Exodus,* ed. by Ritchie Robertson and Edward Timms (Edinburgh: Edinburgh University Press, 1995), p. 125.

[30] Spiel, *Früchte*, p. 90.

[31] Magris, *Der Habsburgische Mythos*, p. 252.

[32] *Ibid.*

[33] Spiel, *Früchte*, p. 132.

[34] Cosima Wagner quoted in Walter Hanak, 'quasi una fantasia. Zur Dramaturgie einer Ausstellung', in *quasi una fantasia. Juden und die Musikstadt Wien,* ed. by Leon Botstein and Werner Hanak (Vienna: Wolke, 2003), p. 24.

[35] *Ibid.*

Imagining Austria: Kohlröserl, Alpenglühen und Patisserie – the Vision of the Exiled Children

Deborah Vietor-Engländer

Eva Ibbotson, born Eva Maria Charlotte Michelle Wiesner in Vienna on 25 January 1925, the daughter of the scientist Berthold Wiesner and the playwright and novelist Anna Gmeyner (1902-1991; also known under the names Anna Wiesner and Anna Morduch and the pseudonym Anna Reiner), was taken to Britain initially as a baby and definitively in 1933, aged eight. This paper wishes to examine the romantic vision of Austria created by Ibbotson in six of her novels and a book of nineteen short stories for adults (1981-1998), and in a book for children (2004), while living in Britain, compared to her realistic portrayal of exile and internment in Britain and of her own childhood as a chronically neglected child.

Biographical elements are vital to the understanding of Eva Ibbotson's work; hence a brief biographical summary is in order. As she herself tells the story, her parents, the dramatist Anna Gmeyner and the biologist Berthold Paul Wiesner met in Vienna. Gmeyner was longing to escape from her family and when, at the age of 22, she encountered a young biology student, weeping at having just finished eating the last pot of strawberry jam made by his mother before she died, it led to their marriage in 1924 and the birth of their daughter in 1925. Eva describes the bond between her parents as 'a mutual unhappiness, a longing to get away from home [...] and of course it was not enough'.[1] Wiesner obtained a research appointment at Edinburgh University and in 1926 Gmeyner followed her husband there and took a great interest in the General Strike of 1926. She interviewed miners and her play *Heer ohne Helden* was the result. According to her daughter Wiesner initially studied the maternal behaviour of rats which he found more satisfactory than his own wife's maternal behaviour.[2] Wiesner and Gmeyner separated in 1927 and Gmeyner returned to Berlin, initially taking her daughter with her. Wiesner evidently remained in Edinburgh and neither parent seemed particularly concerned about the fate of their two year-old daughter. The Wiesners divorced in 1928 when Eva was three. Eva Ibbotson's early childhood was spent shuttling back and forth in trains across Europe from one parent to the other and to her grandparents, as well as living in a 'Kinderheim' in Vienna. Anna Gmeyner's play *Heer ohne Helden* was first performed in Dresden in 1929 and in January 1930 in Berlin.[3] She worked on the film *Don Quichotte* in France with Georg Wilhelm Pabst in 1932 and 1933 and did not return to Germany after the 'Machtergreifung' except for a brief trip through Munich in 1934.[4] In Paris she met and married the Russian-Jewish philosopher Jascha Morduch who had a British passport.

In 1927 a Pregnancy Diagnosis Centre was established in Edinburgh by Zondek and Aschheim where Berthold Wiesner carried out research into gonatrophins. He pioneered fertility treatment (artificial insemination) in the 1930s and probably provided a great deal of sperm himself for donor insemination of the women who were treated. One does not know precisely how many half-siblings Eva Ibbotson may have, though a number have been traced.[5] Wiesner brought his daughter to Edinburgh in 1933; her mother and stepfather arrived in England in May or June 1934 and soon went to live in Belsize Park. Eva again had to shuttle between both parents and basically felt as if she belonged to neither while trying to ingratiate herself with both. Gmeyner wrote the novel *Manja* for which she is best known today between 1936 and 1938, publishing the German version with the Querido Verlag in Amsterdam in 1939 under the pseudonym Anna Reiner (to protect her family, particularly her mother, still in Austria). It also appeared in English in London and New York in 1939, as well as in Dutch, and received excellent reviews in the mainstream press, but was then 'swamped by the war', as Eva Ibbotson puts it.[6] A second novel, *Café du Dome*, also published originally under the name Anna Reiner, was similarly translated into English and published in 1941.[7] Instead of the perpetual tug of war between Belsize Park and Edinburgh, Eva was sent to the progressive boarding school Dartington Hall in Devon. She then studied physiology and later married the ecologist and naturalist Alan Ibbotson who taught at Newcastle University. Whilst bringing up their four children she began writing short stories and, once her youngest son had started school, novels. Her first novel for adults was published in 1981 when she was 56. There are an exceptionally large number of autobiographical elements both in her books for children and in those for adults. In fact they represent a mosaic; she establishes leitmotifs in her early books and develops them in the later ones. According to Eva Ibbotson, at a young age her mother had been the acknowledged story-teller of the neighbourhood[8] with an ability to turn anything into a story. She herself based many of her early stories on her mother's family anecdotes: for example, the carp kept in the bath who refused to become the Christmas Dinner resulted in the early story 'The Great Carp Ferdinand' in 1984, recurring twenty years later in her most recent book *The Star of Kazan*.[9]

In general, romantic novels tend to escape critical attention although Eva Ibbotson did win the Romantic Novelists' Award in 1983. However, her books for children (nine altogether) have received numerous awards and sold over one million copies. Here I have selected six novels and one book of short stories for adults as well as one of her children's books covering the period 1981 to 2004[10] in order to demonstrate how Ibbotson has created a romantic vision of Austria whilst living in England, as compared to her realistic portrayal of exile and internment. Her mother, Anna Gmeyner, once wrote of the 'exciting climate of Berlin [...] so different from the drifting, dreaming charm of backward-looking Vienna';[11] and Ibbotson maintains that, since her mother was never really as happy in Vienna as she was in Paris and Berlin, Vienna was left for her. She created a vision of the Golden City which she had left at the age of eight and where she had in any case not spent much time.

The Vienna connection, as she calls it, is an entirely imaginary vision of the Golden City of Vienna: in Vienna itself, Vienna in Belsize Park, Newcastle on Tyne and Northumberland, and Vienna in Sweden, 'a place of whimsy and schmalz but not only that, I hope'.[12] It is based on the anecdotes of her mother's childhood on which she fell greedily; and it is presented with love though not with knowledge, as a city of the imagination, as something of a cloud cuckoo land, as an imaginary country of the heart. One of the leitmotifs in almost all the novels is an idealized vision of the city itself: of the old Emperor in *Madensky Square* and *The Star of Kazan*, in the pre-First World War era when people loved him: 'Little girls would present him with bunches of flowers and when he bent down to take them, his back would seize up and his aides would have to come and straighten him. [...] All the same, the people of Vienna loved him' (*The Star of Kazan*, pp. 12, 326). Ibbotson had used almost the same words earlier in *Madensky Square* (p. 155). In both these novels about a magic city, the Church of St. Florian plays a romantic role (*Madensky Square*, pp. 6, 10, 130-31; *The Star of Kazan*, p. 6). In *Magic Flutes*, the setting has changed to a post-1918 world, without the emperor, of course, but still with all the enchantment. Guy asks Tessa: 'Is it like that for you? A piece of heaven, this city?', and she replies: 'Yes. Sometimes it is like that for me. Heaven in springtime. Heaven in C major. Yes, sometimes it is like that for me' (p. 61). And *The Morning Gift* begins with the words, 'Vienna has always been a city of myths' (p. 1).

Other elements which make up this idyllic picture are the huge fun fair, the Prater with its Riesenrad, for which Maxi longs so deeply in *Magic Flutes*. To him it represents the joys of ordinary people denied to him:

> How he had yearned to ride up there when he was a little boy, compelled to sit stiffly between his parents in their embossed, gold-wheeled carriage as it rolled relentlessly away from the high hedge behind which the 'hoi polloi' disported themselves (pp. 213-14).

Once he has found the girl of his dreams, 'the Prince and his little dancer gave way to their unquenchable compatibility' (p. 196). In *Madensky Square* the Prater offers enchantment and healing for Sigismund (pp. 173-78) while, at the end of *The Star of Kazan*, Annika's idea of a supreme celebration is a lunch on the Giant Wheel high above the city (pp. 377-79). Vienna is also the city of the Spanish Riding School which represents man's true devotion to horses and genuine interaction between man and animal. The horse in *The Star of Kazan*, which ultimately enters the School, is used to demonstrate the difference – black is black, white is white, there are no shades of grey here – between those who ride for prestige and ill-treat the horse (such as Hermann) and those who feel, as Zed does, that Rocco is a person who happens to be a horse: 'She found Zed in the paddock, schooling Rocco, except that "schooling" did not seem to be the right word because Rocco was so obviously enjoying himself' (pp. 137-38, 354, 215). Zed maintained that horses like Rocco really wanted to learn provided that they were treated well, and that he felt he was betraying Rocco every time Hermann rode him.

But most of all Vienna is the city of music. In *Magic Flutes* – a paean to opera – Tessa the Princess of Pfaffenstein finds happiness working as an unpaid wardrobe mistress for an opera company in order to be part of the process of making music and creating a performance of *The Magic Flute* – 'an opera that was the quintessence of Austrian life' and an opera that permits of no lies (pp. 148, 156). Nerine, the would-be aristocrat, is shown as the outsider when she falls asleep during the performance, remarking afterwards: 'After all, dear, I *am* English. And the English have never been fond of opera, have they [...] all those priests droning on and that rather ridiculous birdcatcher' (pp. 154, 160). *The Morning Gift* contains a spirited description of English aristocratic Philistines and their attitudes to Jews, refugees and music:

> The opera singer from Dresden, I sent him to the dairy because all the indoor posts were filled and it's been a disaster. The dairy maid fell in love with him and he was useless with the cows. [...] I can't help wondering whether some of them go round pretending to be Jews just to get the benefits. [...] Poor Helen – he made her take a man from Berlin to act as a chauffeur and handyman and as soon as he's finished work he gets people in and they play chamber music. It's like lemons in your ears, you know – screech, screech. [...] Not that one likes Jews. When they're rich they're bankers and when they're poor they're pedlars and in between they play the violin (p. 54).

For Ruth Berger, on the other hand, the heroine of *The Morning Gift*, music is essential to her life:

> Ruth's need for music was so much a part of her Viennese
> heritage that no one at first noticed now acute it was. Ever since
> infancy it had been almost impossible to pull her away from
> music-making and she had her own places, music-places she
> called them, to which she gravitated like a thirsty bullock to a
> water hole (p. 6).

In *A Song for Summer* Marek thinks with exasperation of the Viennese at a time of international crisis, to whom nothing else mattered except what was going on at their opera house. Yet, at the same time, he is aware that: 'If the Viennese fiddled while Rome burnt perhaps there were worse occupations' (p. 184).

Food plays a significant role in all Ibbotson's books and many of the food visions are based on her family anecdotes – cutting cucumbers so thinly that you could read a newspaper through the slices (*The Star of Kazan*, p. 17) or visualizing Vienna as a city of patisserie and marzipan animals (*A Song for Summer*, pp. 85-86; *The Star of Kazan*, pp. 13, 224). The unhappy and disturbed children who are 'dumped' in the idealistic madhouse of a school without rules and taboos (pp. 20, 34) in *A Song for Summer* reveal their problems in their choice of marzipan animals: 'I think if I was Professor Freud [...] I'd take them to Herr Fischer's shop and see what they chose' (pp. 151-52). Individual foods indicate emotions: in *Madensky Square*, 'Indianerkrapfen' and a trip to the Prater represent the first real happiness the little Polish boy Sigismund has ever experienced (p. 174); while the 'Guglhupf' baked by Miss Maud and Miss Violet of the Willow Tea Rooms in *The Morning Gift* is their way of letting compassion override principle (they are totally against baking 'Continental' cakes but want to support the refugees). It also enables Ruth's mother Leonie to give way to tears for the first time (pp. 43, 91-92). In *Magic Flutes*, likening someone to 'vanilla kipferl' is the highest praise a child can give: 'Bubi loves Tessa an awful lot. More than vanilla kipferl, Bubi loves Tessa' (p. 222). When Ibbotson described the 80th birthday party she had enjoyed in North Northumberland, she used 'vanilla kipferl' in a similar context to establish the principle of love and the 'Vienna connection': a woman in the village, guided by Eva's daughter, produced absolutely perfect, totally traditional 'vanilla kipferl'. 'And if that isn't a Vienna connection, I don't know what is,' she comments.[13]

Several of Ibbotson's characters – like Mitzi Schumacher in *Madensky Square*, 'who begged to be allowed into her mother's kitchen as other children begged to go to the Prater' (p. 21), or Ellen in *A Song for Summer*, whose first words in her grandmother's kitchen are 'I *have* to help' (p. 8), or Annika in *The Star of Kazan* – find cooking their *raison d'être*. Annika is allowed to make the sauce for the Christmas carp on her own for the first time when she is very young and introduces something completely new into it; later on, in order to keep her sanity and fight her homesickness in a cruel boarding school, 'when she felt misery engulfing her she cooked the Christmas carp [...] if she forgot how to cook everything was lost' (*The Star of Kazan*, pp. 278-79).

Ibbotson's idyllic imaginary vision also included alpine gentians ('Kohlröserl'), the symbol of love for Henny, Marek and Aniella in *A Song for Summer* – 'only in heaven could one find such a scent' (pp. 230-31, 12, 75); and 'Alpenglühen', great peaks turning to rose when the sun sets. Some of the happiest moments in Ruth's childhood in *The Morning Gift* are when they gather at the Grundlsee each summer evening to watch the sun set behind the snow-capped mountains and shriek 'wunderbar' (p. 3).[14] As Anna Gmeyner recorded in her memoirs of her own mother's death, *No Screen for the Dying*, when her mother lay dying in Edinburgh after the war, she persuaded a park keeper in the Botanical Gardens to let her pick a few Alpine gentians so that Eva Ibbotson's grandmother died with them beside her bed.[15]

Ibbotson's books contain many idealized elements; however, when she introduces personal leitmotifs, it is evident that they are based on numerous bitter experiences of her own and have an acid ring of truth. Almost all her books for adults portray anti-Semitic reactions from middle and upper-class English people, one of the most poignant instances featuring in the earliest novel *A Countess below Stairs* (1981):

> Hannah was standing by the window, the letter in her hand. She looked, suddenly, immensely, unutterably weary and as old as one of the mourning, black-clad women in the Cossack-haunted village of her youth. And indeed the hideous thing that had crept out from beneath Muriel's honeyed, conventional phrases was as old, as inescapable, as time itself. [...] but this particular thing ... we make jokes about it but for us it is like a deep black hole, always there. Sometimes we don't wait to be pushed, we jump (pp. 169, 230).

Moisewitch in *A Company of Swans* is deeply humiliated by Harriet's father, the professor (p. 289). In *The Morning Gift* nearly all the Somerville family's upper-class neighbours and the insufferable Placketts at the university have few initial objections to Hitler:

> Hitler seems to have achieved miracles with the German economy. [...] Mother was pleased to hear it [i.e. that Ruth is leaving]. I think she feels that there are too many of them [...] foreigners, refugees. She feels that places should be kept for our own nationals. [...] Well, of course, it doesn't do to say so, but

one can't help feeling they've rather taken over. Of course one
can't entirely approve of what Hitler is doing (pp. 146-47).

Nor does Kendrick Frobisher's equally insufferable mother in *A Song for
Summer* initially disapprove of Hitler:

> Mrs Frobisher had not been very interested in the policies of Herr
> Hitler. She had no particular quarrel with him – indeed with his
> attempts to clear away Jews, homosexuals, communists and
> gypsies she had a certain sympathy – but he was making a lot of
> noise about *Lebensraum* and colonies and that was a different
> matter (p. 102).

It is as English to reject refugees as it is to be proud of a lack of musicality.

However, the assimilated refugees who come to England from
Europe find observing a Judaism they have never known most problematic
and the local religious leaders disapprove of them: 'The poor rabbi in
Belsize Park gets quite cross: all these people being persecuted who don't
even know when Yom Kippur is or how to say kaddish. He doesn't think we
deserve to be persecuted' (*The Morning Gift*, p. 216). There is an extremely
amusing scene in *The Morning Gift* when the refugees in Belsize Park try
unsuccessfully to celebrate Hanukkah: they feel that a Festival of Light is
badly needed but, since they have no idea how to go about it, they ultimately
produce a traditional Austrian Christmas Eve at the Willow Tea Rooms with
a tree, candles and plates of smoked ham and salami (pp. 248-51, 269-70).
Yet in *A Song for Summer* the violinist Isaac Meierwitz's life is saved by
orthodox Jews who see him as a persecuted brother – religious or not:

> He himself had scarcely set foot in a synagogue; his mother had
> been baptised, but Hitler had created a new kind of Jew –
> someone who existed to be hunted and killed – and these
> unknown men had accepted him as a brother (p. 126).

Ibbotson includes very detailed and accurate descriptions of
internment on the Isle of Man in her love story *A Song for Summer* in which
the British authorities, succumbing to press and public pressures, begin to
round up and imprison just those enemy aliens who have the most to fear
from Hitler and Mussolini: 'And each day more confused enemy aliens
arrived – Nobel Laureates, old men with diabetes, social democrats who had
been tortured in the prisons of the Reich and had come to Britain as to
Mecca or Shangri La' (pp. 243-44). Marek, who is an internee, makes it
clear to the authorities that, in retrospect, this will turn out to be a pretty
discreditable episode, and he asks for a piano so that he can organize a
performance of Bach's Mass in B minor. When the order comes for his

release, he insists on remaining in internment until after the performance (pp. 254-57). In real life the composer Hans Gál likewise stayed an extra day in internment in order to be there for the performance of the camp revue *What a Life!*[16] *A Song for Summer* is far more significant than the mere romantic novel it is usually considered to be as Ibbotson genuinely tries to present both points of view with regard to internment. Many of the internees also understand, as Marek does, that a number of those in command are basically humane men. Heini in *The Morning Gift* discovers that his visa is a forgery, but instead of being grateful, as are his fellow-internees, that they are all to be allowed to remain in England – since public opinion has now woken up to the plight of the refugees – he considers that he is being persecuted in being expected to peel three buckets of potatoes under a cold water tap, eat porridge and substitute tea for coffee (p. 243).

There are two figures in the books under consideration who are, on Eva Ibbotson's own admission, entirely autobiographical and bitterly personal: Sidi in the story which bears her name in *A Glove Shop in Vienna* and Sophie in *A Song for Summer*. Sidi's parents divorce in 1935 and from then on she bleeds internally, feels that she is dispatched like a paper parcel between her two parents and is a mere pawn in their machinations, exiled amid the alien corn (*A Glove Shop in Vienna*, pp. 84-85, 89). Love comes from her governess Miss Hogg. Sidi's much-loved and unattainable mother who breaks into films is a finely-etched portrait of Anna Gmeyner as is Sophie's mother, who has left Vienna for Paris and Paris for London to be with her lover, and is now making a film in Ireland from where she fails to write (p. 16). Sophie's terror of abandonment, the images of her warring parents and the letters that do not come are all-encompassing:

> She had been shunted backwards and forwards between her warring parents since she was two years old, never knowing who would meet her or where she belonged. Her homesickness was of that devastating kind experienced by children who have no home [...] Sophie's life had so far been devoid of certainties. The marriage of her beautiful English mother to an austere scientist [...] was a mistake both partners quickly put right. The only thing they had in common was an ego the size of a house and an apparent indifference to the happiness of their little daughter. They separated and Sophie began her travels across the continent of Europe: on the Train Bleu to Paris [...] always trying to please, to change identities as she arrived. To be charming and prettily dressed and witty for her mother; to be serious and enquiring with securely plaited pigtails for her father. Then suddenly the tug of war stopped. Both parents dropped the rope and she was packed off to a school that was unlike any she had known. That it was the beginning of a permanent abandonment, Sophie was sure (pp. 18, 25 and 35).

All Sidi wants is for her father to say one kind word about her mother; this never happens, however, and her governess provides all the security she is ever to know until she meets her future husband. Sophie's security is afforded by her father's laboratory assistant Czernowitz who is the man who feeds the rats (according to Eva Ibbotson, this man, actually named Rabinovitch, died recently in Belsize Park aged nearly 100):

> '[Fitzallan] said I oppressed Czernowitz because he came in on Sunday to feed the rats,' said Sophie coming in [....] in tears, 'but I didn't, honestly, Ellen; I loved Czernowitz. I still do. If it wasn't for him I'd never know where anyone was' (p. 81).

When Sophie forgets to write to her mother it is an indication that she is gradually overcoming her sensation of being lost and is finding security elsewhere – she is more or less adopted by Leon's secure family. Just as Sidi marries a husband from a secure family background, Sophie marries Leon and Tessa in *Magic Flutes* marries Guy who, though a foundling, has found security with his foster-mother Martha Hodge. Tessa receives love from her aunts but not from her parents to whom she is always a disappointment and who force her to suppress her personal feelings of misery and to pursue tedious and interminable duty (pp. 93, 104).

Maxi in the same novel is terrified of his mother. Similarly, Kendrick in *A Song for Summer* and Quin's father in *The Morning Gift* are persecuted by their biological parents for failing to live up to their ideals. Ibbotson insists that people need to be what they themselves want to be and not what other people want to make them into, moreover that real riches come from within. This is particularly true of her portrayal of Daniel Frankenheimer in *Madensky Square* (according to Eva Ibbotson a portrait of her husband, the naturalist Alan Ibbotson). Daniel is the person the 'difficult' children in the children's camp want to be with since he can see them without their past and their problems. He can interact with wild creatures and teaches the children how to observe things in the natural world, suddenly becoming an oak tree or making a grotto for salamanders in order to achieve this (pp. 142-43, 209) as he believes that the natural world can heal them. Marek in *A Song for Summer* (also based on Alan Ibbotson) is a similar sort of figure: he creates a quiet world of trees, water and plants, he can recognize different types of wood when blindfolded, and he is, as Sophie says, 'a person who *found* things [...] mouse's nests and fireflies [...] and when he shows you it's like getting a present' (p. 44). He is the one whom Ellen asks for help to realize her vision of storks at Hallendorf school since she believes that their presence blesses a house (p. 54); his home, Pettelsdorf in Bohemia, where he spent a harmonious and secure childhood, had numerous storks. Indeed, storks are a symbol of happiness in several of Ibbotson's books – in *The Star of Kazan*, for instance, where Annika has likewise been told that they bless the house, storks nest only on the servant's house, although this is almost a hovel, while the storks are absent from the big house where there is no happiness.

As indicated above, Eva Ibbotson tends to favour all-black or all-white figures in her novels, with stark contrasts and very little ground in between, and this applies particularly to the mother-figures. The 'true' mothers are frequently not the biological mothers. Sidi has her governess; while in both *The Star of Kazan* and *Magic Flutes* it is the foster mothers who transmit a sense of security and belonging to the foundlings Annika and Guy. Annika daydreams of her mother, and when her 'mother' comes to claim her she thinks that her dream has come true. She worships the woman she thinks is her mother and is prepared to give her everything; but ultimately she realizes that she belongs to the person who has always cared for her, Ellie. The final betrayal for Annika is her discovery that the woman pretending to be her mother wishes only to deprive her of her property (*The Star of Kazan*, p. 371). Isobel in *A Company of Swans* neglects her son, only concerning herself with him when she can manipulate him. Edith Sultzer's mother in *Madensky Square* neglects her husband while trying to turn her daughter into an intellectual. Edith sobs that she has missed the whole of her father's life and that she never wanted to be clever, nor give her toys to the poor; all she ever wished for was to be ordinary. In the event she happily marries a very ordinary butcher (pp. 132, 226).

Anna's and Rupert's mothers in *A Countess below Stairs* both need their children to protect them rather than the other way round. However, there are also several 'all-white' mother figures: Leonie almost smothers her daughter Ruth with love in *The Morning Gift*, Susanna's mother in *Madensky Square* is as wholesome and loving as Henny in *A Song for Summer* but dies when she is twelve. Susanna has to give up her own illegitimate daughter for adoption but, as a loving mother, is still desperate to see her. In 'A Question of Riches', Jeremy's mother is widowed and remarries, leaving her seven year-old son to the mercies of a 'good' English preparatory school while she herself becomes as distant and longed-for as a mirage (*Glove Shop*, p. 225). His two grandmothers, the superior and wealthy Mrs Tate-Oxenham and his father's mother who lives on her pension, are the black and white contrast Ibbotson is so fond of: Grandmother provides him with luxury but with neither affection nor happiness but Nana with a period in his life when the sun always seems to shine and when he feels that Nana owns the whole of London, if not the world (*Glove Shop*, pp. 223-24). It is to Nana that he writes the real weekly letter unlike the stilted one to his mother and the 'proper' letter to Mrs Tate-Oxenham (*Glove Shop*, p. 225). At Christmas his mother lets him down once again, but he finds an opportunity to be taken to spend the holiday with Nana, the 'rich' grandmother, rich in love, with whom he is happy.

Eva Ibbotson's presentation of marriage in her novels sets out in most cases to communicate the same black and white sense of 'rightness'; nearly all her books share a basic structure. The six couples Anna and Rupert, Tessa and Guy, Harriet and Rom, Ruth and Quinton, Ellen and Marek, Susanna and Gernot all experience misunderstandings within their relationships to each other until they realize whom they are really 'meant' for, to whom they really 'belong'. All six men are initially involved with a 'suitable' partner who during the course of each of the novels proves not to be suitable at all. The real Cinderella-and-the-prince partner is temporarily unavailable in each case. The four heartless and selfish snobs Muriel, Nerine, Isobel and Verena, are only concerned with themselves and their beauty and/or wealth, experience direct rejection but are in each case provided with an appropriate but distinctly inferior partner (Muriel with Dr Lightbody, Nerine with Frith, Isobel with de Larne and Verena with Kenneth).

In *The Morning Gift*, Ruth's initial happiness, despite her exile, is precarious, while the sound of the Schubert quartet in E flat invokes memories of loss (personified by the violinist Biberstein, who jumped out of a fourth-floor window to his death when the storm troopers came) and nearly makes her founder: 'Yet if her happiness was real it could be fractured in an instant by a reminder of the past. [...] Time had not run backward [...] the past was past, and Biberstein was dead' (pp. 134-35). Even in this novel, where the portrayal of exile is so realistic that any of the exiled children find it easy to identify with because it is so intrinsically 'right', Eva Ibbotson insists on a happy ending. 'I must have happy endings whether I write for children or grown-ups', she commented to the *Independent* in July 2004 and to the present writer on the telephone a year later.[17] The Cinderellas find their Ultima Thule and Ruth's beloved husband survives the war. At the end of *The Morning Gift*, imagined Austria even returns in the invisible symbolic presence of the violinist Biberstein as Ruth hears the Schubert quartet again and is comforted for the loss of her home – the romantic vision is complete: 'Perhaps, it had occurred, this miracle. [...] as the ravishing, transcendent music filled the room, Ruth seemed to see a plump and curly-headed figure who leant out from heaven and lifted the bow of his Amati in salute – and smiled' (*The Morning Gift*, p. 361).

Anmerkungen

[1] Foreword to Anna Gmeyner, *Manja* (London: Persephone Books, 2003), p. ix.

[2] Nicholas Tucker, 'Journey of a lifetime', *The Independent*, 23 July 2004, p. 20.

[3] It was directed by Brecht's friend Slatan Dudow, using Erwin Piscator's 'Gruppe junger Schauspieler', including Ernst Busch, on 26 January 1930. See Heike Klapdor-Kops, '"Und was die Verfasserin betrifft, lasst uns weitersehen." Die Rekonstruktion der schriftstellerischen Laufbahn Anna Gmeyners', in *Gedanken an Deutschland im Exil. Exilforschung. Ein internationales Jahrbuch*, vol. 3, 1985, pp. 316-17; and J. M. Ritchie, 'Anna Gmeyner and the Scottish Connection', in Ritchie, *German Exiles. British Perspectives* (New York: Peter Lang, 1997), p. 203.

[4] Her play *Automatenbüffet* (commended for the Kleistpreis) was produced in Hamburg and Berlin in 1932. It was advertised in March 1933 in the *Völkischer Beobachter* but was then produced not in Berlin but by the Zürcher Schauspielhaus, entitled *Im Trüben fischen* (12 September 1933). As late as June 1933 there was an article in the *BZ am Mittag* about her (and presumably written by her). Her presence in Germany in 1934, however, is indicated by a letter she wrote from Munich to Berthold Viertel (thanks to Birte Werner for this information).

[5] On this, see *The Scotsman*, 31 July 2002: 'Every time they got close, for example, trying to get Dr Mary Barton and boffin Berthold Wiesner's natural daughter [Eva Ibbotson] to give a saliva swab to prove what we knew – that Wiesner himself had provided the sperm for all of the kids in a fit of extraordinary egomania – they were thwarted by the understandable wishes of people to hang on to the foundation of their lives.'

[6] However the work reappeared in 2003 in a new English translation, with a preface by Eva Ibbotson (published in London by Persephone).

[7] It was republished by Peter Lang, Berne in 2006 (Exil-Dokumente, vol. 9).

[8] See note 2.

[9] A talk by Eva Ibbotson for Newnham College in 2005 entitled 'The Vienna Connection', typescript in author's possession, p. 1; 'The Great Carp Ferdinand' in *A Glove Shop in Vienna*, first published 1984, here: New York: St. Martin's Press, 1992, pp. 116-27. *The Star of Kazan* (London: Macmillan, 2004), pp. 70-75.

[10] The novels for adults and children were published between 1981 and 2004 (here listed in chronological order): 1. *A Countess below Stairs* (London: Macmillan Futura, 1981), here: London: Arrow edition, 1994; 2. *Magic Flutes* (London: Century, 1982), here: New York: St. Martin's Press, 1984, (both these novels involve a post-1918 wounded hero); 3. *A Glove Shop in Vienna* (London: Century, 1984) (19 short stories), for edition used here see note 9; 4. *A Company of Swans* (London: Century, 1985), set in Cambridge in pre-World War II period (edition used here London: Arrow, 1999); 5. *The Morning Gift* (London: Arrow, 1994), set between 1938 and 1945; 6. *A Song for Summer* (London: Arrow, 1997) recreates Dartington Hall, transplanting it to pre-World War II Austria and then to the Second World War period; 7. *Madensky Square* (London: Arrow, 1998), set in the Vienna of Franz Josef, 1911-1912, and written for children; 8. *The Star of Kazan* (London: Macmillan, 2004), in which Annika is found towards the end of Franz Josef's reign.

[11] Anna Gmeyner, 'A House with two doors', unpublished manuscript, Gmeyner-Nachlass, Deutsches Filmmuseum, Stiftung Deutsche Kinemathek, Berlin, p. 14, by courtesy of Birte Werner.

[12] Newnham typescript, see note 9, pp. 1, 2.

[13] *Ibid.*, p. 5.

[14] See also *A Countess below stairs*, p. 65, *A Song for Summer*, p. 11, and *The Star of Kazan*, p. 54.

[15] Newnham typescript, see note 9, p. 5 and Anna Morduch [i.e. Gmeyner] *No Screen for the Dying* (London: Regency Press, 1964), p. 15, p. 22, pp. 54-56 and p. 68.

[16] Hans Gál, *Musik hinter Stacheldraht. Tagebuchblätter aus dem Sommer 1940* (Berne: Peter Lang, 2003), pp. 144-45.

[17] On 18 July 2005.

Austria Revisited

„Einmal Emigrant, immer Emigrant": Zur literarischen und publizistischen „Remigration" Robert Neumanns 1946-1965

Maximiliane Jäger

Robert Neumann zählte zu den ersten von den Nazis verbotenen Autoren, ging – als Österreicher – schon 1934 ins englische Exil, um erst 1958 ins Schweizer Tessin zu übersiedeln. Von einer „Remigration" dieses bekannten Exilautors kann daher bestenfalls auf dem literarischen und publizistischen Gebiet gesprochen werden. Einigen Stufen dieser „Remigration" möchte ich im folgenden Beitrag nachgehen: Der Wahrnehmung des Exilautors Neumann durch die in Österreich verbliebenen Schriftsteller; den spezifischen Weichenstellungen der Neumann-Rezeption in Österreich und (West-)Deutschland nach dem Krieg; dem Problem des zweimaligen Sprachwechsels und schließlich der Rolle Robert Neumanns in der literarischen und politischen Landschaft (West-)Deutschlands, das spätestens seit dem Ende der fünfziger Jahre im Fokus seines politischen und literarischen Interesses steht.

Unter den österreichischen Schriftstellern im englischen Exil ist Robert Neumann einer der Prominenten. 1897 in Wien geboren, 1927 mit einem ersten Band literarischer Parodien *Mit fremden Federn*, aber auch mit den beiden großen, an der Sprachkritik von Karl Kraus wie der Psychoanalyse Freuds und Adlers geschulten Zeit- und Gesellschaftsromanen *Sintflut* und *Die Macht* (1929 und 1932) berühmt geworden, gehören seine Bücher zu den ersten, die 1933 auf dem Index und Scheiterhaufen der Nazis landen. Bereits 1934 emigriert Neumann nach England, wo er als aktives Mitglied des Austrian Centre, der „Free Austrian Movement" und Mitinitiator der österreichischen „Kulturkonferenzen" sowie als Gründer und späterer Präsident des österreichischen PEN-Club im Exil zu einer wichtigen Integrationsfigur wird. Zudem gehört Neumann zu den wenigen deutschsprachigen Exilautoren, die, wie beispielsweise auch Ruth Feiner, Ernst Bornemann oder Hilde Spiel, auch literarisch den Schritt in die neue Sprache wagen. Neumann wird zum „englische[n] Schriftsteller",[1] schreibt und publiziert zwischen 1942 und 1957 seine Bücher auf Englisch, und das mit nicht unbeträchtlichem Erfolg. Erst mit seinem Umzug ins Schweizer Tessin Ende 1958 kehrt er literarisch wieder ganz zur deutschen Sprache zurück, insbesondere in Deutschland und speziell der Bundesrepublik wieder ein durchaus bekannter und nicht weniger umstrittener Autor und Publizist, dem der in Wien und München ansässige Kurt Desch-Verlag ab 1959 eine Gesamtausgabe (*Gesammelte Werke in Einzelausgaben*) widmet. Seit seinem Tod im Jahr 1975 allerdings ist Robert Neumann sowohl in England als auch in Österreich und Deutschland so gut wie vergessen oder bestenfalls noch als Verfasser jener literarischen Parodien bekannt, mit denen er in den zwanziger Jahren zuerst berühmt geworden war.[2]

Auf die Tatsache, dass diese nunmehr seit rund drei Jahrzehnten andauernde Rezeptionsmisere von Neumanns Werk neben der problematischen und stockenden Aufnahme der Literatur des Exils insgesamt nach dem Krieg nicht zuletzt auch dem zweimaligen Wechsel der literarischen Sprache und damit des Publikationsumfeldes und Lesepublikums geschuldet sein dürfte, hat Richard Dove bereits hingewiesen. Seinen Arbeiten über Robert Neumann ist es auch zu verdanken, dass Neumanns Zeit und vielfältige Aktivitäten im englischen Exil insbesondere in den Jahren von 1934 bis 1946 mittlerweile bekannt, aufgearbeitet und der Forschung zugänglich gemacht worden sind.[3] Ich möchte mich daher in meinem folgenden Beitrag auf die Zeit nach dem eigentlichen Exil, auf die Jahre zwischen 1946 und 1965 konzentrieren, literarisch markiert einerseits von dem 1946 in englischer Sprache geschriebenen Buch *Children of Vienna*,[4] in dem Neumanns Heimatstadt Wien ja wieder den titelgebenden Handlungsschauplatz darstellt, andererseits von dem 1965 erscheinenden kritischen Gegenwartsroman *Der Tatbestand oder Der gute Glaube der Deutschen*,[5] mit dem Neumann auch literarisch wieder ganz in der deutschen Gegenwart ankommt. Das freilich immer unter der Bedingung seiner ihm sowohl von außen immer wieder zugeschriebenen als auch, im positiven wie im negativen Sinn, von ihm selbst immer wieder für sich reklamierten Außen- und Außenseiterposition, die sich auch in der aus seinem 1964 geschriebenem Tagebuch *Vielleicht das Heitere* stammenden Feststellung: „Einmal Emigrant – immer Emigrant" spiegelt, welcher der vorliegende Beitrag seinen Titel verdankt, an welche sich aber im Textzusammenhang bezeichnenderweise die Bemerkung anschließt: „Mitternachtsnachrichten aus Deutschland. Einem Lande der Barbaren, dem man hassend und liebend verbunden bleibt, trotz allem."[6]

Wie sehen Robert Neumanns Überlegungen, seine biographischen und literarischen Weichenstellungen nach Kriegsende im Einzelnen aus? Zunächst deutet nichts darauf hin, dass er – im Unterschied etwa zu Hilde Spiel, Franz Theodor Csokor, Hans Weigel, Felix Braun oder Hans Flesch-Brunningen, die sich auf größeren oder kleineren Umwegen wieder nach Österreich orientieren – je ernsthaft mit dem Gedanken einer möglichen Rückkehr nach Österreich umgegangen wäre. Immerhin findet sich in seinem Nachlass ein Schreiben an Dr. Karl Renner, den späteren österreichischen Bundespräsidenten, dem Neumann im Juli 1945 mitteilt, dass er großes Interesse an den Schriftstellerorganisationen in Österreich habe und regelmäßig den österreichischen Rundfunk verfolge. Der Brief schließt mit der Bitte an Renner, über ihn, wenn er „dienlich sein" könne, „zu verfügen".[7] Das hier geäußerte Interesse an den „Schriftstellerorganisationen" hängt sicher unmittelbar mit Neumanns Funktion als Präsident des „Free Austrian PEN" zusammen, in der er zwischen 1945 und 1947 ganz entscheidenden Einfluss auf die Reorganisation des österreichischen Pen-Zentrums ausüben wird. In seiner Darstellung des österreichischen PEN-Clubs hat Klaus Amann nachgezeichnet,[8] wie sich, unter Neumanns energischer Federführung, der neue, dann auf dem internationalen PEN-Kongress in Zürich 1947 offiziell gegründete österreichische PEN-Club in direkter und ausschließlicher Nachfolge des österreichischen PEN-Club im Exil konstituiert hat, so dass neben der literarischen Qualifikation die, wie es in den von Neumann formulierten Richtlinien hieß, „einwandfrei antifaschistische Gesinnung" seit 1933 zum Hauptkriterium für die Auswahl der aufzunehmenden Mitglieder erklärt wurde. In den Gründungsstatuten des neuen Wiener PEN wird es heißen:

> a) Sämtliche Mitglieder des Austrian-London-P.E.N. werden automatisch Mitglieder des Wiener P.E.N.
>
> b) Die seinerzeit aus dem österreichischen P.E.N. aus politischen oder opportunistischen Gründen Ausgetretenen werden in den neuen P.E.N. nicht wieder aufgenommen.[9]

Es ist leicht vorstellbar, dass diese von Neumann maßgeblich betriebene eindeutige und ausschließliche Orientierung am Exil-PEN zu Spannungen mit den in Österreich verbliebenen Schriftstellern führen musste. Denn „ist es nicht Entmündigung", schrieb zum Beispiel Rudolf Jeremias Kreutz noch am 8. Mai 1947 an den Kollegen Oskar Maurus Fontana,

> wenn man uns bei der Restituierung des österreichischen Penklubs keine freie Hand lässt, als ob wir unfähig wären, uns selbst frei und von außen unbeeinflusst zu konstituieren? [...] Ich finde das, gelinde gesagt, beschämend [...]. Es geht [...] nicht an, uns nicht viel anders als ein Kolonialvolk minderer Sorte von London aus zu gängeln.[10]

Neben dem hier anklingenden Ressentiment gegenüber den „diktatorisch" in die inneren Angelegenheiten eingreifenden emigrierten Kollegen, treffen jedoch im Zusammenhang der nach der Befreiung Österreichs fälligen Rekonstituierung und Neuformulierung der österreichischen Literatur auch unterschiedliche Auffassungen von literarischer und kultureller Kontinuität aufeinander – welche zumal unter den gegebenen Umständen vom Thema der Politik nicht zu trennen sind. Anders als in Deutschland, wo, vertreten durch die Gruppe 47, der Ruf nach einer „Stunde Null" der Literatur nach dem „Kahlschlag", einem völligen Neubeginn ohne Traditionsanbindung jeglicher Form zur prägenden Forderung an die neue Literatur werden wird, versucht man in Österreich, Eigenart und Aufgabe der Nachkriegsliteratur im Sinne der kulturellen Kontinuität und der Fortsetzung einer spezifisch österreichischen Tradition zu formulieren. Alexander Lernet-Holenia, Grandseigneur der österreichischen Literatur und ab 1967 Präsident des österreichischen PEN-Club, schreibt im November 1945 in einem Brief an die österreichische Monatszeitschrift *Der Turm*, man müsse doch jetzt „nur dort fortsetzen, wo uns die Träume eines Irren unterbrochen haben, in der Tat brauchen wir nicht voraus- sondern nur zurückblicken [...] wir sind im besten und wertvollsten Verstande, unsere Vergangenheit."[11] Beide Positionen, die des radikalen Bruchs wie die der ungestörten Fortsetzung einer zwischenzeitlich nur „unterbrochenen" Vergangenheit, kollidieren natürlich mit den Erfahrungen und Erinnerungen der Emigranten. Man muss allerdings sagen, dass gerade der österreichische PEN-Club in den ersten Jahren nach seiner Neuetablierung unter Führung von Franz Theodor Csokor und Alexander Sacher-Masoch Etliches unternommen hat, um die zur Emigration gezwungenen, im Exil verstorbenen oder in KZs umgekommenen Autorinnen und Autoren wieder im öffentlichen Bewusstsein in Österreich präsent zu machen.[12] Im Fall Robert Neumanns, der nach 1947 weiter als Ehrenpräsident des Wiener PEN fungiert, ist allerdings eine Reintegration in die österreichische Literatur so gut wie vollständig ausgeblieben.[13]

Biographisch gesehen, stellt Neumann selbst die Weichen seines Lebens in dieser Zeit auch in geradezu umgekehrter Richtung. Im Sommer 1947 übergibt er die Präsidentschaft des österreichischen PEN an Franz Theodor Csokor, im gleichen Jahr wird seinem (bereits 1939 zum ersten Mal gestellten) Antrag auf britische Staatsangehörigkeit statt gegeben und, ebenfalls in diesem Jahr 1947, erwirbt Neumann das „Pest House" in Cranbrook in der Grafschaft Kent, wo er bis zu seinem Umzug in die Schweiz Ende des Jahres 1958 wohnen wird – ein „englischer Schriftsteller" nun auch hinsichtlich der Staatsbürgerschaft. Mit einer Art wehmütiger Ironie hat Neumann selbst zu diesem Hauskauf angemerkt: „Erster Schritt auf dem großen Heimweg. Zurück zur Scholle. Heimweh, im Grunde. Ein jüdischer Charakterzug."[14]

Und doch war Robert Neumanns erstes Buch nach dem Krieg, *Children of Vienna*, der Heimatstadt Wien gewidmet, wenngleich der Autor in seiner Vorbemerkung schrieb, es handle sich um ein „book of fiction [...] in a ficticious setting which I call Vienna, but which could be anywhere east of the Meridian of Despair".[15] Trotz dieser Einschränkung, des Hinweises auf das Recht der Fiktion gegenüber der Faktizität, schlägt Neumann hier, nach dem Krieg, doch einen literarischen Bogen, knüpft an seine beiden großen Wien-Romane von 1929 und 1932 an, an *Sintflut* und *Die Macht*, zwei Bände eines ursprünglich als Trilogie geplanten, großdimensionalen Querschnitts durch alle Gesellschaftsschichten in der bewegten Zeit der Inflation und Nachinflation, in denen er mit geradezu Balzacscher Opulenz und Detailkenntnis bekannte Wiener Korruptionsskandale, die ersten Arbeiteraufstände und schließlich die Verflechtungen der Großfinanz mit den erstarkenden Deutschnationalen aufs Korn genommen hatte; dieses Letztere hatte schließlich den ersten Ausschlag für Verbot und Verbrennung von Neumanns Büchern durch die Nazis gegeben.[16] Nach Krieg und Exil nun also wiederum ein Wien-Roman, aber jetzt verengt auf einen Keller in der von Bomben verwüsteten Stadt, zentriert auf ein kleines Häufchen von aus KZ, Erziehungsheim, Flüchtlingstreck und Hitlerjugend übrig gebliebenen Kindern, die hier Zuflucht gefunden haben und ihr von Besatzungssoldaten, Zuhältern, Dieben und Spekulanten umstelltes Auskommen suchen, bis ein schwarzer Militärgeistlicher sich ihrer annimmt, dessen Rettungsversuch jedoch von der amerikanischen Militärpolizei wegen Verstoßes gegen das Fraternisierungsverbot zunichte gemacht wird.

Obgleich *Children of Vienna* auch ein anspruchsvolles literarisches Experiment ist, in dem Neumann in einer kruden, mit amerikanischen, polnischen, jiddischen, russischen und deutschen Versatzstücken durchsetzten Sprache die Zerstörung und Korruption der Lebenszusammenhänge auch sprachlich umzusetzen versucht, wird das Buch – und das entspricht auch seiner Intention – vor allem unter humanitären Gesichtspunkten ein publizistischer Erfolg. Gleich nach seinem Erscheinen wird es in mehrere Sprachen übersetzt, eine Verfilmung wird schon 1947 ins Auge gefasst, allerdings nicht realisiert. Die österreichische Schriftstellerin Elisabeth Freundlich berichtet, sie habe

> Robert Neumanns *Kinder von Wien* unmittelbar nach dem Krieg auf den Schreibtischen von Unitariern und Quäkern, in den Händen vieler jener Männer und Frauen gesehen, an die das Buch sich ausdrücklich richtete, und die Hilfsaktionen für das besiegte und zerstörte Europa leiteten.

Mit diesen knapp 160 Seiten habe „der Autor das Gewissen der Welt aufgerüttelt".[17]

Insgesamt ist Neumanns neuer Wien-Roman in Österreich allerdings alles andere als ein Erfolg. Als 1948 bei Querido in Amsterdam die deutsche Übersetzung von Franziska Becker erscheint – die allerdings, so ist

anzumerken, kaum etwas vom sprachlich experimentellen Charakter des
englischen Originals wieder zu geben vermag – bezeichnet der Rezensent
des *Neuen Österreich* die *Kinder von Wien* schon im Titel seiner Rezension
als „missratenes Buch" voll von „angehäufte[n] Geschmacklosigkeiten, das
ein mit einer „Überfülle von Widerwärtigem [...] verzerrtes Bild von Wien
und seiner Jugend" gebe, eine weder literarisch noch politisch zu
rechtfertigende „hemmungslose Verzeichnung", die gerade von einem
österreichischen Autor nicht hinnehmbar sei. Nicht „zärtliches Heimweh"
nach Wien, nur das „grelle J´accuse" stehe Neumann zur Verfügung, der
seine Informationen ja auch nur aus „schlechten Rückübersetzungen
hassentstellter Berichte" beziehe. Mit ihrem Schlusssatz exponiert diese
Rezension denn auch die Konstellation von „Dem (oder Denen) da draußen
vs. Wir (die wir die Realität des Kriegs und Nachkriegs kennen) hier
drinnen", eine für das Verhältnis zwischen Emigranten und Nichtemigranten
in den Jahren nach dem Krieg sicher insgesamt charakteristische
Konstellation:

> Wir haben den Krieg, seine Not, den Straßenkampf, die Befreiung
> und alle Wehen der Wiedergeburt eines neuen Lebens getragen.
> Man muß die Härte dieses Lebens täglich am eigenen Leib spüren,
> um zu ermessen, wie sehr mit den „Kindern von Wien" den
> Kindern und Wien Unrecht geschieht.[18]

Es ist mir nicht bekannt, ob Neumann diese Rezension zur Kenntnis
genommen hat, denkbar ist es allerdings schon. Jedenfalls ist sie ein
interessantes Dokument für die Art und Weise, wie er, neben seiner
„Diktatorenrolle" als Reorganisator des PEN, unmittelbar nach dem Krieg
als Autor in Österreich wahrgenommen wurde. Ein österreichischer Verlag
hat sich nicht um ihn bemüht, in dieser Hinsicht wendet sich Neumann nach
Deutschland. Im Sommer 1947 schließt er einen Vertrag mit dem Curt
Weller Verlag in Konstanz mit siebenjähriger Lizenz über eine „Deutsche
Gesamtausgabe".[19] Doch geht der Weller-Verlag bereits 1948 in Konkurs.
Ab 1950 verlegt Neumann seine Bücher dann bei dem Münchner Verlag
Kurt Desch, der ihm, wie schon gesagt, ab 1959 *Gesammelte Werke in
Einzelausgaben* widmet. Doch geht auch der Desch-Verlag 1973, zwei Jahre
vor Neumanns Tod, in Konkurs, ein Faktor, der die weitere Rezeption von
Neumanns Werk natürlich nachhaltig beeinflussen musste und der um so
schwerer wog, als auch Neumanns sehr viel jüngere Frau und Mitarbeiterin
Helga Neumann schon kurze Zeit nach Robert Neumann überraschend
verstarb,[20] so dass praktisch niemand mehr übrig blieb, der sich um die
Publikation und Pflege des Werkes gekümmert hätte. Die „literarische

Remigration" Robert Neumanns ist damit natürlich insgesamt recht unvollständig geblieben.

Wie sieht aber zunächst die Rückkehr auf den deutschen Buchmarkt im Einzelnen aus? Was liegt dem deutschsprachigen Lesepublikum vor, wie wird der Exilautor Neumann hier wahrgenommen? Ein wichtiger Faktor ist, dass Neumann in der Zeit nach dem Krieg seine neuen Bücher weiterhin auf Englisch schreibt, was bedeutet, dass sie in Deutschland als Übersetzungen erscheinen müssen. Entweder in fremder Übersetzung, wie die *Kinder von Wien* (1948), wie *Bibiana Santis* (1950; d. i. *The Inquest,* London: Hutchinson, 1944), ein Buch über Flucht und Exil zwischen den faschistischen Systemen in ganz Europa, zentriert auf die Figur der jungen Emigrantin Bibiana und die Rekonstruktion ihres Lebens bis hin zu ihrem Selbstmord oder plötzlichen Tod im Londoner Exil),[21] wie *Die Puppen von Poshansk* (1952; d. i. *Insurrection in Poshansk*, London: Hutchinson, 1952) über den stalinistischen Gulag. Obgleich man seine von Georg Goyert besorgte Übersetzung das Erscheinen dieses Buches nicht anders denn als hölzern bezeichnen kann, gab in Deutschland Anlass für eine mehrseitige Coverstory, die der *Spiegel* über Neumann herausbrachte. Solch ein prominenter Artikel in einer der wichtigsten politischen Wochenzeitschriften ist sicher ein wichtiger Schritt hin zur neuerlichen Präsenz Neumanns im Bewusstsein der bundesdeutschen Öffentlichkeit gewesen. Doch zeigt er auch die Verwerfungen und nachhaltig wirkenden Rezeptionsschienen, denen die Aufnahme Neumanns in Deutschland unterworfen bleibt. Unter einem ganzseitigen Fotoporträt Neumanns titelt der *Spiegel*: „Mit fremden Federn. Jagd auf Menschen und Gespenster: Robert Neumann" und lenkt damit über die Zeit des Nationalsozialismus und Krieges hinweg die Aufmerksamkeit grundsätzlich zurück auf den Autor der Parodien von 1927.[22] Wenn im Artikel selbst von Neumanns Leben und Schicksal seither durchaus die Rede ist, so bannt ihn doch zugleich der gleich zweimal bemühte Vergleich mit dem „ewigen Juden" gleichsam ins „ewige" Exil, schreibt seine Existenz als Exilautor affirmativ fest. Zudem eröffnet der Verfasser des Artikels seine Darstellung mit der nicht ganz ohne Häme geäußerten Erwartung, dass angesichts der neuen sowjetkritischen *Puppen von Poshansk* ja nun Robert Neumanns Freundschaft mit den beiden DDR-Autoren und -Literaturfunktionären Arnold Zweig und Johannes R. Becher endgültig in die Brüche gehen müsse.[23] Diese sofortige Einbindung von Buch und Autor in den Diskurs des Kalten Krieges weist *ex negativo* auf ein weiteres Problem nicht nur der Neumann-Rezeption in der Nachkriegszeit hin. Neumann, der sich selbst Zeit seines Lebens als Sozialist bezeichnet und schon 1946, in den *Kindern von Wien*, die Symptome des kommenden Kalten Krieges angeprangert hat, vertritt eine stets kritische, unabhängig von politischen Lagern bleibende Position, die ihn unvereinnahmbar, aber eben zugleich auch heimatlos zwischen den politischen Blöcken bleiben lässt. Darüber hinaus „passt" er aber auch nicht zu den jungen Autoren, die ja, vor allem in der späteren Zeit der Gruppe 47, den kritischen Standpunkt für sich reklamieren werden. Hier wiederum ist er zu „alt", bringt eine Tradition politischer und literarischer Erfahrung mit, die vom Neubegründungsimpetus der jungen bundesdeutschen Literaturszene kaum gewünscht und die ihn selbst auch mit nicht unbeträchtlichem Vorbehalt auf sie reagieren lässt.[24] Über ein Treffen mit Rudolf Walter Leonhardt anlässlich eines Besuchs bei der Frankfurter Buchmesse notierte Neumann beispielsweise in seinem Tagebuch:

> – und dazwischen, grüßend nach allen Seiten, von allen Seiten gegrüßt oder bedeutungsvoll ungegrüßt, aß man mit diesem R. N. zu Mittag, eigentlich gehörte er ja dazu. (Der brillante Jens hatte es erst vorgestern in einem Interview gesagt: „Ein Schriftsteller über sechzig gehört erschossen, er paßt mir nicht ins literarische Bild.")[25]

Und noch in dem erst postum veröffentlichten „Bericht über mich selbst" schreibt Neumann nicht ohne Bitterkeit über die „jungen Dichter in Deutschland":

> Es waren junge Menschen nach meinem Herzen, aber sie kannten mich kaum noch, sie verstanden mich nicht mehr. Es bedurfte einer ganzen Weile, bevor ich begriff: Da stand ich, jünger im Herzen als sie, und lebensdurstig und triumphal und war nicht krepiert – und war für sie doch nur ein unbequemerweise Nochimmerlebendiger, ein weißhaarig Umsichschlagender, der die Fotografie verwackelte.[26]

Tatsächlich bewegt sich Robert Neumann trotz oder gerade wegen seiner Unabhängigkeit von den politischen Lagern in extremeren, im Rahmen der Literaturlandschaft bisweilen unkonventionelleren Bahnen als so mancher Nachwuchsautor. Seit den späteren fünfziger bis in die siebziger Jahre schreibt er, der auch in der *Zeit*, im *Spiegel* und der *Tribüne* veröffentlicht, als eine Art Hausautor regelmäßig in der Linkszeitschrift *konkret*, wo seine politischen und literaturkritischen Artikel nicht selten zwischen damals noch außerordentlich skandalösen, emanzipatorisch gemeinten Nacktfotos zu stehen kommen. Auf dem Gebiet der Literatur wird er nicht nur den ersten deutschen Roman, nämlich den *Tatbestand* (1965), verfassen, der in zuvor unbekannt zugespitzter Form den deutschen, aber auch den deutsch-deutschen, den amerikanischen, sowjetischen und israelischen Umgang mit der Nazivergangenheit in der Gegenwart fokussiert – auf ihn komme ich unten noch zu sprechen –, er ist auch Verfasser des ersten Romans, nämlich *Festival* (1962), der das gesellschaftliche und literarische Tabuthema lesbischer Liebe in der anspruchsvollen deutschen Literatur verankert und ebenfalls mit einer weit ausgreifenden politischen Dimension verknüpft.[27] Sein kleiner Hochstapler-Roman *Olympia* von 1961, ein heiteres Seitenstück zu Thomas Manns *Felix Krull*, bringt Neumann einen zähen Plagiatsprozess mit dem S. Fischer-Verlag und Thomas Manns „Erbdamen" ein[28], nicht nur ein Kuriosum, sondern wohl auch ein Symptom der veränderten literarischen Landschaft und der Konkurrenz unter den einstmals Exilierten (und ihren Nachlassverwaltern). Nicht zu vergessen sind die langwierigen und zähen Plagiatsanschuldigungen, die Claire Goll seit 1953 gegenüber Paul Celan erhebt und die Celans folgende Lebensjahre nachhaltig verbittern.

Doch noch einmal zurück zur literarischen „Remigration" im Einzelnen. Neben den genannten Fremdübersetzungen ins Deutsche, die oftmals recht wenig von der literarischen und stilistischen Eigenart der englischen Originale wieder zu geben vermögen und insofern natürlich auch ein Problem für eine qualitative Rezeption des Neumannschen Werkes darstellen, erscheinen ab 1948 auch ursprünglich im englischen Exil noch auf Deutsch geschriebene Bücher neu: So die Zaharoff-Biographie, Neumanns erstes Werk im Exil, die ihm in England einen Gerichtsprozess wegen Verunglimpfung der Person des Waffen-Tycoons Sir Basil Zaharoff beschert hatte; das schon im Titel als solches markierte „klassische" Exilbuch *An den Wassern von Babylon* über das universale jüdische Exil (1939 zuerst in englischer Übersetzung erschienen, eine erste deutsche Ausgabe veranstaltete die East and West Library in Oxford 1945, bei Desch erscheint es 1954), der historische Struensee-Roman *Der Favorit der Königin* (1953), ursprünglich 1935 bei Querido in Amsterdam, und der ebenfalls historische Roman *Eine Frau hat geschrien* (Titel der Neufassung von 1958 *Die Freiheit und der General*) über den ungarischen 48er-Aufstand, den 1938 der Züricher Humanitas-Verlag veröffentlicht hatte. Und es erscheinen auch Neumanns eigene Übersetzungen, oder besser: Übertragungen bzw. Neufassungen von auf englisch verfassten Büchern: 1948, noch bei Curt Weller, der Emigrantenroman *Scene in Passing* von 1942, Neumanns erstes englisch geschriebenes Buch, jetzt unter dem wenig aussagekräftigen Titel *Tibbs*, spät, 1974, auch eine deutsche Neufassung der *Kinder von Wien*, die deren sprachlich und stilistisch experimentellen Charakter nun noch einmal im Deutschen nachzuschaffen versucht und, im veränderten Kontext der 70er Jahre, dann auch in dieser Hinsicht einige Beachtung findet.[29]

Mit dem 1957 erscheinenden autobiographischen Bericht *Mein altes Haus in Kent* kehrt Neumann literarisch in die deutsche Sprache zurück,

1958 übersiedelt er in die Schweiz. Dieses wie auch das folgende Buch, *Die dunkle Seite des Mondes* von 1959, besteht grundsätzlich in zwei Fassungen, einer englischen und einer deutschen. Von *Olympia* (1961) an wird Neumann in England wieder ein übersetzter Autor sein, dessen Bücher nach und nach vollständig aus dem Druck verschwinden. Unübersetzt aus dem Englischen bleibt der 1949 erschienene, in Österreich vor und nach dem Zweiten Weltkrieg spielende Roman *Blind Man's Buff* (1949),[30] nur in einer französischen Übersetzung erscheint der Roman *Sur les pas de Morell* (*In the Steps of Morell*, 1952), einer von mehreren Roman- und Dramenentwürfen, in denen Neumann sich literarisch mit dem Tod seines Sohnes auseinander zu setzen versucht. Heini Herbert Neumann war 1944 im Alter von zweiundzwanzig Jahren überraschend an einer Sepsis verstorben, Robert Neumann versuchte dieses – wie man seinem im Nachlass befindlichen Tagebuch von 1944 und den Erwähnungen auch in sehr viel späteren autobiographischen Schriften entnehmen kann – für ihn im Wortsinn traumatische Ereignis literarisch zu bewältigen, indem er ein autobiographisches Romanfragment seines Sohnes überarbeitete, zunächst mit dem Ziel, es unter dem Titel *Journal and Memoirs of Henri Herbert Neumann* zu veröffentlichen, dann, indem er es in immer weiteren Fiktionalisierungsschritten in eigene Romanprojekte einarbeitete (*The Pillar of Absalom, In the Steps of Morell*). In dieser literarisch wie psychisch äußerst quälenden Auseinandersetzung mit dem autobiographischen Text seines Sohnes liegt letztlich auch der Ursprung von Robert Neumanns eigenen autobiographischen Schriften, die – angefangen vom *Alten Haus in Kent* über die große Autobiographie *Ein leichtes Leben* (1963) und das Tagebuch *Vielleicht das Heitere* (1968) bis hin zu einem späten, nicht mehr gedruckten autobiographischen Projekt *Bericht von Unterwegs* in seinem Werk immer breiteren Raum einnehmen werden.[31]

Angesichts der Vielzahl von Büchern und Themen ist es erstaunlich, wie schnell und hartnäckig sich gleich nach dem Krieg ein einziger Strang in der Wahrnehmung des Autors Robert Neumann durchgesetzt hat, nämlich der parodistische. In der Tat hatten seine literarischen Parodien ihn 1927 berühmt gemacht, selbst im Exil, in englischer Sprache, versuchte er sich in diesem Genre und nach dem Krieg, ab der ersten Neuausgabe von Desch im Jahr 1950, sind alte und neue literarische Parodien in den verschiedensten Ausgaben eindeutig ein Neumann-Verkaufsschlager. Nicht selten jedoch bleibt der – durchaus richtige – Hinweis auf das parodistische Element in Neumanns gesamtem Schreiben, dessen Komplexität als Medium einer gesellschaftskritisch eingesetzten, psychologisch geschärften Sprach- und Stilkritik[32] nur in speziellen Rezensionen reflektiert wird, ein Schlagwort, das als eine Art „Neumann-Markenzeichen" die gesamte Lektüre bestimmt und dazu tendiert, den Blick sowohl für die feinen psychologischen und humanen Aspekte von Neumanns Büchern als auch für ihre tatsächliche gesellschaftliche Brisanz zu verstellen und den politischen Kritiker und Aufklärer Robert Neumann in der Rezeption zu entschärfen.

Von Beginn, d. h. vom Ende des Krieges an stand Robert Neumann sowohl aufgrund persönlicher Erfahrungen als auch aufgrund politischer Beobachtungen der politischen Entwicklung in Deutschland äußerst skeptisch gegenüber. Im Frühsommer 1949 notierte er in seinem Tagebuch:

> R's [d. i. Rolly's] mother met at Dover [...] An incurable German, never heard of concentration camps, convinced of Germans' absolutely correct behaviour in Russia, etc. Easier to find common platform with Mars men.[33]

Und in der Autobiographie heißt es rückblickend:

> Der Krieg vorüber, der Nazi vernichtet, die Deutschen selbstanklägerische Philosemiten, jeder von ihnen hatte heimlich einen Juden gerettet und von den Konzentrationslagern hatten sie nichts gewußt – das war das Bild, das einem angeboten wurde, als man zum erstenmal wieder nach Deutschland kam [...] Was ging es mich noch an [...] Ich war ein englischer Schriftsteller und lebte in England.[34]

Doch mit der Orientierung zurück auf den Kontinent Ende der 50er Jahre und dem (zunächst aus Geldnot betriebenen) Ausbau seiner Kontakte zu den deutschen Medien rücken auch die deutschen Verhältnisse wieder in Neumanns Blick. Waren seine ersten Beiträge im Wiener *Forum* und in der bundesdeutschen *Zeit*, entsprechend dem Interesse der Auftraggeber, Fragen der Parodie gewidmet, bringt Neumann nun Ende 1959 und Anfang 1960 im Norddeutschen Rundfunk, der *Süddeutschen Zeitung* und der *Zeit* drei Beiträge über „Die furchtbarste Fälschung der Geschichte", das antisemitische Machwerk *Die Protokolle der Weisen von Zion* heraus. Diese Beiträge eröffnen die lange Reihe von politischen Artikeln, Polemiken und Streitschriften, die Robert Neumann von hier an in Presse und Rundfunk veröffentlichen und in denen er unermüdlich den deutschen Umgang mit der nationalsozialistischen Vergangenheit beleuchten und durchleuchten wird, stets aber – das ist das Ungewöhnliche und Provozierende dieser Beiträge, was ihm sicherlich am meisten Feinde gemacht hat – mit dem Hauptaugenmerk auf den Zustand der und den Umgang mit der Vergangenheit in der Gegenwart. So beispielsweise in der dreiteiligen Rundfunksendung mit dem Titel „Ausflüchte unseres Gewissens. Dokumente zu Hitlers ‚Endlösung der Judenfrage' mit Kommentar und Bilanz der politischen Situation" von 1960, die auch in den *Heften für*

Zeitgeschehen erscheint und lange vor der großen „Wehrmachtsausstellung"
nicht zuletzt die Mitwisser- und Mittäterschaft breiter Kreise der deutschen
Bevölkerung thematisiert. Zum Beispiel, ebenfalls 1961, mit der über
Tonbandaufnahmen in Marburg und Ost-Berlin in Gang gebrachten ost-
westdeutschen Diskussion über die Frage „Was geht uns Eichmann an?",
mit der Neumann das deutsche Geschichtsbewusstsein in eine gesamtdeutsche
Kontroverse zu bringen versucht.[35] Zum Beispiel mit dem Dokumentarband
Hitler. Aufstieg und Untergang des Dritten Reiches von 1961, dem, unter
Regie von Paul Rotha, ein zwar gekürzter und entschärfter, aber doch einer
der ersten bundesdeutschen Dokumentarfilme über das Dritte Reich folgt.

Und schließlich, 1965, folgt auch ein fiktives Werk zu diesem
Thema, nämlich der schon genannte Roman *Der Tatbestand oder der Gute
Glaube der Deutschen*, mit dem ich diesen Versuch einer Darstellung von
Neumanns literarischer und publizistischer „Remigration" in notwendiger
Kürze beenden möchte. Denn mit dem *Tatbestand*, mit dem er noch einmal
zu dem Genre des kritischen Zeitromans zurück kehrt, führt Neumann beide
Stränge: Fiktion und politische Reflexion, am Gegenstand der deutschen
Gegenwart zusammen – in der er damit, so könnte man sagen, auch
literarisch wieder zur Gänze „ankommt".

Der Tatbestand schildert ein fiktives Geschehen am Rande des
Frankfurter Auschwitz-Prozesses, den Neumann während der Niederschrift
selbst besucht hat und dessen Materialien er hier verwendet. Im Zentrum
steht ebenfalls ein – allerdings fiktiver – Prozess, nämlich der Strafprozess
gegen den jüdischen Journalisten Sahl-Sobieski, der im Ghetto von Łódź
(Litzmannstadt) Angehöriger der jüdischen Lagerverwaltung war, das KZ
Auschwitz überlebt hat und sich nun, 20 Jahre nach dem Ende des Krieges,
selbst als Kriegsverbrecher anklagt, weil er in den letzten Kriegstagen zwei
jüdische Mitflüchtlinge verraten und so ihren Tod verschuldet habe. Im
Vorfeld dieses Prozesses, der, je nach Position der Beteiligten, skandalisiert,
bagatellisiert oder pathologisiert wird, lässt Robert Neumann ein ganzes
Kaleidoskop unterschiedlichster Personen aufeinander treffen – Zeugen und
Journalisten, angereist aus Israel, den USA, aus West- und Ostdeutschland,
Verteidiger,   Staatsanwalt,   Nebenkläger   und   einen   von   der
Selbstbezichtigung Sahl-Sobieskis als ehemaliger SS-Mann schwer
belasteten einheimischen Bürgermeisterkandidaten. Es sind nicht nur die
Fakten der Vergangenheit, die Neumann im wechselnden Aufeinandertreffen
der Personen, sozusagen in einem diskursiven Prozess vor dem Prozess, ans
Licht bringt, es ist vor allem auch die Art und Weise, wie sich die daran
Beteiligten seither mit diesen Fakten arrangiert, wie sie sie umerzählt,
umgeschrieben, handhabbar gemacht, wie sie sich ihren „guten Glauben"

zurecht gerückt haben – bis es einem von ihnen, eben dem Journalisten Sahl-Sobieski, das Schweigen verschlägt. Als Beispiel dafür nur ein Zitat:

> „Diese Krähen hacken einander kein Auge aus" hieß der Artikel, auf den hin der Bonner Minister über den französischen Gesandten bewirkte, daß die Agence ihn nach Südamerika versetzen wollte. Worauf er seine Kündigung nahm und in Deutschland blieb, als freier Schriftsteller und Journalist. Denn es faszinierte ihn, er reiste kreuz-quer, seine Nerven zitterten von Meldung zu Meldung. Der Vertriebenenminister, der selbst ein Blutrichter gewesen war. Diese Heimatvertriebenen selbst. Kameradschaftstreffen der SS, da, dort und überall. Das Soldatenblatt, die Soldatenverlage, die Groschenhefte, würg stich und schieß, und wie hoch der Prozentsatz der Beamten des Außenamts übernommen von Ribbentrop, und wie viele vom Major aufwärts in der Kriminalpolizei die nicht vorher in der Gestapo gewesen waren? Laß einen Staatsanwalt nur den Gedanken hegen, einen getarnten Kriegsverbrecher zu fangen – wie groß die Chance, daß der nicht schon binnen vierundzwanzig Stunden von der Kripo den vertraulichen Tip hat und sich nach Argentinien absetzt, nach Peru Brasilien nach Südafrika nach Ägypten? Kam es trotzdem zu einem Prozeß – wie war die Bilanz der Prozesse? Die Quersumme, von den Staatsanwälten selber errechnet: vor diesen deutschen Richtern war ein massakrierter Jude durchschnittlich zehn Minuten Gefängnis wert. Massakrier tausend Juden mit Weib und Kind – du kommst billiger weg als wenn du beim nächsten Grünkrämer einbrichst und zehn Mark aus der Kasse raubst [...].[36]

Über dieses Buch, das Neumann selbst als eines seiner wichtigsten, sogar als eine Art Vermächtnis angesehen hat, wäre vieles zu sagen: Über die aufklärerische Funktion der Verschränkung von Opfer- und Täterrolle in der Figur des Protagonisten Sahl-Sobieski; über das Verhältnis von Satire und Dokumentation oder dasjenige von Realität und Fiktion insbesondere hinsichtlich des Schlüsselroman-Charakters, den es ebenfalls besitzt. Nach seinem Erscheinen wurde *Der Tatbestand* äußerst kontrovers in den Feuilletons diskutiert, ist aber heute, ebenso wie fast alles Andere von Robert Neumann, so gut wie vollständig vergessen. Mir scheint jedoch, dass *Der Tatbestand* eines derjenigen Bücher Robert Neumanns ist, die unbedingt wieder den Druck und die Regale gehören würden: als ein gewichtiges und in seiner Art einzigartiges Dokument im Rahmen vieler Diskussionen, die auch aktuell noch über die Frage nach dem tatsächlichen wie dem literarischen, dem vergangenen wie dem gegenwärtigen Umgang mit der Nazivergangenheit und mit Auschwitz geführt werden.
Im Jahr 1947 hatte der Wiener Professor Ferdinand Kögl an der Universität Wien um einen Professorentitel für Robert Neumann eingereicht. Man gab

ihm den Bescheid, dass solche Ehrenprofessuren nur an österreichische Staatsbürger verliehen würden.[37] Anfang der 70er Jahre bemühte sich der Abendroth-Schüler Friedrich-Martin Balzer an der Marburger Philipps-Universität um einen Ehrendoktortitel für Neumann.[38] Das scheiterte an den aufgeheizten politischen Animositäten: Neumanns Freund, der Marburger Politologie-Professor Wolfgang Abendroth, war an der Universität als Kommunist verschrien, seine Kinder wurden in der Schule geschnitten,[39] kein passender Bürge also für einen Ehrendoktor. Im Januar 1975 forderte Klaus Rainer Röhl in der Zeitschrift *das da* den Nobelpreis für Robert Neumann.[40] Doch war der *konkret*-Herausgeber und Ehemann der späteren RAF-Terroristin Ulrike Meinhof natürlich kein Fürsprecher, auf den die literarische Elite oder gar ein Nobel-Komitee hätten hören können. Abgesehen aber von nicht vergebenen Preisen und verflossenen politischen Lagern: Dreißig Jahre nach seinem Tode wäre es wieder und immer noch an der Zeit, Robert Neumann wieder zu lesen. Schließlich schrieb Rudolph Walter Leonhardt schon 1976 in dem nach Neumanns Tod erschienenen Band *Typisch Robert Neumann* im Vorwort:

> Der Generation der heute Zwanzig- bis Vierzigjährigen sei es überlassen zu entscheiden, welche Rolle dieser Robert Neumann gespielt und was er bewirkt hat. Dafür freilich müssen diese Jungen seine Bücher lesen. Und das gerade wollte er – mehr als alles andere.[41]

Anmerkungen

[1] So Neumann selbst in seiner Autobiographie *Vielleicht das Heitere. Bericht über mich selbst und Zeitgenossen* (Wien/München/Basel: Desch, 1963), S. 529. Vgl. dazu Richard Dove: „Almost an English Author: Robert Neumann's English-Language Novels", in *German Life and Letters*, 51 (1998), S. 93-105.

[2] Vgl. auch ebd., S. 104 f.

[3] Neben dem genannten Aufsatz zum Beispiel Richard Dove, „ ‚Ein Experte des Überlebens': Robert Neumann in British Exile 1933-45", in *Aliens – Uneingebürgerte. German and Austrian Writers in Exile*, hrsg. von Ian Wallace (Amsterdam/Atlanta: Rodopi, 1994), S. 159-73. Ders.: *Aliens: Authors and Others. German-speaking Refugees in Britain 1933-1945* (University of Greenwich: Inaugural Lectures Series, 27th January 2000) sowie ders., *Journey of No Return. Five German-speaking Literary Exiles in Britain, 1933-1945* (London: Libris, 2000).

[4] (London: Gollancz, 1946).

[5] (München: Desch, 1965).

[6] Robert Neumann, *Vielleicht das Heitere. Tagebuch aus einem anderen Jahr* (München/Wien/Basel: Desch, 1968), S. 142.

[7] ÖNB Ser. n. 22.479. Für den Hinweis auf diesen Brief danke ich Herrn Dr. Franz Stadler (Wien). Von einer Resonanz auf diesen Brief Neumanns ist allerdings nichts bekannt.

[8] Klaus Amann, *P.E.N. Politik, Emigration, Nationalsozialismus. Ein österreichischer Schriftstellerclub* (Wien/Köln/Graz: Böhlau, 1984).

[9] Zit. nach ebd., S. 92.

[10] Kreutz an Fontana, 8.5.1947. Zit. nach ebd., S. 89.

[11] *Der Turm. Österreichische Monatsschrift für Kultur*, 4/5, (Jg. 1, 1945), S. 109. Vgl. zu dieser Thematik auch den Beitrag von Anthony Bushell im vorliegenden Band.

[12] Vgl. nochmals Amann: *P.E.N.*, insbes. S. 95 ff.

[13] Noch 1976 stellt Volker Kaukoreit fest, Robert Neumann, „obwohl gebürtiger Wiener", sei „selten für Österreich reklamiert worden" und merkt an: „Der Große Österreichische Staatspreis hätte Robert Neumann ebenso gut angestanden wie etwa Johannes Urzidil", in *Die zeitgenössische Literatur Österreichs*. Hrsg. von Hilde Spiel. Zürich/München 1976, S. 150 (= *Kindlers Literaturgeschichte der Gegenwart. Autoren, Werke, Themen, Tendenzen seit 1945*).

[14] Robert Neumann, *Ein leichtes Leben*, (Wien/München/Basel: Desch 1963), S. 188.

[15] Robert Neumann, *Children of Vienna*, (London: Gollancz 1946), S. 4.

[16] „1933 verbrannten und verboten die Nazis meine Bücher – ich hatte sie bekämpft und verhöhnt und gehaßt und war ein Jude und Sozialist. Ich ging ins Exil, nach England" erinnert sich Neumann in seinem postum erschienenen „Bericht über mich selbst", in *Typisch Robert Neumann. Eine Auswahl*, hrsg. von Helga Heller-Neumann (München: Desch, 1976), S. 16.

[17] Elisabeth Freundlich, „Die Welt Robert Neumanns", In: *Robert Neumann: Stimmen der Freunde. Der Romancier und sein Werk. Zum 60. Geburtstag am 22. Mai 1957*. (Wien/München/Basel: Desch 1957), S. 63-131, hier S. 76 und 77.

[18] „Mißratene Kinder? – Mißratenes Buch! Notwendige Korrektur eines verzerrten Bildes von Wien und seiner Jugend", in *Neues Österreich*, 6. Mai 1948, S. 3 f.

[19] ÖNB Ser.n.21.634.

[20] Vgl. den Brief von Ruth Stock-Rother an Friedrich Martin-Balzer vom 15. April 1976 aus München: „Sie werden Verständnis dafür haben, wenn ich nicht viel Worte verliere und denke, daß Sie nicht weniger erschüttert sein werden, wie gute Freunde von Helga es bis heute noch sind. Helga ist letztes Jahr am 18. Mai innerhalb weniger Wochen an einer unheilbaren Krankheit gestorben."

[21] Zu Bibiana Santis vgl. die interessante Interpretation von Nicole Brunnhuber in ihrem Buch: *The Faces of Janus. English-language Fiction by German-speaking Exiles in Great Britain, 1933-45* (Oxford u.a.: Peter Lang 2005; = Exil-Studien Bd. 8), S. 90-111.

[22] Vgl. auch Scheck, *Die Prosa Robert Neumanns* (1985), S. 75 f.

[23] „Mit fremden Federn. Jagd auf Menschen und Gespenster: Robert Neumann", in *Der Spiegel*, 27. August 1952, S. 29-33.

[24] Vgl. zu diesem Thema übergreifend zum Beispiel Stefan Braese, *Die andere Erinnerung. Jüdische Autoren in der westdeutschen Nachkriegsliteratur* (Berlin/Wien: Philo, 2001).

[25] Neumann, *Vielleicht das Heitere* (München 1968), S. 64 f.

[26] Robert Neumann, „Bericht über mich selbst", in *Typisch Robert Neumann. Eine Auswahl.* Mit einem Vorwort von Rudolf Walter Leonhardt, S. 13-19, S.18.

[27] Vgl. dazu Anne Maximiliane Jäger: „ ‚Eine so vielfältige Verwechslung ...' – Frauenliebe und Eros der Macht in Robert Neumanns Roman *Festival* (1962)", *LiLi. Zeitschrift für Literaturwissenschaft und Linguistik,* 135, Jg. 34 (2005), S. 87-109.

[28] Vgl. Holger Pils, „Die Begegnung der Hochstapler oder: von der Vertracktheit der Aggression. Robert Neumanns *Olympia* als Parodie auf Thomas Manns *Bekenntnisse des Hochstaplers Felix Krull* ", in *Germanica,* 35 (2004), S. 91-104.

[29] Vgl. zum Beispiel die umfangreiche und außerordentlich positive Besprechung von Hartmut von Hentig, „Vom Wert der Umwertung. *Die Kinder von Wien* des Robert Neumann", in *Merkur. Deutsche Zeitschrift für europäisches Denken,* 32/3 (1975), S. 287-93.

[30] Vgl. dazu demnächst Jörg Thunecke, „Täuschung und Selbsttäuschung: Variationen über ein Thema in Robert Neumanns Roman *Blind Man's Buff* ", in Anne Maximiliane Jäger (Hg.), *„Einmal Emigrant – immer Emigrant"? Der Schriftsteller und Publizist Robert Neumann (1897-1975),* (München: Edition text&kritik 2006).

[31] Zumal im Rahmen der Autobiographieforschung wäre es außerordentlich lohnend, diesen Zusammenhang einmal nach zu zeichnen und den Ursprung der Autobiographie aus der literarischen Trauerarbeit zu verfolgen – ein anderes und eigenes Thema.

[32] Vgl. dazu Anne Maximiliane Jäger: „ ‚Was uns interessiert, ist: der Hörer lacht' – Lachen, Witz und Parodie bei Robert Neumann", in Arnd Beise/Ariane Martin/Udo Roth (Hg.): *LachArten. Zur ästhetischen Repräsentation des Lachens vom späten 17. Jahrhundert bis zur Gegenwart* (Bielefeld: Aisthesis, 2003), S. 213-34.

[33] 29. März und 24. April 1949. ÖNB Ser.n. 21.609.

[34] Robert Neumann: *Ein leichtes Leben.* (Wien/München/Basel: Desch 1963), S. 528 f.

[35] Sie ist dokumentiert in dem Band von Reinhard Hübsch/Friedrich-Martin Balzer (Hg.), *„Operation Mauerdurchlöcherung". Robert Neumann und der deutsch-deutsche Dialog* (Bonn: Pahl-Rugenstein Nachf., 1994).

[36] Robert Neumann, *Der Tatbestand* (München: Desch, 1965), S. 291f.

[37] Hinweis von Dr. Franz Stadler (Wien), dem ich dafür herzlich danke.

[38] Für die persönliche Mitteilung danke ich Dr. Friedrich-Martin Balzer (Marburg).

[39] Wolfgang Abendroths und seiner Familie Situation in Marburg schildert Neumann in seinem Tagebuch *Vielleicht das Heitere,* S. 267.

[40] Klaus Rainer Röhl, „Nobelpreis für Robert Neumann!", in *das da,* Nr. 1 (1975), S. 52.

[41] *Typisch Robert Neumann* (1976), S. 12.

Many Happy Returns? Attitudes to Exile in Austria's Literary and Cultural Journals in the early Post-war Years

Anthony Bushell

This article seeks to shed light on the manner in which exile was regarded in immediate post-war Austria by those who had remained in the country. The future reception of those émigrés attempting to re-establish themselves in Austria after 1945 was shaped in large measure by the initial and far from uncritical stance of those in positions of influence who in many cases had not belonged to the exile community. The article concentrates principally on the experience of Austrian writers and the debates conducted in the broad spectrum of the country's early and influential literary journals.

The significance of the role of Austria's literary and cultural journals immediately following the collapse of the Third Reich in 1945 has long been acknowledged.[1] This position of influence was to be short-lived, as were indeed many of the titles, but for a few years after the Second World War these journals exercised considerable influence not only in the domain of literary taste but also in forming and directing public opinion. Despite the restrictions of allied censorship, paper shortages and the problems of production and distribution amidst the privations of post-war Austria, these journals enjoyed a brief moment of prominence helped by an apparently insatiable appetite for information from a population now free of the obvious distortions of National Socialist propaganda. Until the currency reform of November 1947 and the gradual restoration of industrial production to meet the material needs of the population these journals found a ready market amongst a population whose meagre purchasing power had few other commodities available to it.

It is therefore illuminating in the context of 'Austria in Exile' to see how these journals responded to the theme of exile and the extent to which they acknowledged – or failed to acknowledge – the experience of exile. Certainly for those Austrians considering returning to Austria after May 1945 the handling of the issue of exile in these journals was to give an early indication to the sort of reception they might expect, whilst, with the benefit of hindsight, those who are now researching the complex issue of exile can see how the points were being set for the emerging debate.

An initial consideration of attitudes towards exile and to those who had been forced to flee Austria might invite the assumption that exile would be an unchallenged and even perhaps a dominant theme in these early publications, especially in those journals devoted to the literary and cultural restoration of an independent Austria. It was, after all, especially for writers that exile had been particularly painful. Whereas musicians, scientists, architects, painters and many other categories of intellectuals were free – in theory at least – to continue to practise their professions when once established in their new world, writers with few exceptions could not. Their lifeblood was the German language and it was only within a German-speaking world that they, with few exceptions, could ply their trade. And the position and status of Austrian writers in exile had been markedly difficult for it has been claimed that no land occupied by the fascists, not even the German Reich itself, could show a higher proportion of its writers forced into involuntary exile than Austria.[2] For this reason there was a particular urgency, from their perspective, to have their years spent outside of Austria acknowledged and to be awarded some form of status that could constitute a platform for restoring or resuming their careers in a post-war, denazified Austria. Supporting such an expectation was the fact that a number of the dominant personalities and editors behind these publications, such as Hermann Hakel, editor of *Lynkeus*, Bruno Frei of the *Österreichisches Tagebuch* and the sedulous and ubiquitous Hans Weigel, were themselves returnees from exile. Yet the treatment of exile in the early post-war journals was to be far from simple or clear-cut. And in this paper I hope to demonstrate both the range of responses and the implications of the position taken in these various publications.

The immediate problems were naturally of a very fundamental, material nature. In the chaotic circumstances following the collapse of the Third Reich it was often impossible to establish any reliable information about the men and women, the writers and artists who had left Austria. Their whereabouts, or simply news that they were still alive, were matters of conjecture. This uncertainty even extended to artists who had enjoyed some degree of prominence before the Anschluss. Typical of the tone of uncertainty, almost a year after the war had ended, is the following short gloss devoted to Oskar Kokoschka in a 1946 issue of Otto Basil's journal *Plan:*

> Zehn Jahre ist es her, daß eine letzte große Kollektivausstellung in Wien von seinem Schaffen Kunde gab. Seitdem tröpfelte es nur noch ab und zu einmal spärliche Nachrichten über ihn, die bald nach der Besetzung Österreichs ganz aufhörte. Auch heute weiß man noch kaum mehr von der Entwicklung dieses Künstlers während des letzten Jahrzehnts.[3]

The nature of the challenge, however, for those Austrians who had remained in the country throughout the Anschluss years, of coming to terms with the host of Austrians who had gone into exile was more than one of merely filling in the information gaps. And in many respects the issues were compounded by factors that were not present in the two post-war Germanys. It was clear from which Germany and for what reasons many Germans had fled after 1933 – and in opting to return after 1945 to either East or West Germany it was also often evident in a rudimentary way to which type of Germany those who had been in exile were hoping to return. By contrast, the issue in Austria was far from straightforward. Those Austrians in exile were not all refugees from the Nazi invasion in 1938, for some had left the country during the Dollfuß and Schuschnigg regimes when both socialists and communists had been forced underground. And in the early years after 1945 the status of post-war Austria was still to be clarified – was it to be a legal restoration of the Austria invaded by Hitler, or of the corporate state of 1934, or some pre-Republican evocation, or perhaps a new Danubian structure such as favoured by Churchill? It was therefore a matter of speculation which Austria would have the task of beckoning back many of its leading intellectuals and artists, and there was a natural and understandable reluctance amongst many Austrians in exile to consider returning until these matters had been resolved.

It is for this reason that the tone set by the journals in their treatment of exile was to be so important and for many in exile the debate must have proved disappointing since it quickly became apparent that the fate of those in exile was not of paramount concern within Austria.

It is widely agreed that the position of Austrians in exile had not been helped by the lack of a formally acknowledged and effective Austrian government in exile similar to those that spoke for many other states overrun by the Nazis. The absence of such a government in exile meant that power in post-war Austria never passed out of the hands of those who had remained in the country throughout the war years and into the hands of those who had not. An Austrian government in exile with the backing of the Allies would have shifted the balance of power in favour of those who had been in exile and on returning to a liberated Austria it is wholly conceivable that the status and patronage awarded to those who had left Austria would have been very different to the attitudes displayed by Renner's and Figl's early administrations. But it was not only the lack of a government in exile that undermined the status of exile in the eyes of those who had remained in Austria; more recently there has been justified speculation at the absence of a specific Austrian *Literaturwissenschaft* in exile and the implications this had on the fortunes of writers who had left Austria.[4] The existence of a self-conscious and vocal scholarly community abroad recognizing and promoting the work of Austrian writers during and after the occupation of the country would have done much to enhance their status and their claim for a place in the new Austrian order after 1945. That such a discipline did not emerge had much to do with the state of Germanistik in Austrian universities in the years before the war. Many departments of German, and certainly many prominent Austrian academics in the field of German literature at Austrian universities, moved very closely to the position encountered in German universities, and a notion of a specifically Austrian tradition was jettisoned in favour of ethnic concepts of a literary community, which placed Austria firmly within the greater Reich. By the time of the great exodus from Austrian universities a generation of younger Germanists had been trained without a sense of the specifically Austrian tradition. Perversely the restoration of an independent Austria in 1945 with its understandable and urgent desire to establish a concept of Austrianness to the exclusion of all things German – a cultural trend that was to disconcert Hans Weigel so much – only served to diminish yet further the status of German literature written in exile for if Austria distanced itself from Germany then it followed that Austrian literature need not take particular heed of the work and achievement of German writers in exile since their work belonged to a German literature and to a German canon and was consequently of no pressing concern to a restored Austria.

The concern for many of these early journals was first and foremost to establish a sense of continuity with the Austria from before the Anschluss. Continuity went hand in hand with a claim to legitimacy for those who had not left Austria and this brought into immediate and stark relief a point of conflict between those who had gone into exile and those who had not. In countless articles and manifestos of intent the various literary and cultural journals invoked an earlier Austria with which post-war Austria must now reconnect. Characteristic of the intensity of feeling was the conclusion to an article in one of the earliest editions of *Der Turm* entitled 'Die Zukunft der Geisteswissenschaften':

> ... die österreichische Forschung [knüpft] an ihre alten, traditionellen, organisch gewachsenen, aus ihrer Geschichte und Lage entspringenden, in die glanzvolle Barockperiode zurückreichenden universalen Ausblicke und Beziehungen an.[5]

There is no mention at any point in this article of any possible enrichment that Austrian scholars in the Diaspora might bring to this restitution of an Austrian tradition. This emphasis on a seamless reconnection with a pre-1938 Austria found its most notorious expression in the very next edition of *Der Turm* at the close of 1945. This was Alexander Lernet-Holenia's infamous letter to the editor, Egon Seefehlner, which sought to see the years of Hitler's occupation as nothing more than an irksome interruption: 'In der

Tat brauchen wir nur fortzusetzen, wo uns die Träume eines Irren unterbrochen haben.' More tellingly within the context of attitudes to exile and the value of the experiences of those in exile were Lernet-Holenia's following words:

> In der Tat brauchen wir nicht voraus-, sondern nur zurückzublicken. Um es vollkommen klar zu sagen: wir haben es nicht nötig, mit der Zukunft zu kokettieren und nebulose Projekte zu machen, wir *sind*, im besten und wertvollsten Verstande, unsere Vergangenheit, wir haben nur zu besinnen, daß wir unsere Vergangenheit sind – und sie wird unsere Zukunft werden. Auch das Ausland wird kein neues, es wird, im Grunde, das alte Österreich von uns erwarten.[6]

If the years of the Anschluss could be eradicated from Austrians' consciousness as the country re-grafted itself onto the body from which it had been momentarily severed then such an act brought with it the prospect that the experience of exile could also be forgotten since a direct line of continuity could be re-established with the Austria before the Anschluss. A note of maliciousness enters the argument concerning the most illustrious of all German writers in exile: Thomas Mann. Even for the Austrian journals the debate concerning his return was of intense importance. Mann was regarded as the flagship of German cultural integrity in the world's eyes. Many felt that his continued absence from Europe was an unspoken condemnation of the German-speaking world, whilst his return from America would be regarded as a signal that the odium of National Socialism had been lifted. Whilst many readers' letters to the various journals argued for Mann's return other voices condemned the debate as humiliating pleading. Lernet-Holenia appears at first sight to acknowledge Mann's achievements. He praises the Nobel Prize winner's earlier work, yet his article is undeniably barbed for he suggests in an aside that exile can diminish an artist's abilities: 'Es ist hier nicht der Ort, um zu untersuchen, ob ein Dichter nur inmitten seines eigenen Volkes Bedeutendes leisten könne oder ob etwa das intensive Zusammenleben mit einem anderen Volk seinen Hervorbringungen schade.' The article concludes with a suggestion that the experience of the war years has left a division between those who experienced them in Austria and those who had not, and Lernet-Holenia's article leaves the impression that although he and his fellow Austrians did not begrudge the physical and material safety of those like Mann who had gone into exile, nevertheless those who remained were left with the greater task: 'Was uns anlangt, die wir diesseits des Weltmeeres geblieben sind, wollen wir bemüht sein, die Last, die uns auferlegt ist, auf unsere Art weiterzutragen, wenngleich sie ins Enorme gewachsen ist.'[7]

The passions enflamed by the debate concerning Mann's possible return from exile were, however, muted when set against the debate centred on Josef Weinheber, the most popular of Austrian poets in the inter-war years. His early flirtation with National Socialism had led him in the final days of the war to take his own life, conscious of the degree to which he had compromised himself as an artist. No debate about an émigré writer or poet and the privations and hardships they had endured in exile matched the intense argument for or against Weinheber's literary rehabilitation that took place within the pages of these journals.

It had been the common experience of many who returned to Austria after 1945 to be told that they had had the easier lot, having being spared both the Allied bombings and the atrocities of the invading Red Army. In the pages of these post-war journals it is even possible to find those returning from exile, or simply writing from exile, pandering to this popular conception held by locals of the life led by those who had fled the country. Clemens Holzmeister, who had spent the war years as a distinguished architect in Istanbul begins his 'Brief nach Österreich' in a 1946 edition of *Der Turm* with words that are little short of an apology:

> Sosehr es mein Herz bewegt, nach langer Nacht über Österreich
> mit diesem Brief wieder in den altvertrauten Kulturkreis treten zu
> dürfen, so erfaßt mich nach acht Jahren völliger Abtrennung von
> ihm doch jenes Unbehagen, das ich kurz so ausdrücken darf: Mir
> ist es immer gut gegangen, Euch allen aber schlecht.[8]

A yet more remarkable reversal of perceptions was surely that offered by a member of the British Council in Vienna writing in late 1945 in *Der Turm* on 'Britische Kultur im Krieg'. It must have pleased and flattered Austrian readers to learn that the six years of war had not meant Austria's cultural isolation but rather Britain's: 'Für englische Kunstliebhaber war die fast sechs Jahre während Trennung von der kulturellen Tradition des Festlandes und insbesondere von der Heimat der modernen Musik, Wien, eine der ganz großen Tragödien des Krieges.'[9]

Several of the early post-war journals were associated strongly with a conservative and Catholic stance. In its opening programme of May 1946 the journal *Austria*, which bore the sub-title *Die Welt im Spiegel Österreichs. Zeitschrift für Kultur und Geistesleben*, acknowledged the Christian values upon which Austria's renewal would be based. In such a context it is difficult to see how Austrians of the Jewish faith, who had made up, of course, a significant element of those writers in exile, could feel that this new Austria was opening up to receive them. The journal *Austria* did not turn its back on Austrians in exile. It ran a number of articles on distinguished Austrian artists and scholars abroad, yet even these pieces followed a certain pattern. Either in their own words or in articles about them these pieces demonstrated these artists' continued loyalty to Austria and the Austrian idea, thus a piece on the composer Karl Weigl entitled 'Ein österreichischer Musiker in Amerika' concludes with the words: 'Es wäre gewiß die Pflicht der österreichischen Heimat, dieses bedeutenden Musikers, der ihr auch in der Ferne die Treue bewahrt hat, des öfteren in Aufführungen zu gedenken.'[10] In an article published in the same year the composer and musicologist Egon Wellesz, who had studied with Schönberg and had associated with Berg and Webern, wrote a personal reminiscence from his college at Oxford, where he had found refuge after leaving Austria abruptly in 1938. His conclusion must have corresponded closely to the journal's preferred view of Austrians in exile for Wellesz expresses gratitude for the life he has been able to lead at Oxford but simultaneously expresses his indebtedness and continued allegiance to his home: 'Und ich betrachte es als ein Glück, daß ich in der großen österreichischen Tradition aufgewachsen bin und jetzt hier, dem Zentrum des englischen geistigen Lebens, wirken kann.'[11] The journal *Austria* certainly had no misconceptions concerning the nature of that tradition for immediately following Egon Wellesz's contribution the journal printed an article by the discredited Germanist Josef Nadler devoted to Grillparzer. Nor was the journal slow to denounce what it perceived to be the destructive influence of Austrians in exile. It claimed that the British public's critical if not hostile view of Austria was in part the result of émigré groups fighting internal squabbles to the detriment of Austria as a whole:

> Abgeschnitten vom wirklichen Geschehen in der Heimat, erging man sich in überspitzten Debatten, wie sie meist zum psychologischen Typ der Emigration gehören. In Sonderheit geisterte das unselige innenpolitische Krisenjahr von 1934 fort und trübte immer wieder die Atmosphäre.[12]

That all was not well amongst Austrian émigré circles was clear for any reader to see, and the literary émigrés themselves contributed to this picture of internal divisions and rivalries. The poet Ernst Waldinger, writing from New York for the journal *Plan*, pulls no punches in the introduction to his article, proclaiming: 'Der innere Zwiespalt der Vertriebenen ist verständlich. Ihre enttäuschte Liebe zur ursprünglichen Heimat hat sich in einen verkrampften und neurotischen Haß verwandelt.' Waldinger is anxious to inform his readers back in Austria of the existence of stark social differences between the various contingents of emigrants and takes the opportunity in his article from America to attack both Thomas Mann and Franz Werfel.[13]

For those Austrians who had been denied access to the outside world for so many years impressions of life in countries from which they were still debarred after 1945 by virtue of travel restrictions or lack of funds were of great importance and many of the journals offered variations of letters from abroad. But with the onset of cold-war politics these impressions from those who had been or were still living abroad served more than informational purposes. Readers of the *Österreichisches Tagebuch*, which had pronounced communist sympathies, could learn that life in the capitalist west was far from attractive. Describing her return to Austria after eight years of exile in London one correspondent told her readers of her last tour of London before her return to Vienna:

> Diese Arbeiterviertel im Süden Londons sind alle einander gleich. Dieselben einförmigen Straßen, mit Häusern, die eins wie das andere sind, erbaut von demselben Bauspekulanten; mit spielenden Kindern im Rinnstein, weil es keine Gärten und keine Parkanlagen gibt für sie; und Schmutz und Verfall, von dessen Trostlosigkeit man sich keine Vorstellung machen kann.[14]

Negative views of life in the supposedly better-off West were reinforced by negative connotations in the vocabulary to describe exile. The Catholic-orientated weekly *Die Furche*, founded in December 1945 by Friedrich Funder and a major outlet for the energetic young historian Friedrich Heer,[15] was attacked by the *Österreichisches Tagebuch* for its printing of an article by Wenzel Jaksch on the position of ethnic Germans in Czechoslovakia. *Österreichisches Tagebuch* denounced the author as a member of the 'notorious' London 'Emigrantenkomitee des Faschistengenerals Prchala'.[16] Increasing this distancing from countries in the West that had given shelter to many Austrian emigrants were articles by the *Österreichisches Tagebuch* such as one devoted to the Portuguese resistance, which reminded its readers that the dictatorship of Salazar was propped up by Washington and London.[17] It is difficult to resist the conclusion that in drawing such a negative picture of life in the capitalist west doubts were being sown about the validity and usefulness of any insights brought back by Austrians who had spent their years of exile in those countries and who might express some form of positive commitment to the values they had encountered there.

The real value of exile for the early post-war journals becomes particularly apparent in three recurring topics. The first was the heartfelt issue of the 'Heimkehrer'. The topic is raised on countless occasions and it invariably referred not to those who were in exile but to those Austrians who were still detained by the Allies, especially by the Soviets, after having served in the armed forces of the Reich. The journal *Austria* in a plaintive article entitled 'Laßt sie heimfinden!' called for the return not of the émigrés but of the Austrian soldiers who had fought in Hitler's army, suggesting that each man, now shorn of all illusions, will be the carrier of the new Austrian identity;

> Aus der Sinnlosigkeit des Dritten Reiches wuchs sein Sinn für und sein Glaube an Österreich. Die moderne Sklaverei der Kriegsgefangenschaft ließ diese Männer alles Leid des Menschentums durchmachen. Die Heimat rief und lockte mit tausend Stimmen. So ist ihre Heimkehr der Schlußakt der Tragödie eines ganzen Volkes.[18]

It is difficult to find impassioned pleas of a similar nature for the return of those in exile. Indeed one contributor to a 1946 edition of *Plan* succeeds in uniting the issue of the Heimkehrer with a concept of collective guilt and thus eradicating any special status that might be given to those who had gone into exile as an act of resistance:

> Gibt es heute einen Menschen in Österreich, egal ob er die Jahre nationalsozialistischer Herrschaft im Zuchthaus, KZ oder an der Front verbracht hat, der nicht irgendwie für das nazistische System mitverantwortlich ist? Selbst diejenigen, welche aktiv am Kampf gegen den Faschismus teilgenommen haben, sind von dieser Mitverantwortung nicht loszusprechen, weil es ihnen nicht gelungen ist, die Kräfte unseres Volkes gegen die damalige reaktionäre Regierung zu mobilisieren.[19]

The second area in which the relative insignificance of exile became apparent was the many reviews of Austria a year or so on from the downfall of the Reich. The Vice-Chancellor of the University of Graz, Professor Josef Dobretsberger, who before the war had been a minister in Schuschnigg's government but had been too open to the left to remain in office, wrote a long essay in the *Österreichisches Tagebuch* published on 2 November 1946 reviewing the 'Probleme des Wiederaufbaues in Österreich'. As with many similar reviews looking at what had been achieved and what had still to be done Dobretsberger makes no mention of the Austrians in exile. They do not appear either as a resource of new ideas or as possible ambassadors that could bring about Austria's renewal through closer cooperation with the countries in which they had found exile during the Anschluss period and they form no part of Dobretsberger's analysis of the problems facing Austria or the new order that is needed:

> Hinter diesen Fragen steht jedoch die viel tiefer gehende
> Gesamtproblematik unserer Wirtschafts- und Gesellschafts-
> ordnung. Sie hatte sich schon vor dem Krieg in Spannungen und
> Bürgerkriegen angekündigt, sie ist aber heute vollends
> offentsichtlich. Wir stehen an einem jener Wendepunkte der
> Geschichte, die immer wieder, wenn ein Zeitalter zu Ende geht,
> zu neuen Formen des Erwerbslebens, Kulturschaffens und
> Staatsgefüges überleiten. Es sind dies die Zeiten schmerzhafter
> Krisen, in denen eine neue Gesellschaft geboren wird.[20]

Dobretsberger's own exile had been spent in the Near and Middle
East yet he could find no place for that experience in Austria's renewal. In
that same month in 1946 *Österreichisches Tagebuch* printed a review of the
state of Austrian literature and the challenges that faced it. The author, Eva
Priester, although born in Russia and standing close to the Communist cause,
had spent her exile in London. Her long article describes the present parlous
state of Austrian literature and Austrian publishing and declares Marxism to
be the only possible way for writers not only to understand the world but to
find the basis for being a good writer. As in the case of Dobretsberger's
article, exile itself is not offered as a potentially significant intellectual
reservoir for the new Austria nor is there any mention of any works of
literature produced by Austrians in exile. For Priester the experience of exile
is almost dismissed in the renewal of Austrian literature:

> Ein kleiner Sektor [...], der vom Ausland her im Rahmen der
> Möglichkeiten der Auslandbewegungen und jedes einzelnen darin
> am Kampf gegen Nazideutschland teilnahm, ist zahlenmäßig zu
> gering und, vor allem noch immer geographisch so zerstreut, daß
> er kaum in Erscheinung tritt.[21]

Yet it was in a third domain that the low status of the experience of
exile could be clearly and painfully felt and with telling implications for the
immediate future. Many of the early journals made an effort to attract a
young readership and to engage with young Austrians both as readers and as
possible contributors to the new Austria. Amongst those contributions there
is a striking failure to acknowledge those in exile or the validity of the
experience of exile. In Otto Basil's *Plan*, under the rubric 'Tribüne der
Jungen', Peter Rubel proclaimed 'Wir alle sind schuldig!', thus according
the émigrés no special status nor acknowledging them as a source of
inspiration for the younger generation. Rubel's article implies that the
generation above his, without any differentiation, constitutes an impediment
and the young must now replace them if Austria is not to stagnate: '*Heute*
können wir noch die ältere Generation für die Katastrophe der

Vergangenheit haftbar machen. *Ab morgen* sind aber wir Jungen für das Weltgeschehen verantwortlich!'[22]

Not all young contributors would accept any sense of guilt falling on their own generation but nevertheless they would share the conviction that a division now stood between the generations. The young Walter Toman, one of the most productive of the younger generation of writers immediately after 1945, was given room to express these opinions in the journal *Theater der Jugend* a journal which was subsequently retitled *Neue Wege*. Under both titles this publication was responsible for promoting many of Austria's first post-war generation of authors. In an article entitled 'Was wir jungen Menschen brauchen?' Toman, who was born in 1920, claims the older generation has little to offer his. The younger generation would have to work out its own concept of what Austria is to be and Toman pays not even passing attention to the possible contribution of those who went into exile for the sake of Austria :

> Unsere Väter sind müde geworden unter den schweren Hieben der letzten Jahre. Wir junge Menschen, wir sind es nicht. Wir haben keine Schuld an dem letzten Jahrzehnt [...] Unsere Väter sind noch zu nahe an der tiefen Vergangenheit, am zusammengebrochenen Imperium Österreich. Wir Jungen haben nichts mehr davon erlebt. Wir haben nur mehr die Zukunft.[23]

A year later, when the journal had beome *Neue Wege*, a dedicated section for the younger generation of readers entitled 'Der Jugend das Wort' showed that exile as a concept and as possible inspiration had still failed to impinge itself upon the young. Indeed the experience of exile lost any claim to uniqueness when one contributor under this rubric began his article with the words, 'Wir alle sind Heimkehrer aus dem Kriege'.[24]

It would be misleading to assert that individual writers returning from exile were ignored by these early post-war journals, although exile as a collective or abstract concept is rarely encountered. Admittedly, the return from exile of distinguished writers from amongst the older and established generation of writers such as Franz Theodor Csokor or Felix Braun was duly noted by these journals and space was often found for them to write their initial impressions of post-war Austria. Yet often these contributions followed a formula that amounted to a ritual: they express the emotional impact of returning to Austria after so many years of separation; they acknowledge the physical and spiritual suffering that Austrians have endured. Yet there is a noticeable lack of concrete proposals being brought back from exile or a sense that Austrians have been awaiting their return. But as one historian noted pointedly: 'Als die Exilgroßen wieder in

Österreich auftauchten, hatten die Österreicher selbst ihr Haus schon bestellt; die Kommandoposten waren vergeben.'[25]

Notes

[1] Rüdiger Wischenbart, Der *literarische Wiederaufbau in Österreich 1945-1949* (Königstein/Ts.: Hain, 1983), p. 8; Elisabeth Weber, *Österreichische Kulturzeitschriften der Nachkriegszeit 1945–1950* (Frankfurt am Main: Lang, 1988), p. 9.

[2] Siglinde Bolbecher and Konstantin Kaiser, *Lexikon der österreichischen Exilliteratur* (Vienna: Deuticke, 2000), p. 7.

[3] Anon., 'Oskar Kokoschka', *Plan*, 1, 5 (1946), p. 431.

[4] Wendelin Schmidt-Dengler, 'Literaturwissenschaft und Exil' in *Vertriebene Vernunft II: Emigration und Exil österreichischer Wissenschaft*, ed. by Friedrich Stadler (Vienna: Jugend und Volk, 1988), pp. 520-22 (p. 520).

[5] W. Sas-Zaloziecky, 'Die Zukunft der Geisteswisschenchaften', *Der Turm*, 1, 3 (1945), p. 56.

[6] Alexander Lernet-Holenia, 'Brief an den Turm', *Der Turm*, 1, 4/5 (1945), p. 109.

[7] Alexander Lernet-Holenia, 'Der Fall Thomas Mann', *Der Turm*, 1, 7 (1946), p.172.

[8] Clemens Holzmeister, 'Brief nach Österreich', *Der Turm*, 1, 12 (1946), pp. 374-77 (p. 374).

[9] J. H.Vinden, 'Britische Kultur im Krieg', *Der Turm*, 1, 4/5 (1945), pp. 110-11 (p. 110).

[10] Anon., 'Ein Östereichischer Musiker in Amerika', *Austria*, 2, 7 (1947), p. 278.

[11] Egon Wellesz, 'Gelebtes Leben', *Austria*, 2, 10 (1947), pp. 368-71 (p. 371).

[12] Dr. W. R-n [= Wilhelm Reinermann, editor of the journal], 'Österreichs politischer Kurswert – gestern und heute', *Austria*, 1, 6 (1946), pp. 37-38 (p. 38).

[13] Ernst Waldinger, 'Briefe aus der Heimat und ihre tiefere Bedeutung', *Plan*, 1, 12 (1946/47), pp. 949-52 (pp. 951-52).

[14] Anna Hornik, 'Reisebilder London-Wien', *Österreichisches Tagebuch*, 7 September 1946, p. 7.

[15] *Geschichte der Literatur in Österreich: Das 20. Jahrhundert*, ed. by Herbert Zeman (Graz: Akademische Druck- u. Verlagsanstalt, 1999), p. 555.

[16] J. Kostmann, 'Bemerkungen zur Woche', *Österreichisches Tagebuch*, 27 April 1946, pp. 2-3 (p. 3); Jenö Kostmann, journalist and Communist functionary, had spent his exile in London where he was editor-in-chief of *Zeitspiegel*, the newspaper published by the Austrian Centre.

[17] Lucien Corosi, 'Der portugiesische Widerstand', *Österreichisches Tagebuch*, 3 August 1946, p. 17.

[18] Carantanus, 'Laßt sie heimfinden!', *Austria*, 2, 12 (1947), pp. 475-76 (p. 474).

[19] Kurt Hirsch, 'Das Heimkehrerproblem', *Plan*, 1, 9 (1946), pp. 775-76 (p. 776).

[20] Josef Dobretsberger, 'Probleme des Wiederaufbaues in Österreich', *Österreichisches Tagebuch*, 2 November 1946, pp. 2-3 (p. 3).

[21] Eva Priester, 'Die Aufgaben der österreichischen Literatur', *Österreichisches Tagebuch*, 16 November 1946, pp. 3-5 (p. 3).

[22] Peter Rubel, 'Wir sind alle schuldig!', *Plan*, 1, 9 (1946), pp. 781-83 (p. 783).

[23] Walter Toman, 'Was wir jungen Menschen brauchen?', *Theater der Jugend*, 22, 8 April 1947, pp. 1-2 (p. 1).

[24] Franz Robert Mayer, 'Arbeiten, nicht verzweifeln!', *Neue Wege*, 35, 15 May 1948, p. 193.

[25] Helmut Andics, *Österreich 1804-1974*, vol. 4, (Munich: Goldmann, 1984), p. 79.

Index

Yearbook of the Research Centre for German and Austrian Exile Studies, Volume 9 (2007)

Volume 9 of the Yearbook will publish a selection of Papers from the Conference 'Refugee Archives: Theory and Practice' to be held at the Centre for German-Jewish Studies, University of Sussex, Brighton, 11-13 April 2007 An International Conference to mark the launch of the Online Database of British Archival Resources Relating to German-speaking Refugees, 1933-1950 (BARGE). A call for papers was issued in August, but the names of contributors are not available at the time of going to press. The volume will be edited by Anthony Grenville and Andrea Hammel.

The editors welcome contributions relating to any aspect of the field of German-speaking exile in Great Britain, not limited to the refugees from Hitler in the mid-twentieth century. Articles should be sent on disk and in hard copy to: the Hon. Secretary, Research Centre for German and Austrian Exile Studies, Institute of Germanic and Romance Studies, Senate House, Malet Street, London WC1E 7HU. A style sheet is available from the Hon. Secretary.